Special Problems in Corrections

JEFFREY IAN ROSS, PH.D.

Associate Professor
Division of Criminology,
Criminal Justice and Social Policy Fellow,
Center for Comparative and International Law
2003 Distinguish Chair in Research
University of Baltimore

PEARSON

Prentice
Hall

Upper Saddle River, New Jersey 07458

Library of Congress Cataloging-in-Publication Data

Ross, Jeffrey Ian.
  Special problems in corrections / Jeffrey Ian Ross.
    p. cm.
  Includes bibliographical references and index.
  ISBN-13: 978-0-13-113874-2 (alk. paper)
  ISBN-10: 0-13-113874-X (alk. paper)
  1. Prisons.   2. Corrections.   3. Prison administration.   I. Title.
  HV8665.R66 2008
  365.068—dc22

                                                    2007031592

Editor-in-Chief: Vernon R. Anthony
Senior Acquisitions Editor: Tim Peyton
Associate Editor: Jillian Allison
Editorial Assistant: Alicia Kelly
Marketing Manager: Adam Kloza
Production Liaison: Joanne Riker
Cover Design Director: Jayne Conte
Cover Design: Rob Aleman
Full-Service Project Management/Composition: Integra Software Services, Ltd.
Printer/Binder: RR Donnelly & Sons

Credits and acknowledgments borrowed from other sources and reproduced, with permission, in this textbook appear on appropriate page within text. Page xxvi, "Footsteps" by Dixie J-Elder. Reprinted courtesy of Dixie J-Elder.

Pearson Education LTD.
Pearson Education Singapore, Pte. Ltd
Pearson Education, Canada, Ltd
Pearson Education–Japan

Pearson Education Australia PTY, Limited
Pearson Education North Asia Ltd
Pearson Educación de Mexico, S.A. de C.V.
Pearson Education Malaysia, Pte. Ltd

10 9 8 7 6 5 4 3 2 1
ISBN-13: 978-0-13-113874-2
ISBN-10:   0-13-113874-X

Dedication

To Mark J. Rochon, Michele A. Roberts, William P. Barry, and all the other criminal defense lawyers and public defenders who, on a daily basis, struggle to protect the rights of defendants against overzealous prosecutors, district attorneys, judges, and juries.

Contents

Foreword

Sentenced to federal prison for Conspiracy to Distribute Marijuana, I got out in 1987. I am an ex-convict, although I have never considered myself to be a criminal. Shortly after completing my Ph.D. and landing my first tenure-track position, I was introduced to Jeffrey Ian Ross. Over time, I learned that Jeff, a former courier, cab driver, journalist, and correctional worker, was a young criminologist, with a phenomenal amount of energy and a single-minded need to conduct research and write about issues that he felt passionate about.

In the early 1990s, Jeff was finishing off an edited book that later became *Controlling State Crime.* He asked me if I would be willing to provide an anonymous review of the chapters and make suggestions for improving that manuscript. After reading my reviews, he invited me to write a chapter on community corrections for another volume, *Cutting the Edge: Current Perspectives in Radical/Critical Criminology and Criminal Justice.* I submitted a chapter entitled "Critical and Radical Perspectives on Community Punishment: Lesson from the Darkness." He made me do a dozen or more revisions, spending many late night hours with me on the phone reading the chapter aloud word by word. I guess he thought with a lot of help, I might actually write something worth reading. Jeffrey taught me that writing is like sculpture, add a piece here, remove a piece there, the work takes shape and comes alive. He forced me to write a quality chapter, for which I have received many professional compliments.

Thus began our professional collaboration and eventual friendship that over the past 17 years produced numerous pieces of writing including essays, articles, chapters, and books. Meanwhile, Jeffrey has written or edited numerous books on subjects such as police violence, state crime, criminal and political violence, radical and critical criminology, political crime, and Native Americans in the criminal justice system. Most of these I have read, some I have reviewed, contributed to, or provided commentary and suggestions. His research is widely cited and referenced by academics and adopted for university courses. Jeff is one of the most prolific academics I know. I have done my best to try to keep up with him. At times I do, and yet he always seems to have more work on the back burner, projects that even I knew little about, that somehow appear out of nowhere. Where he gets his energy I don't know. But it is not uncommon for him to e-mail me at 1:00–2:00 in the morning trial ballooning some sort of new idea. In fact, this is the time of day when we wrote some of our best work together.

In addition to our scholarly work, for better or worse, we have also made numerous appearances on public and commercial television and radio shows, sometimes together, or one after the other. I remember one day appearing on five different television programs myself, with Jeff taking his turn being interviewed before or after me. As "newsmaking criminologists," we were just trying to educate the public as best we could about some crime or corrections hot topic. After each media blitz, the alphabet soup ABC, NBC, CBS, MSNBC, CNN, NPR ringing in my head, despite doing our best, I knew we had made little progress overcoming the fear and trepidation most Americans feel about criminals and convicts.

Of course, Jeff and I are probably best known for our work helping, along with many other prominent criminologists, to create and organize the "New School of Convict Criminology." This includes the edited book *Convict Criminology* (2003) and associated articles. The Convict Criminology group consists of an informal coalition of ex-convicts and "noncon" critical and progressive graduate students and professors of criminology, criminal justice, social work, and related disciplines. This group has been concerned with how the problem of crime is defined, the solutions proposed, the devastating impacts of those decisions on the men and women "labeled" criminals, the record high rates of incarceration, overcrowding of penal institutions, and a lack of meaningful programming inside and outside of prison.

Over the past two decades, as the prison population grew, a small but significant number of convicts managed to get educated, to find their way out of prison and into graduate programs. Even more remarkable, some of these former prisoners are now working as professors around the country at different universities, where they have made considerable progress prodding academia to open its doors to prisoners returning home after many years in prison. At the same time, the scholarly contributions of the ex-convict professors and their growing number of allies have served to update and better inform the intellectual debates on crime and corrections.

The public desperately requires education on prisons. Prison is the distant country of this twenty-first century, strange worlds where people live in cages, doing time confined behind the walls and fences of security perimeters. Since 1970, the jail and prison population of the United States has increased tenfold, from approximately 200,000 to over 2.2 million today.

The driving force behind this horrific increase in imprisonment has been the war on drugs. We are all too familiar with how the war on drugs has contributed to the dramatic increases in prison population counts. Since 1980, when President Regan officially started the war on drugs, millions of Americans have been busted for possession or sale of illegal recreational chemicals. By some estimates 70 percent of federal prisoners are serving time on drug convictions. State prisons are also filled with people serving time for simple possession or small-time drug sales. Meanwhile, state prisons are also receiving increasing numbers of men and women convicted of drunk driving and sex offenses.

Given the proliferation of films and television series, we also know the public is fascinated by prisons. Not only is this knowledge achieved through the mass media, but given the astronomical rate of incarceration in this country, sooner or later they or their loved ones may have personal experience with incarceration. We live in a democratic country where nearly anyone, unless they rarely venture beyond their front porch, have a chauffer, or live in a mansion protected by wealth and lawyers, can be a guest of the state for running afoul of some law. Today, one no longer needs to be a "criminal." Unfortunately, if somebody in their family experiments with illegal substances, has a serious traffic accident, or illegal teenage romance, they may be off to prison for many years. It all depends upon the state, the jurisdiction, and how criminal justice authorities decided to enforce the law.

Maybe if one doesn't smoke pot, take too many prescription drugs, drink intoxicating beverages, drive a car fast, or have sex with anyone besides their spouse, they are safe. By the way, one better hope they have no mentally ill or challenged individuals in their family, as statistically they are the most likely to be charged with sex crimes. No wonder prison has become the home of "special populations." And these special populations create unique challenges for prison staff and other prisoners. This "transcarceration" of vulnerable and indigent people has redeployed or shifted a large population of mentally ill, retarded, impoverished, and developmentally challenged individuals to prison. Some of the people who used to live in mental hospitals, metal health facilities, and homeless shelters now reside in prison.

Today, unbeknownst to most people, the United States is being transformed into a convict nation. The American landscape is literally littered with jails, prisons, and correctional facilities of various configurations, built here or there over the last 20 years. We have special prisons for men, women, juveniles, even drug offenders, traffic offenders, and sex offenders. There are so many prisons that now a pilot can literally navigate a plane at low altitude across the country at night guided by the high security lighting of correctional institutions and penitentiaries. Nevertheless, unless one is absolutely blind, nobody can miss them, and still the public knows so little about what happens behind the razor wire and fences, inside the walls, where men and women live in absolute peril and quiet desperation.

Many states now spend more tax money on prisons than on university systems. New prisons are built while education budgets are cut. The net result is as we spend more on prisons we will have fewer dollars left to devote to the important social issues including education, employment, health, and various economic and community problems that generate the populations that fill prisons. If they build it, they will come, let's build one on your block, next door to the school we cannot afford to maintain or repair.

Meanwhile, criminal justice programs continue to grow at colleges and universities as more students realize the career opportunities in corrections. The question becomes, What might we want these students to study before they enter prison careers? At the very least, I want mine to know that, despite all the difficulties encountered in prison work, many hard-working people enter correctional facilities every day because they are devoted to the custody and care of prisoners. They are serious professionals who want to help convicts turn their lives around. The best correctional workers are the ones who could sell ice cream to an Eskimo. They somehow find a way to market hope to men and women who have almost given up on themselves. Some may even dream that when they arrive at the prison the gates are open and the place has emptied. Hopefully, the education our students receive at university will provide them with the intellectual skills to "do corrections" and reduce our prison population.

This brings us back to the current book *Special Problems in Corrections*. Here, Jeff's research and writing builds upon his previous work and is consistent with the use of the Convict Criminology perspective as a means to better explore and understand the prison problem. Ross' conceptualization of special problems and concern for prisoners and correctional workers as human beings sets this book apart from most of the other tomes on the market that approach prisoners, correctional workers, jails, and prisons primarily from a managerial or administrative perspective.

Special Problems in Corrections explores the issues inherent in correctional systems that are overbuilt, overcrowded, and especially "well planned" to drain scarce public resources. But Jeff's book does not stop there. It reviews the solutions that have been proposed, many that have failed, the few that have worked, and then tries to suggest which might be tried in the future. As we have come to expect, Ross' research is thorough and his writing style is engaging.

Because Jeff is not only a researcher but also a teacher, he includes thoughtful review questions that challenge and provoke students to understand the materials included in the chapters. In short, this is a text that is well worth reading and adopting.

Stephen C. Richards, Ph.D.
Former federal prisoner
Associate Professor of Criminal Justice,
University of Wisconsin–Oshkosh

Preface

The average person is not likely to be too concerned about corrections, incarceration, or prisoners. But I am. The problem of jails and prisons has intrigued me since the early 1980s, when I took my first and only job in a correctional facility. My interest in this topic has since ebbed and flowed due to a variety of life and career circumstances.

Nevertheless, now that I have been teaching corrections for close to a decade, I have become increasingly curious to identify the most important problems within this field as well as their solutions. I am under the belief, misguided as it may seem, that this information will help us focus our efforts at meaningful reform. I am not alone. At any given time, correctional consultants, alone or part of a team, are crisscrossing the country providing all sorts of evaluations of correctional policies and practices. I'm also aware of the politically charged atmosphere that prison reform exists, which can significantly effect meaningful efforts for change. Suggestions may be ignored because they rub politicians, practitioners, and the public the wrong way and poorly researched programs may be funded simply because they have temporary political cache.

REFLEXIVE STATEMENT

I wrote this book because of the limitations I found with standard nuts-and-bolts texts on corrections. Although most corrections books used for introductory college and university courses provide an overview of the history and practices and mention some of the problems of jails, prisons, and community corrections in the United States, too often this field of study and practice is approached in an uncritical (i.e., politically conservative) fashion. This is understandable.

Most prison research and writing tends to reflect the language and special interests of the prison bureaucracy. After all, the government typically funds the studies and

An earlier version of this preface was presented at the American Society of Criminology Meetings, Denver, November 2003.

therefore sets the agenda, limits the parameters, and often decides if the final report will collect dust on a shelf or be distributed widely and used to inform old and new policies and procedures (Ross and Richards, 2003).

Regardless of whether the research is state-sponsored, foundation-sponsored, or self-funded, the methodology that many researchers use can often be also faulted because it consists disproportionately of complicated statistical analyses. This typically means that investigators do not have to "get their hands dirty" by interacting with convicts, ex-cons, or correctional professionals to have a better contextual understanding of their subject matter and findings. Until recently, very little good qualitative research has been done on prisons that use this approach (e.g., Liebling, 1999).

It must be noted that this book is not an anticorrections text per se. Many correctional officers and administrators will find many of the things I have to say in this book hard to swallow. My prose might seem overly opinionated, ideological, and "political." Or that I editorialize too much. I attribute these impressions to a number of factors. These include a poor understanding of what constitutes an opinion in academic discourse, what ideology and politics exactly means, and their relationship to policy and practice. I also point the finger at the socialization process that most correctional professionals are subjected to, which I believe fosters a kind of tunnel vision, an us-versus-them mentality, and seeing anyone critical of the practice of corrections as having an axe to grind. Indeed, there are often large perceptual gaps among inmates, correctional professionals, and scholars in which they seem like they are operating in separate worlds. On the other hand, many of my critical criminology colleagues may fault me for not taking a more radical stance. For example, the book does not advocate the abolishment of jails and prisons, despite being familiar with this position (e.g., Mathiesen, 1974), having covered the very first prison abolition conference as a reporter for *Now Magazine* in Toronto (Ross, 1983), and having worked for almost four years in a correctional facility.

HOW TO IDENTIFY THE PROBLEMS

In any given field, there are several different ways and perspectives from which to identify and judge the severity of a problem. Difficulties can be determined and examined at the micro or macro level, albeit at several levels of analysis in between too. Caution, however, must be exerted in this task. The method investigators use to identify problems will naturally impact the findings. One must also be sensitive to who is going to use this information.

Looking at root causes versus outcomes to determine problems is also an issue of concern. Investigators need to acknowledge who is doing the evaluation, as well as any biases they may bring to the research. For example, is the person or entity an insider or an outsider? The goal here is to determine who has the appropriate knowledge, skills, and who is most objective. Insiders may have considerable knowledge, but they can suffer from undue bias.

In order to minimize these problems during the course of my research, I spoke to a wide variety of individuals. I interviewed, observed and/or corresponded with numerous convicts, ex-cons, correctional, probation, and parole officers, and administrators and visited several correctional facilities, both private and public, not only in the United States but elsewhere. I also relied on and integrated the relevant literature, contextualized the numerous problems (citing statistics where appropriate), and proposed what I believe are realistic solutions. Some of the problems—like too much red tape, which is an all-too-familiar complaint of all bureaucracies—were too ambiguous and not given much attention.

Micro Level

At the institutional level (individual jails and prisons), for example, one way to identify and judge the severity of a problem is to thoroughly review performance indicators (e.g., Logan, 1993). One such example is the *Key Facility Report*. This document lists the various incidents that have occurred in a correctional facility over a period of time, and provides a statistical summary of how many verbal and physical altercations have occurred among concerned parties (e.g., staff and inmates). These numbers can be compared with those from previous days, weeks, months, or years to determine if things are improving, remaining the same, or in fact worsening.

Another way to get a handle on the problems is to review the number and kinds of *Administrative Remedy Reports* that have been turned in to a coordinator. Typically, these items, much like a complaint form, are submitted by inmates in a secured ballot-type box. The coordinator is usually a high-ranking correctional officer, and the investigation is conducted by another officer. Some of the complaints are legitimate while others are of questionable merit; they cover the gambit from poor medical treatment to the poor haircuts by unqualified barbers.

Prisoners can and do complain. However, if this is perceived to be a nuisance or the convict a "troublemaker," inmates may incur retribution from correctional officers and management. This can involve bringing an inmate up on disciplinary charges (i.e., often referred to as receiving a *shot*), no matter how minor they are, sending the convict to solitary confinement, special management, or administrative segregation (or in prison argot, the *hole*), or transferring (almost perpetually) the inmate to another facility (known as riding the bus or diesel therapy). There are countless ways that correctional officers and managers can retaliate against convicts who are perceived to complain excessively or unnecessarily. That is why many inmates are reluctant to complain through official mechanisms. Likewise, this state of affairs may contribute to learned helplessness or surplus powerlessness where after numerous rejections the person simply does not try to address their grievances.

Additionally, the performance of officers can be determined through activity reports or periodic personnel evaluations (Freeman, 2000: 329–332). In most organizations this process is done on an annual basis. But this sort of bureaucratic information is typically very superficial and sanitized. It generally does not go into enough detail for investigators to draw meaningful conclusions.

Finally, gathering anecdotal or confirming evidence by interviewing sources, experts, or "key informants" such as convicts, correctional officers, administrators, and prison scholars is often done. The correctional officers and prisoners are probably the best sources to provide this kind of information because they are on the front lines every day (Conover, 2001; Ross and Richards, 2002; 2003). Preferred by journalists and ethnographic researchers, this method provides information that is typically current and rich in detail, but also potentially biased because it is difficult to judge the veracity of the information. Sources may lie, embellish, or forget critical material. Thus, it is essential that several individuals from the same institution be consulted and observed over a sufficient period of time, because often workers are on their best behavior, but have difficulty sustaining this demeanor over time. Alternatively, key personnel may be on vacation, on a leave of absence, or out sick. Finally, this does not accommodate to the problem in gaining access, which for some facilities is next to impossible.

Macro Level

There are approximately five methods by which researchers, practitioners, and policy-makers can obtain a larger picture of the problems within the corrections field (Welsh and Harris, 2004). They are listed from least to most useful.

First, thoroughly review journal articles in the field of corrections. This method provides researchers with an idea of academics' perceptions of the most dominant problems and also editors' and reviewers' judgments of which papers are the most worthy of journal publication. However, just because journal editors decide to publish an article on a specific topic, does not mean that this issue is the most important for practitioners or convicts; it could simply be a reflection of the kinds of manuscripts that have been submitted, the availability of space, or the current editor's (or editorial board's) predilections.

Second, perform a content analysis of news media, such as television and/or radio news broadcasts as well as newspaper and magazine reporting, to see which corrections-related issues are cited most frequently (e.g., Krippendorf, 1981). The drawback here is that these reports may simply be snapshots in time and suffer from the same constraints as scholarly journals.

Third, collect so-called social indicators (i.e., data on such factors as crime rates, victimization patterns, and incarceration rates) located in diverse sources like the *Correctional Compendium*, or the Uniform Crime Reports, through the *Sourcebook of Criminal Justice Statistics* (www.albany.edu/sourcebook).

Fourth, some value may be gained by holding a community forum. The downside here is that they tend to simply be opportunities for people to vent, and geographically constrained to the region in which they were held. One way around this is to hold public forums where considerable thinking has gone into their organization, and in different parts of the country. This is similar to the method of the 2005–2006 National Commission on Safety and Abuse in Prison (www.prisoncommission.org) (hereafter Commission on Safety and Abuse), which on June 8, 2006, released its final report on conditions in correctional facilities throughout the United States.

Finally, systematically administer a survey to a broad constituency of individuals who have a strong interest and/or expertise in the field of incarceration (i.e., officers, administrators, and convicts). A method involving experts in the field is commonly referred to as a Delphi study and has been perfected in several branches of the criminal justice system (e.g., Tafoya, 1986). Unfortunately, this method is like a snapshot in time and may not be useful for long-term planning.

In the end, although each method has advantages, almost all have drawbacks. Instead, combining all these methods may be the most useful and would come closest to achieving a balanced approach. To do this properly, however, researchers need adequate resources.

SOLUTIONS TO PROBLEMS

Few of the solutions proposed for the field of corrections are easy to implement, and all may lead to unintended consequences (e.g., Merton, 1936; Clear, 2001; Preston and Roots, 2004). It might be easiest to achieve success at the institutional level rather than at the state or federal level of corrections. There is also a realization that many problems seem to simply snowball. Problems can be linked together and affect each other, and the population interviewed or surveyed may not be able to disentangle them. It is also recognized that the history of prison reform is fraught with problems (Sullivan, 1990). Moreover, solutions to correctional problems may be initiated or may originate from several sources. They include the state or government, the private sector, religious bodies, self-help organizations for convicts, or inmates themselves. Finally, some of the more extreme suggestions like prison abolition are not widely held and perhaps impractical at this point in history.

So what? Given that I do not have the kind of resources to conduct the more comprehensive kinds of studies, almost each semester I survey my students and ask them to rank in order what they think are the most important problems facing the field. Not all the responses fit into distinct categories, but over the years I have discovered a number of consistent themes. Indeed, the problems will not strike the reader as anything new, but the organization and rendering in this book should. Additionally, to the extent possible, the problems identified in each chapter are presented from least to most important in terms of how they affect corrections. Certainly, there will be disagreements among correctional officers, administrators, and inmates and other corrections experts, with respect to what they think is most important. But I believe that an author's most important job is to contextualize things. Some may also question the utility of students' perceptions as an organizing tool. Most students have not yet been exposed to the realities of the criminal justice system; however, the reader should understand that my approach should serve as a benchmark or pedagogical starting point for communicating the problems with corrections to them and not an end in itself.

One set of difficulties I've identified focuses on the problems for convicts and correctional facilities, and the other difficulties encountered by correctional officers and administrators. It is with this knowledge that I organize my courses, lectures, and this book. As I have argued in my other books (Ross 1995/2000; 2000), while it is important to discuss problems (and, in general, most people are reasonably good at doing this), it is more important to propose and implement realistic solutions to address or solve these difficulties. The reader should also realize that some of the solutions proposed in one part of the book reappear frequently because they are capable of solving more than one difficulty.

Mention should also be made of the social justice (Arrigo, 1999) or restorative justice approach (e.g., Braithwaite, 1989). Many observers of corrections, including myself, recognize the limitations with the current criminal justice system, particularly its emphasis on retributive justice, and its inability to address the higher order societal goals of human respect and dignity. That is why the criminal justice system and corrections in particular should be working in this direction. To the extent possible, this book emphasizes these themes.

It must also be understood that corrections is ultimately a system in which each component has a part or role to play,[1] and like systems theory suggests, if you tinker with one aspect of the organization, it will have an effect somewhere else. It is like a domino effect and the ripples are felt in many places that are often not immediately apparent or easy to distinguish. What do I mean by this statement? In simple terms, some of the solutions implemented by practitioners can and do have negative and unintended consequences that correctional planners failed to account for or originally minimized in terms of the impact they may have. Nothing in life is perfect. But some of the negative effects might be controlled. The trick in proper criminal justice planning is to adequately predict and prepare for this possibility with contingency plans (Welsh and Harris, 2004).

Another issue that should be addressed is the best practices approach. Over the past two decades in policy circles, there has been a tendency to admire what works in institutional settings. What the supporters of this phenomenon often fail to recognize is the diversity of agencies or transferring methods, without much consideration of context from the private sector into the public sector and assuming they do not have to be tinkered with is fraught with problems.

Additionally, the reader will notice that some problems were not included (or at least in any great detail). These are the death penalty, juvenile corrections, racism in prison, and reentry. This is not to suggest that these issues are not problematic, but reflect the consensus of those to whom I have administered my survey.[2]

Finally, a note on terminology is in order. To the extent possible, and apologies if I sound too politically correct, this book avoids using the term *offender*. In normal usage, most people do not think twice about uttering this word as a synonym for "prisoner," "inmate," or "convict." But, on closer examination, "offender" is derived from the same set of words that includes the term *offensive*. Granted, many of the things convicts have done or do are or appear offensive. Yet, because of the fallibility of our criminal justice system, it should come as no surprise that some people are wrongfully committed (Christianson, 2004). In addition, some things that individuals have done which land them in jail or prison are so minor (e.g., possession of small amounts of recreational drugs) that we might question why they are there in the first place. Thus to call all convicts offenders is probably unnecessarily derogatory. Likewise, to the extent possible, the labels *boss, bull, cap, guard, hack,* or *screw* are avoided as these synonyms for correctional officers are also perceived to be pejorative, as it neglects the professional nature of this occupation. True, many correctional officers act in a deviant manner, but in a scholarly text such as this, nuance should be observed. That is why I will strive to use the term *correctional officer*. Finally, there are few synonyms for jails, prisons, and correctional facilities outside of institutions. I have refrained from using the colloquial words *can, hoosegow, joint, and pokey.*

In order for students to better appreciate the subject matter of each chapter, and to break up the flow of the text, I have included exhibit boxes that provide overviews of a well-known piece of relevant research and/or a movie that they may wish to see or instructor may wish to screen. These can be identified by the subhead "Classics in Corrections."

Finally, corrections is not only an American problem but a global one. However, for the sake of focus, the majority of examples marshaled within this book are rooted in the United States. In sum, my book reviews and examines the critical, longstanding, and emerging issues that affect the way correctional facilities are operated, and how convicts, correctional officers, and administrators experience this unique setting.

Jeffrey Ian Ross, Ph.D.

Notes

1. See, for example, the theoretical literature on structural functionalism and systems theory.
2. For a good review of the death penalty, see, for example, Bohm (2003). For research connected to race in prison, see, for example, Carroll (1988). For the graying prison population, see, for example, Aday (1994). For Native Americans behind bars, see, for example, Archambeault (2003; 2006).

Acknowledgments

In any given project there are many people to thank and this one is no different. I would like to extend my appreciation to Frank Mortimer of Prentice Hall for signing this book and the patience he demonstrated during the management of this project. Susan Beauchamp was essential for marshaling an initial slate of reviewers for the proposal and championing my cause when this was needed. Mayda Bosco was instrumental for sending the earlier drafts out to reviewers and keeping this project near the top of my priority list. Margaret Lannamann also stepped up to the plate and served a similar role. Mellisa Orsborn in the marketing department helped me organize my marketing strategy. I would also like to thank Tim Peyton, former sales manager, and current senior acquisitions editor for capably picking up where Frank left off and helping me to make it across the finishing line; Louise Sette, Project Manager, and Joanne Riker, Director of Central Publishing, Pearson/Prentice Hall Higher Education, for getting this book ready for production; and Shiny Rajesh, Project Manager, at Integra Software Services Pvt. Ltd. in Pondicherry, India, who worked at breakneck speed to produce the book.

I would like to thank Catherine Leidemer who tidied up my prose when it was clear that my thoughts were a bit scattered. My gratitude is extended to my students, many of whom are former or current correctional, probation, and parole officers and administrators, including Ginger Duke-Miller, Alicia Peak, and Dana Valdivia, for enduring many of these chapters as lectures and/or required readings. I would further like to express my thanks to Christine Bevans, a former Maryland State Trooper and stellar graduate student in our department, who periodically acted as an informal research assistant.

I'm also indebted to Bradley Chilton, Francis (Frank) Cullen, David Curry, Ernest J. Eley Jr., Burk Foster, Richard Hogan, Jay Hurst, Mike Johnson, David Vandiver, Angela West Crews, and Miguel Zaldivar who volunteered to take a look at selected chapters, and the anonymous reviewers who forced me to rethink many of the ideas I initially presented while writing this book. Thanks to Stephen C. Richards for writing the foreword, and Dixie

J-Elder for preparing the poem. Finally, I would like to thank numerous convict crimi-nologist colleagues including, but not limited to Bill Archambeault, Bruce Arrigo, Preston Elrod, Marianne Fisher-Giorlando, John Irwin, Richard Jones, Alan Mobley, Greg Newbold, Dan Murphy, Barbara Owen, Stephen C. Richards, and Chuck Terry, and prison activists, like Charlie and Pauline Sullivan of National CURE who provided a supportive community of sorts.

Finally, I extend my thanks to Natasha J. Cabrera, my wife and fellow scholar, who provided encouragement and feedback at several critical times, served as a sound-ing board for my ideas, and tries to keep my feet firmly planted on the ground, and to Keanu and Dakota Ross-Cabrera, our children, a source of inspiration, who tolerated their father's divided attention more times than necessary.

About the Author

Jeffrey Ian Ross is Associate Professor, Division of Criminology, Criminal Justice, and Social Policy, and Fellow, Center for Comparative and International Law, University of Baltimore. He has conducted research, written, and lectured on national security, political violence, political crime, policing, and corrections for over the past two decades. His work has appeared in many academic journals and books, as well as in articles in popular magazines.

Dr. Ross is the author, coauthor, editor, or coeditor of 11 books. As a sole author, he has published, *Making News of Police Violence* (Praeger, 2000), *The Dynamics of Political Crime* (Sage, 2002), *Political Terrorism: An Interdisciplinary Approach* (Peter Lang, 2006), and *Will Terrorism End?* (Chelsea House, 2006). He is the coauthor (with Stephen C. Richards) of *Behind Bars: Surviving Prison* (Alpha Books, 2002) and the editor of *Controlling State Crime* (Transaction, 1995/2000), *Violence in Canada* (Transaction, 1995/2003), *Cutting the Edge: Current Perspectives in Radical/Critical Criminology and Criminal Justice* (Praeger, 1998), and *Varieties of State Crime and Its Control* (Criminal Justice Press, 2000), and coeditor (with Stephen C. Richards) of *Convict Criminology* (Wadsworth, 2002) and (with Larry Gould) of *Native Americans and the Criminal Justice System* (Paradigm, 2006).

Ross is a respected and frequent source of scholarly and scientific information for local, regional, national, and international news media including interviews with newspapers, magazines, and radio and television stations. More specifically, he has commented on crime and policing issues in Baltimore, the 9/11 attacks, the Beltway sniper incidents, the Laci Peterson disappearance/Scott Peterson trial and conviction, the Columbine (Colorado) shootings, and the Columbus (Ohio) sniper incidents. In terms of live appearances on national television shows, Ross has been on CNN, including Jack Cafferty's "In the Money," and "Larry King Live," and on Fox national news, including "Hannity and Colmes" and "The O'Reilly Factor." Additionally, Ross has written op-eds for *The (Baltimore) Sun*, *The (Maryland) Daily Record*, *The Gazette* (weekly community newspapers serving Maryland's Montgomery, Frederick, Prince Georges, and Carroll counties), the *Baltimore Examiner*, and the *Tampa Tribune*.

Ross received his Ph.D. in political science from the University of Colorado and from 1995 to 1998 was a social science analyst with the National Institute of Justice, a division of the U.S. Department of Justice. During the 1980s, Ross worked almost four years in a correctional facility. In 2003 he received his college's Distinguished Chair in Research Award. Most recently (2005–2006) he was a member of the Prisoner/Prisoner Advocate Liaison Group for the National Academy of Sciences' Institute of Medicine Committee examining ethics and research with prisoners. His Web site is www.jeffreyianross.com.

There is not—there is never silence here.
It's like back home, where sirens broke
into our half-sleep, dreams were peppered by
gunshots—in this dark, loud place, prayers
bang into cement ceilings & armed guards
keep us walking in circles, following the shoes
in front of ours, looking down at the dirt
where ants in hot weather scramble for safety.
I trusted my own innocence until they bashed
down my door, tore open drawers, threw
me onto the floor, hands behind head & now
I know that anyone from anywhere could
end up in this loud place, walking in circles,
blinking at a blaring sun after days in solitary.

Dixie J-Elder

PART I
Laying the Groundwork

Chapter 1

What Is Corrections and What Are Its Problems?

INTRODUCTION

It bears mentioning that criminology is primarily the study of the causes and effects of crime, and that criminal justice consists of the analysis of organizations responsible for monitoring, investigating, and responding to crime, and processing those who have been charged or convicted of a crime. The criminal justice system, in particular, is composed of four interconnected branches: law enforcement, the courts, corrections, and juvenile justice. Corrections, in particular encompass jails, prisons, and a variety of community-based programs and sanctions (e.g., probation, parole, and the like). The term *corrections* usually means "the institutions, policies, procedures and other nuts and bolts of the system" (Welch, 1996: 3). It also encompasses "the great number of programs, services, facilities and organizations responsible for the management of people who have been accused or convicted of criminal offenses" (Cole, 1994: 544). Corrections are typically divided into two parts: institutional corrections, which is the brick-and-mortar side with jails and prisons, and community corrections, which encompasses such programs and practices as probation, parole, and intermediate sanctions. Additionally, it must be understood that the practice of corrections is generally supposed to have three objectives: punishment, community safety, and rehabilitation. Sometimes the system achieves these goals, while at other times it falls short. A side benefit of jails and prisons is that they are supposed to deter individuals from committing crime.

This chapter has benefited from comments by Richard Hogan.

Another important distinction should be made between the state and federal correctional systems. Those who are sentenced to state prisons have violated a state criminal
code. People who have committed a relatively minor crime are often given some form of
community corrections. If, on the other hand, they are sent to jail, depending on the sentencing
structures of the state in which they were convicted, they may be incarcerated in one of
these types of facilities up to 18 months. Individuals sent to federal prisons, run by the Federal
Bureau of Prisons (FBOP), have engaged in a select number of crimes like income tax
evasion, counterfeiting, trafficking across state lines, kidnapping, bank robbery, political
crimes, and crimes on a federal property.

RELEVANT STATISTICS

Over the past four decades, America has experienced one of the largest expansions in its
jail, prison, and community corrections populations. This phenomenon has alternatively
been called "the imprisonment binge" (Austin and Irwin, 2001) or the "race to incarcerate" (Maur, 2006). In the United States (for the year 2005), 6.48 million people were under
the control of the criminal justice system. Approximately 2.3 million were behind bars
in jails or prisons, 4.16 million on probation, and 784,408 on parole (Glaze and Bonczar,
2006; Harrison and Beck, 2006). State and federal correctional systems (not to mention
private prisons) employ roughly 650,000 people who work as administrators, correctional
officers (COs), case managers, classification officers, probation and parole officers, counselors, and social workers. It currently costs approximately $112 billion a year to fund
the correctional systems in the United States (Austin and Irwin, 2001: 13), and the number
of individuals entering correctional facilities is increasing exponentially.

WHY HAS THIS OCCURRED?

Approximately four reasons account for the increase in the number of people being
sentenced to jails and prisons:

1. the construction of new facilities;
2. sentencing guidelines (particularly "truth in sentencing" legislation, mandatory
   minimums, and determinant sentencing);
3. new laws (e.g., "three strikes you're out" legislation);[1] and, the most important,
4. the war on drugs.

These factors include several ironies. Why? The bulk of individuals who are sentenced
to jail or prison are there because they were convicted of nonviolent, drug-related crimes.
On the other hand, violent criminals are being released back into the community to
make way for first-time nonviolent criminals. Most of those who are let out are angry,
leave with few marketable skills, or have not received any special vocational training.

The majority who are released come out worse than when they entered. This is why prisons have often been called a revolving door or turnstile justice (Gido and Alleman, 2002). Those entering the system are also disproportionately minorities: African Americans, Hispanics, and Native Americans. They are usually drawn from lower socioeconomic segments of society and are either unemployed or underemployed (Miller, 1996; Welch, 1996; Austin and Irwin, 2001: 3).

Moreover, there is no proven relationship between the crime rate and the number of people who are locked up. One might assume that an increased rate of incarceration might ultimately result in a lower rate of crime. And many individuals take comfort in this assumption. Unfortunately, this has not been the case—our crime rate increases and decreases in a cyclical fashion, and rarely is this connected to the number of people we incarcerate (Blumstein, Cohen, and Nagin, 1977; Blumstein et al., 1981).

Finally, "[b]ecause of the ongoing imprisonment binge, the United States currently locks up more prisoners per capita than does South Africa [under the former apartheid system] and the former Soviet Union" (Welch, 1996: 4), regimes that were previously considered to be repressive. Although the United States champions itself as a democratic country, putting a disproportionate number of people behind bars restricts the civil liberties of an unnecessarily large number of its citizens. Also it is quite bizarre when you compare the United States with countries such as Denmark, Sweden, and Holland where the crime rates per capita basically match that of the United States, but they have a lower incarceration rate (Christie, 1993).

WHAT HAS BEEN THE RESPONSE?

The prevailing impression among many correctional administrators, officers, experts, and activists is that the jail and prison system is failing. One of the classic statements echoing this idea is Reiman's *The Rich Get Richer and the Poor Get Prison* (1979/2003). This book argues that the criminal justice system encourages the existence of a criminal class and promotes the notion that the poor are disproportionately responsible for the majority of crime. That is why Reiman and "other critics focus on the class bias inherent in the criminal justice system" (Welch, 1996: 5). This approach is taken by the critical perspective that involves

> [q]uestioning, challenging and examining all sides of various problems and issues. Instead of uncritically accepting punishment and corrections as, a natural extensions of society, the critical approach delves under the surface of punishment to explore corrections at greater depths . . . it dispels many myths and misconceptions surrounding corrections . . . it demystifies the objectives, processes and outcomes of correctional intervention and offers alternative interpretations and solutions. (Welch, 1996: 6)

This kind of ideology and methodology typically looks for the hidden meanings behind myths and explores their utility, purpose, and function in an effort to better inform the subject matter under investigation (e.g., Taylor, Walton, and Young, 1973; Lynch and Groves,

1986/1989; Ross, 1998b). I do not suggest that one *needs* to adopt a critical perspective to examine issues at a deeper level, but this is a central feature of such an approach.

CRIME AND CORRECTIONS AS SOCIAL PROBLEMS

Not only are there special problems with selected aspects of jails, prisons, and community corrections, but there are also a number of difficulties with the American correctional system as a whole. Over the past few decades, because of our inability to solve many of the problems with corrections, some analysts believe that the field in and of itself is a problem (Welch, 1996: 8). It has been called a social problem (Welch, 1996) or a "national tragedy and disgrace" (Austin and Irwin, 2001), while others have suggested that the way we incarcerate people is part of a correctional industrial complex, an informal network of correctional workers, professional organizations, and corporations that keep the jail and prison systems growing (Christie, 1993; Hallinan, 2003). In the state of California, for example, jails and prisons are the largest state employer. Moreover, the California Correctional Peace Officers Association is one of the most powerful unions in the state, and California Public Employees' Retirement System (CalPERS), the benefit coordinators for jail and correctional workers, is a multibillion-dollar entity. Therefore, those seeking changes to these systems are always up against powerful lobbying interests.

Some correctional observers and critical criminologists have said that although conditions are problematic, they will not be solved until the underlying causes of crime are addressed. They argue that until we eradicate the conditions and processes that lead to and reinforce inequality, poverty, and racism, and guarantee universal access to housing, health care, and education, we will not be able to solve the prison crisis (Richards, 1998). Thus, it could be argued that requiring COs to have more training or improving classification, for example, is simply tinkering with the symptoms, rather than dealing with the root causes. Undoubtedly, jails and prisons are the consequence of enduring and underlying systemic problems in society.

While addressing, minimizing, and even solving the underlying issues that cause crime are extremely important, this book is primarily intended to sort out the present-day problems affecting corrections.[2] It recognizes that many of these difficulties have endured for a long time, and their relative importance is subject to change over time. In order to bring us up-to-date, however, a brief history of corrections should at least be provided.[3]

THE LAY OF THE LAND: A SHORT HISTORY OF THE CORRECTIONS IN THE UNITED STATES

The history of corrections in the United States can probably be traced back to colonial times. In general, during this period deviance and law breaking was primarily dealt with through the process of shaming.

The Puritans in New England used correctional punishment as a means to enforce their strict Puritan codes. They viewed the deviant as wilful, a sinner, and a captive of the devil. Informal community pressures, such as gossip, ridicule, and ostracism, were found to be effective in keeping most citizens in line. Mutilations, hangings, burnings, and brandings were used to punish serious crimes. Fines, confinement in the stocks and the public cage, banishment, and whippings were other frequently used methods of control, and any citizen who was not a respected property owner was rejected from the town. The jail, which was brought to the colonies soon after the settlers arrived from England, was used to detain individuals awaiting trial and those awaiting punishment. (Bartollas, 2002: 46)

One of the earliest jails was built in 1790 in Philadelphia by the Quakers (i.e., a religious order also known as the Society of Friends). They believed that deviants and law breakers should be left in isolation, preferably with a copy of the King James Version of the Bible by their side, to reflect on the sins they committed. This approach was called the Pennsylvania or *silent but separate system*. No sooner than the first prison was built, there were efforts to change prisons—ranging from architecture to the programs they provide. After several reforms were proposed, larger and more comprehensive structures were built as part of the Pennsylvania correctional system such as Western Penitentiary (built in 1818) and Eastern State Penitentiary (built in 1829).

Later, as the country grew in population, a competing corrections philosophy and practice developed at the prison in Auburn, New York. The administration of this prison believed that a military regime where convicts live and work together but remained silent would have a rehabilitative effect on them. This alternative was called the New York, or *silent but congregate system*.

During the late 1800s, most states began building their "big house" prisons (e.g., Sing Sing, San Quentin, Joliet, etc.), also known as penitentiaries. These facilities, many of which were large structures, typically constructed out of local stone, built by convicts, and partially resembling castles, were usually located in a rural or remote parts of their respective state.[4] Why? The farther the facility was located from the major urban locales, the cheaper was the land. If there was an escape, it would take the convict a long time to reach "civilization." It would also increase the possibility that they would be caught on their way home and minimize urbanites' levels of fear. And to some extent the construction of correctional facilities in rural and remote areas can maintain or spur economic growth (see Exhibit 1.1).

Physically, penitentiaries had high walls, large tiers, a yard, shops, and industries. "The prisoners, averaging about 2,500, came from both urban and rural areas, were poor, and outside the South, were predominantly white. The prison society was essentially isolated; access to visitors, mail, and other kinds of communication was restricted. Prisoners' days were strictly enforced by guards. . . . In the big house there was little in the way of treatment programs; custody was the primary goal" (Cole, 1994: 579). This was generally known as the custodial model.

In 1876, in a sharp departure from the Auburn and Pennsylvania correctional systems, New York State opened the country's first "reformatory" in Elmira. Under its new warden, Zebulon Brockaway, the facility geared to younger inmates (ages 16–30)

EXHIBIT 1.1

Classics in Corrections

Foucault's *Discipline and Punish*

French historian and philosopher Michel Foucault's (1926–1984) seminal book (1977) focuses on how powerful entities, initially the church, then the state, punished heretics and individuals who violated the law. It also suggests how punishment has shifted from the body of a person to their mind and/or soul. In so doing, Foucault looks at the power relationships among those in control and those who have to submit to the control. He begins his famous book with a description of an execution that takes place in the mid-seventeenth century. Foucault points out that after the French Revolution punishment changed from death and torture to the imprisonment of people. Central to prisons and the penitentiary is the process of surveillance embodied in Jeremy Bentham's notion of the Panopticon. Increasingly powerful entities controlled people through the process of surveillance. Foucault believes that surveillance has spread beyond prison and into society.

emphasized rehabilitation that was tailored to each inmate and indeterminate sentencing based on the inmates. This included courses taught by "inmates, college professors, public school teachers, and lawyers teaching a wide range of general subjects, as well as sports, religion, and military drill" (Stone, 2005). Over the next 35 years, the Elmira Reformatory served as a model for the construction of similar correctional facilities in different states in the United States and elsewhere.

During the 1940s and 1950s, more jails and prisons were built and corrections became recognized as a profession. Big houses were becoming obsolete, and the architecture of prisons started changing as did their locations. This was also the beginning of a number of experiments in the field. One noticeable change was the introduction of classification of prisoners into different levels of security (i.e., minimum, medium, and maximum). Another experiment was the beginning of rehabilitative programs that were couched in the medical model (e.g., Rothman, 1980). Crime was perceived as a disease, and convicts afflicted with this malady were to be cured. In this context, a variety of psychological and drug and alcohol treatment programs were introduced. This was also the beginning of the professionalization of corrections. COs needed to take tests to work in jails and prisons and increasingly so for more senior positions in their facility and with their state department of corrections (DOC).

In the 1960s, correctional experts and practitioners experimented with various community corrections programs. These initiatives went beyond simply probation and parole and included innovations such as diversion, work and educational release, and house arrest (McCarthy and McCarthy, 1997). The attempt here was to keep people out of jail and prison who would be best treated, rehabilitated, or monitored in the community.

During the 1980s, however, as a response to the public's fear of crime and sim-plistic interpretations or bad science connected to previous crime-reducing experiments (Austin and Irwin, 2001: xiii–xiv; Austin, 2003), an increasingly conservative agenda took hold of criminal justice research, policy, and practice. Many of the gains that were part of the so-called community corrections era were scaled back. Congress and state legislatures passed draconian criminal laws that reversed such time-honored practices as indeterminate sentencing and ushered in a whole host of laws that made prisoners spend more time in custodial facilities. Politicians also enacted legislation that enabled states to build more correctional facilities. In short, prisons and jails were to be more harsh and punitive. Many people with progressive agendas, on the other hand, advo-cate social and restorative justice as higher-order alternatives to our current criminal justice system that focuses disproportionately on retributive justice (e.g., "an eye for an eye").

In the meantime, the jail and prison-building boom increased with towns and cities lobbying their state legislature for the building of a new correctional facility to make up for the job loss that happened as a result of businesses closing and in some cases moving away (Welch, 1998; Hallinan, 2003). Hallinan states, "These communities profit most from the prison boom: from the construction jobs and the prison jobs and all the spin-off business that prisons create. Yet it is hard to ignore that those getting rich are usually white and those in prison are usually not" (p. xii).

In the 1990s, one the most significant changes in the growth of prisons is the build-ing and use of Supermax facilities (see Chapter 5). These controversial facilities are used to house the most violent and escape-prone prisoners. At the federal level they include political prisoners and organized crime and gang leaders. Prisoners are locked up 23 out of 24 hours a day and over time often suffer problems associated with sensory deprivation.

CURRENT GOALS OF INCARCERATION

As the number of people being sent to jail and prison has doubled and the system has become more punitive, additional challenges face the American correctional system. For example, the events of 9/11 have had an effect on both the state and federal prison systems. In the field of criminal justice, money has been disproportionately spent on law enforcement. In times of budgetary crunches, the justice system has cut back in several areas and jails and prisons feel the brunt of these changes. Correctional workers are leav-ing the profession at alarming rates because in some DOCs they don't believe the risks are worth the rate of pay, they are not allowed to work overtime, or they come into work overtired or exhausted because they may now be holding down another job to make ends meet. Whereas jails and prisons are supposed to punish convicts, keep the community safe, and rehabilitate inmates, rehabilitation is rarely attempted when money is scarce. These and other challenges face the correctional system of today. Before exploring them in greater detail, the following chapter reviews some of the myths of jails, prisons and convicts, and how and why these are created. These misperceptions stand in the way of rational debate, analysis, and policy creation.

KEY TERMS

big house

corrections

critical criminology

custodial model

department of corrections (DOC)

Federal Bureau of Prisons (FBOP)

jail

prison

reformatory

Reiman's hypothesis

sentence

silent but congregate system

silent but separate system

REVIEW QUESTIONS

PART 1: MULTIPLE-CHOICE QUESTIONS

Choose the most appropriate answer.

1. When sent to jail, how long is an inmate expected to stay?
   a. as long as the judge tells them
   b. less than a year
   c. more than a year
   d. weekends
   e. approximately a year

2. What is meant by "The Big House?"
   a. large jails in the country
   b. large penitentiaries located in a remote location
   c. boot camps
   d. all of the above
   e. none of the above

3. What is the name given to the term that includes institutions, policies, and procedures by which we provide a sanction for a criminal offense?
   a. penology
   b. corrections
   c. jails
   d. all of the above
   e. none of the above

4. What is Reiman's hypothesis?
   a. Don't do the crime if you can't do the time.
   b. The criminal justice system is designed to fail.
   c. You get as much justice as you can afford.
   d. If you increase the penalty, you decrease the propensity for crime.
   e. If you build a prison, you will fill it.

5. Most of those currently incarcerated are

    a. convicted of drug violations
    b. nonviolent criminals
    c. lower-class minorities
    d. all of the above
    e. violent criminals

6. What is the new model of criminal justice that shifts from a punishment perspective to one that focuses on community safety and the quality of community life?

    a. retributive justice
    b. distributive justice
    c. restorative justice
    d. all of the above
    e. none of the above

7. What is the term for a sentence in which an offender serves the entire time for which they were sentenced?

    a. determinant sentencing
    b. intermediate sentencing
    c. indeterminate sentencing
    d. tourniquet sentencing
    e. split sentencing

8. Which of the following is NOT a concept of critical criminology?

    a. The American corrections is structurally biased.
    b. The incarceration industry is big business.
    c. More focus on the individual (counseling, treatment, and services) is needed.
    d. Unemployment, crime, and poverty are products of capitalism.
    e. None of the above.

9. Which of the following has been an implication of the growth in corrections over the past four decades?

    a. the construction of new facilities
    b. sentencing guidelines (particularly "truth in sentencing" legislation, mandatory minimums, and determinant sentencing)
    c. "three strikes you're out" legislation
    d. the war on drugs
    e. none of the above

10. What are the two dominant ideological perspectives that guide corrections?

    a. Democrat and Republican
    b. radical and critical
    c. liberal and conservative
    d. quantitative and qualitative
    e. racial and sexist

11. In the United States, what is the approximate number of people in the criminal justice system (either incarcerated or on some form of community corrections)?

    a. 1 million
    b. 5 million
    c. 7 million
    d. 10 million
    e. 15 million

12. Which of the following is an example of microlevel research on corrections?

    a. analyzing the key facility report
    b. content analysis
    c. administering surveys
    d. reviewing scholarly articles
    e. interviewing journalists who cover prisons

13. Which correctional system required prisoners to live in solitary conditions, and be reformed by reading the bible, and engage in quiet reflection?

    a. Pennsylvania system
    b. Auburn system
    c. Elmira system
    d. Community corrections system
    e. Progressive system

14. Which correctional system made prisoners work in total isolation and promote silence and penitence?

    a. Auburn
    b. Newgate
    c. Pennsylvania
    d. Walnut Street
    e. Maryland

15. During the 1960s what type of policy did correctional departments emphasize?

    a. vocational programs
    b. deterrence
    c. incarceration
    d. community corrections
    e. b and c only

16. Which political party generally advocates building more prisons, extending the death penalty, and mandating longer sentences?

    a. Democrats
    b. Republicans
    c. liberals
    d. conservatives
    e. libertarians

17. Community corrections programs that require only part-time incarceration include
    a. intern programs
    b. educational release programs
    c. house arrest
    d. all of the above
    e. b and c only

18. What are the two major types of sentences?
    a. drug related and violence related
    b. individual and group
    c. long and short
    d. state and federal
    e. determinant and indeterminate

PART 2: SHORT-ANSWER QUESTIONS

Answer each question. Be as detailed and specific as possible.

1. List two special interest groups that affect corrections.
2. Why has there been a shift toward conservativism in corrections?
3. List two macrolevel and two microlevel approaches that can be used to identify problems in the field of corrections.
4. What are four reasons why so many people are currently incarcerated in American jails and prisons?
5. List two reasons why prisons have historically been constructed in remote settings.
6. List four crimes that would land a person in the FBOP.
7. What are four different types of items that a content analysis might analyze?
8. What was the Auburn system?
9. What are three different levels of prison security?
10. What is the difference between probation and parole?

PART 3: ESSAY QUESTIONS

Present a logical argument with supporting facts that takes into consideration multiple interpretations. Answer in paragraph form. Be as specific and detailed as possible; avoid generalizations.

1. Briefly review the dominant ideologies and how they apply to the study and practice of corrections.
2. How useful is the critical criminological approach to understanding corrections?
3. Why do we incarcerate people, and what are the ironies that occur as a result of these factors?

4. In the 1980s, in response to the growing public fear of crime, the federal government developed a more conservative agenda. Why did this occur and what was the response?

5. In the 200-year history of corrections in America, what would you say are the three most significant changes that have occurred and why?

6. How has the criminal justice system been affected by 9/11?

7. In your opinion, what is the best way to analyze the special problems in corrections? Why is the method you chose superior to the others that currently exist?

NOTES

1. In 1984, Congress passed the *Violent Crime and Control Law Act*, which enabled tougher sanctions for those accused of particular kinds of crimes. Shortly after the federal system implemented its changes, most of the states followed suit. In 1986, Congress passed mandatory sentencing laws (i.e., mandatory minimums), which instructed judges to sanction those convicted of a crime to fixed lengths of time behind bars.

2. Those wishing an insight on solving the underlying causes of crime might turn to a number of introductory textbooks on the more general field of criminology.

3. Several capable histories of corrections in America have been written. Readers should be directed to these works if they want a more in-depth treatment (e.g., Rothman, 1971/2002).

4. Obviously there are exceptions. The Maryland Penitentiary, the second oldest state facility of its kind in the United States, was built in 1804 and is located in downtown Baltimore. Additionally, other variations exist like industrial prisons and the plantation model in the South.

Chapter 2

Myths of Corrections

INTRODUCTION

The correctional systems in the United States and elsewhere suffer from numerous problems (Welch, 1996; Austin and Irwin, 2001). One of the most pressing issues is that it is hard to obtain accurate information about jails, prisons, incarceration, correctional officers and prisoners. More importantly, many individuals, organizations, and institutions tend to develop misconceptions and stereotypes about correctional systems and convicts.[1]

This chapter identifies the dominant common falsehoods about corrections, reviews the most important cultural industries responsible for developing these misconceptions, and provides examples that demonstrate how these myths are created, perpetrated, and perpetuated.[2]

More specifically, in this chapter I examine the importance of mythmaking about crime, criminal justice, and corrections; look at why myths are often believed and taken as fact; and review the important role of cultural industries. I conclude with some thoughts on remedying this problem.

An earlier version of this chapter appeared as Ross (2003).

THE IMPORTANCE OF MYTHMAKING ABOUT CRIME, CRIMINAL JUSTICE, AND CORRECTIONS

Introduction

Most people have never been inside a holding cell, jail, or prison as an arrestee, inmate, CO, support staff, administrator, teacher, or visitor. Thus, the general public depends on secondary sources of information and their own (often inadequate) inferences about correctional facilities and the individuals who live and work within (e.g., Freeman, 2000: 3). Too often, the information on which the general public relies is a myth (Pepinsky and Jesilow, 1985; Kappeler, Blumberg, and Potter, 1996). Myths are not always false, but they exaggerate reality or ordinary experiences.

A myth is not necessarily arbitrary, false, or the result of poor research or differences of opinion. Rather it is "a traditional story of unknown authorship, with a historical basis [that] . . . explain[s] some event." Myths are "nonscientific, spoken or written fiction used as if it were a true account of some event" (Kappeler, Blumberg, and Potter, 1996: 2). Kappeler et al. add, "These crime fictions often take on new meanings as they are told and retold—and at some point . . . [are accepted as] truth for many people" (1996: 2). Myths are powerful windows into the beliefs of a society.

The average person is exposed to numerous myths on a regular basis. We have myths about certain individuals, professions, places, and experiences. Most of us do not stop to question the veracity of these stories; otherwise, we might be unnecessarily scared and possibly immobilized, afraid to do almost anything. We also don't have the time to evaluate every single piece of information we are presented with. We also have limited attention spans, we lack the desire, and we have competing pressures.

We accept myths for a variety of reasons. Myths make our lives easier. We do not question the truth behind many things in our lives. Myths are also presented as if they are true, told by someone who typically has some expert status. They are repeated on a frequent basis. And we manage to function reasonably well with this system of myths even though they are faulty. And almost each time they are told, they are slightly changed, by incorporating new information, in order to make them more believable. They take on new meanings and are believed by an increasing number of people.

The notion that the criminal justice system (e.g., Reiman, 1979/2003; Pepinsky and Jesilow, 1985; Kappeler, Blumberg, and Potter, 1996; Anonymous, 1997), corrections in general (e.g., Freeman, 2000), and various dimensions of corrections (e.g., Klofas and Toch, 1982; Schicher, 1992; McAuley, 1994; Saum, Inciardi, and Bennett, 1995; Peterson and Palumbo, 1997) have their fair share of myths is not new. Needless to say, what we know about the criminal justice system has some basis in fact and reality. Indeed, "[m]any of our contemporary issues of crime and justice are the product of some real event or social concern. Whether or not these events are based on 'truth' is largely irrelevant" because they gain a "larger than life" reality (Kappeler, Blumberg, and Potter: 2).

Perhaps nowhere is mythmaking more prominent than in the field of corrections. According to Roberts (1994: 1), "Prisons, as debated in political campaigns, dissected in university classrooms, and portrayed in newspapers and motion pictures, are often a caricature. The truth about prisons is at once less dramatic, less fixed, less utopian, less dystopian, and less frightening than stereotypes would suggest." To expand upon these ideas, I examine the interrelated topics of the existing myths within the crime and corrections arenas, as well as their creation, effects, and perpetrators.

What Are the Myths?

There are at least 16 interrelated myths about prisons, convicts, and COs, including but not limited to, and loosely ordered from least to most damaging:

- the extensiveness of library holdings;
- the viability of mandatory minimums;
- all convicts are guilty of a crime;
- the effectiveness of community corrections;
- the cost of certain amenities;
- the frequency of sex in prison;
- the physical appearance of convicts;
- the quality of health care behind bars;
- the access to free education;
- the violent nature of prisoners;
- the uncaring disposition of COs;
- the relationship between prison and crime rates;
- the kind/amount of punishment that convicts receive;
- the quality of the facilities that house prisoners;
- the utility of punishment as a deterrent; and
- the deterrent nature of incarceration.[3]

In short, these issues deal with facilities, processes, prisoners, correctional personnel, and sentences. Although each of the myths themselves deserve special attention, the focus of this chapter is on their creation and on the means through which this is accomplished.

How Are the Myths Created?

Myths have deep roots in our beliefs about people, society, institutions, including folklore and cultural expectations; they are often timeless. Stories are passed on from one person to another, from one community to another, from generation to generation, and are often accepted without much regard to (or knowledge about) the evidence that challenges them.

Several factors enable the development of myths, particularly those about crime and criminals. These include proper presentation and dissemination; following certain well-known themes; presentation by a credible source, particularly someone or an organization that is respected; targeting unpopular groups in society as perpetrators; making victims appear helpless and innocent; and, most importantly, using a variety of dissemination vehicles (e.g., the mass media).

All this is facilitated through a process usually referred to as the importation/exportation hypothesis (Irwin and Cressey, 1962). Here ideas, attitudes, behaviors, fashions, and styles (i.e., elements of a particular lifestyle) that originate in prison make their way into the streets, ghettos, and barrios and those that begin on the outside enter into the correctional facilities. We do not know exactly where this transmission belt starts, but this is not really important. This idea suggests that a complex and important relationship exists between attitudes and behaviors that come into the jail and prison and those that go out. It is not certain which precedes which, almost like the classic chicken-and-egg scenario.

In sum, ideas and beliefs are socially (Berger and Luckmann, 1966) or culturally (Heiner, 2001) constructed.[4] Orientations do not exist in a vacuum but are shaped by a variety of individuals and organizations. They occur in a context. The end result is similar to what happens in the game of "broken telephone," where the original communication often bears little resemblance to the final utterance. With reference to information about corrections, in general, our lack of firsthand knowledge makes it understandable that our opinions are based upon mediated truths (Jones and Schmid, 2000).

Effects of Crime Myths Concerning Corrections

Crime myths "have numerous effects on our perceptions; we may not even be conscious that they are at work." There are six main purposes of crime myths, and these are also applicable to corrections. First, myths "organize our views of crime, criminals, and the proper operation of the criminal justice system" (Kappeler, Blumberg, and Potter: 3).

Second, they "support and maintain prevailing views of crime, criminals, and the criminal justice system" (Kappeler, Blumberg, and Potter: 3).

Third, these misrepresentations "reinforce the current designation of conduct as criminal, support existing practices of crime control, and provide the background assumptions for future designation of conduct as criminal" (Kappeler, Blumberg, and Potter: 3–4).

Fourth, the myths are "convenient[ly] used to fill gaps in knowledge and to provide answers to questions social science either cannot answer or has failed to address" (Kappeler, Blumberg, and Potter: 5).

Fifth, the stereotypes "provide for an outlet for emotionalism and channel emotion into action" (Kappeler, Blumberg, and Potter: 5). In general, they "seem[s] to follow a series of recurrent patterns. These patterns allow a disproportionate amount of . . . attention to be focused on a few isolated criminal events or issues" (Kappeler, Blumberg, and Potter: 5).

Finally, with respect to corrections, myths prevent rational discussion about related issues and usually contributes to the same types of mistakes continuing to be made in this policy arena.

Who Perpetrates the Myths?

By all means, criminals, convicts, ex-cons, and COs play a role, when they provide us with war stories, particularly when we ask them questions like "What was it really like when you did time?" or "How was it like when you worked in the prison or guarded so and so?"

Powerful groups with vested interests, however, are mainly responsible for developing, crafting, shaping, disseminating, and perpetuating the majority of myths about corrections. Many of the misrepresentations originate or are reinforced in the media, government (through various politicians and bureaucracies), correctional institutions, interest groups, universities, and consulting companies by reporters, broadcasters, editors, elected and appointed officials, bureaucrats, public relations specialists, information officers/specialists, prisoners and COs alike, wardens, experts, academics, and consultants. These interests can have either competing or complementary agendas.

These actors disseminate myths about jails, prisons, COs and convicts and to try and promote policies and practices that are favorable to their own objectives and consistencies. Their efforts are typically done to minimize external involvement in their programs, in the operation of facilities, and also to help sell products or services to increase their firms' revenues. This provides a greater degree of autonomy than they would otherwise have.

WHY MYTHS ABOUT CORRECTIONS ARE SUCCESSFUL?

There are roughly four interconnected reasons why myths about crime and corrections are so effective. They include, but are not limited to, the power of those creating the myths, the costs involved in obtaining accurate information about jails and prisons, the apathy of the public, and the convincing nature of the myths.

Many who promote myths about corrections possess a considerable amount of resources (i.e., money, personnel, expertise, and access). Membership organizations like the American Correctional Association (ACA) and the American Jails Association (AJA) (the largest professional associations for correctional practitioners in the United States) can and do perpetrate myths about corrections. The ACA, for example, is a large dues-paying organization with many influential members. Although the goal of the ACA is to "improve the image of those who work in corrections . . . [through] . . . improving the conditions of corrections professionals and those who are incarcerated through the development of standards" (Gondles, 1999), it also shapes dialogue on prisons. It is probably less biased because it tries to enhance the professionalism of correctional workers in particular. The government at the local, state, and federal level, to whom jails and prisons are accountable, and many media outlets are also well funded, respectively, through tax revenues and the sales of their products (i.e., advertising).

One way to gather important information about corrections is through qualitative research, especially ethnographic studies. This typically means face-to-face interviews and/or observation of subjects under investigation. Conducting research inside prisons is extremely difficult, and one of the biggest problems is access. Complex and protracted negotiations with prison officials often needs to occur before researchers can interview convicts and correctional workers. Even if this opportunity is granted, gaining the trust and cooperation from prisoners and COs is still a challenge.

Because many correctional facilities are usually located in relatively remote areas, researchers, policymakers and the media are rarely motivated or have the opportunity to conduct independent research and learn firsthand about prison conditions. Gaining access is very difficult. Unless you know someone inside, usually the visit you are allowed is very short. The average person has too many time constraints; thus, they typically have to rely on inaccurate information (Ross, 2000c: 119–120). The lion's share of the public are simply overburdened with the problems of making a living, taking care of children, and so on; thus, attention to many social problems becomes a luxury, especially when it involves taking the time to find accurate information (pp. 119–120). Most correctional officers and administrators do not want to talk to outsiders (i.e., researchers or journalists) because they are worried that they will uncover some sort of problem, reveal this to the public, unnecessarily embarrass them or their correctional facility, and then they will ultimately be sanctioned (i.e., suspended, demoted, fired, etc.) by their organization. Convicts who you want to speak to can be moved around quite frequently. With respect to the federal correctional system, the person who is convicted in New York City can be moved to Alabama or Oklahoma or Alaska if the FBOP wants to. Finally, myths appear to be convincing. Mythmakers are very skilled at getting the message across and tapping into issues that the public feel are important (Beckett and Sasson, 2003).

The public forms its knowledge of corrections through a complex interaction of mythmakers (i.e., initiators, sources, propagandists, and gatekeepers), mediums, and recipients. This knowledge is predicated on shared or misinterpreted meanings among convicts, reporters, researchers, prison information officers, and the public, and these messages are spread through a vast array of cultural industries.

THE CONTRIBUTION OF CULTURAL INDUSTRIES

Introduction

Some businesses exploit the styles and images of deviant subcultures or make references to these groups to generate income (Lopiano-Misdom and De Luca, 1997; Klein, 2000: Chapter 3). This process, referred to as the commodification of culture, uses images and symbols about jails, prisons, COs, and incarceration to convey a particular lifestyle, sell their products and services, and—consciously or unconsciously—perpetrate and perpetuate the myths about corrections.

Cultural industries do not simply exist in a vacuum; they function within a social context and have ideological implications. Schiller (1989) identified cultural industries that "provide symbolic goods and services" (p. 30) and divides them into two tiers. The first one he categorizes as "publishing, the press, film, radio, television, photography, recording, advertising, sports, and . . . the information industry" (p. 30). The second category, on the other hand, consists of "services, . . . displayed in relatively permanent installations," like "museums, art galleries, amusement parks . . . , shopping malls, and corporate 'public spaces' " (pp. 30–31). The former is more transitory and the latter is more permanent. Schiller notes that "all economic activity produces symbolic as well as material goods. In fact, the two are generally inseparable" (p. 31).

Cultural industries reflect and shape public opinion. They can influence policymakers and legislators, ultimately impacting the laws that are debated, introduced, and passed. In some cases cultural industries glamorize or romanticize jail and prison life. The settings, individuals, and issues are typically dramatized for entertainment value. For instance, the camaraderie with or conflict between correctional officers/administrators and prisoners is often romanticized or exaggerated, giving the public a false impression of the range of relationships that exist inside correctional facilities.

Cultural industries are important in constructing the popular culture of corrections, a culture that is "the product of a complicated, ongoing evolutionary process organized around the creation and consistent reinforcement of a core set of negative stereotypes and their associated imagery. This core of negative stereotypes imagery defines the constructed image template of corrections" (Freeman, 2000: 10).

There are eight primary cultural industries that perpetuate myths about incarceration.[5] Organized from least to most important, they are fashion, advertising, music, fiction, documentaries, television, motion pictures, and the news media. Needless to say, these cultural industries are periodically interwoven.[6] Understanding that the styles of deviant or criminal subcultures are often glorified may increase the appeal of jail or prison to those who have never served time.

Fashion

It has long been recognized that clothing, jewelry, and accessories—and, by extension, the fashions and styles we wear or adopt—consciously or unconsciously reflect our values, moods, personality, or self-image, and provide us with a sense of belonging or identity. Clothing can also be used to separate people and categorize them into groups, thereby providing a type of psychological and, later, physical distance among real, imagined, or potential antagonists. It should be noted that fashions are not simply embedded in dress but can extend to speech, hair, and body customization (Goffman, 1959; Miller, 1996). Scholars have long recognized that particular subcultures wear unique styles of clothing (e.g., Tunnell, 2000: 48–51). Over the past four decades, prisoners' clothing styles have been copied by mainstream clothing manufacturers.[7]

Because certain articles of clothing are seen as hip, they are adopted into mainstream culture, by consumers who feel that the fashion does something for them. In turn, this connection can make prison seem acceptable and those who wear the articles some-what radical or rebellious.

Advertising

Prisoners and prisons are often used in advertising campaigns for shock and/or enter-tainment value. By grabbing the public's attention, commercials enable corporations and political organizations to gain attention, sell products and services, and promote and gather support for certain points of view. Although convict and correctional themes are traditionally used in sales of security-related products in mediums that sell prod-ucts to the Correctional Industrial Complex (e.g., Christie, 1993), four relatively recent efforts include either display or television advertisements run by Pot Noodle, Benetton, Camel Cigarettes, and the Republican National Party.

The potential to incorporate jails, prisons and corrections for advertising campaigns and branding is limitless. This process largely depends on the creativity and ability of commercial artists and copywriters to link the symbols and images of this environment with the products and services to be sold.

Music

The connection between music and prisons is hardly new (Fisher-Giorlando, 1987). Several famous musicians have done time, and many individuals formerly incarcerated have gone on to successful musical careers after being released. Moreover, a handful of musicians have been granted access to correctional facilities to play concerts and a number of well-known musicians have written popular protest songs focusing on the plight of the incarcerated. Some of these musicians draw upon their own jail or prison experiences as they write and record songs. Naturally, this prompts the question of why these individuals become successful musicians and what kind of role prison played in their career. In short, did it help or hinder their success? These musicians might have turned their prison experiences into something positive, but this does not necessarily imply causality.

The music-prison phenomenon is prevalent across a number of different music genres including country and western, rock and roll, blues, and bluegrass rap, and hip-hop (Tunnell, 1992; 1995; Hamm and Ferrell, 1994). Additionally, we have successful record labels such as Death Row records, founded by the late and controversial Suge Knight, that draw on the convict theme.

Fictional Treatments

Each year, an increasing number of fictional treatments—including poems, short stories, and novels with prison settings—are written and published (Franklin, 1982; 1998; Massey, 1989). Perhaps the most important fictional medium is the novel because of the possibility that it can be used as the basis for a movie, video, or television series. In general, "the prison novel balances attention on the bureaucratic or institutional setting or atmosphere with a focus on the character caught up in it" (Massey: 3). "Some, like *Cool Hand Luke* by Donn Pearce or Edward Bunker's *No Beast So Fierce*, received recognition when movies based on the novels became popular. Unfortunately, the vast majority of these novels appear briefly, often only in paperback, and then . . . [go] out of print" (Massey: 2).

Fictional books based on prison can be divided into two camps: those written by "professional writers who have not served extensive time behind bars" and those produced by convicts or ex-convicts (Massey: 2). The first category includes Stanley Elkin's *A Bad Man*; John Cheever's *Falconer*; Stephen King's *The Green Mile* series that includes *The Two Dead Girls*, *The Mouse on the Mile*, *Night Journey*, *Coffey's Hams*, *The Bad Death of Eduard Delacroix*, and *Coffey on the Mile*; and Tim Willocks' *Green River Rising*.[8]

There are also a growing number of well-known books written by American convicts or ex-cons, including Jack London, Malcolm Braly, and Edward Bunker. Massey (1989), who performed an in-depth study of these books, said that there is "a progression of experiences found in virtually all prison novels": entry, the world of prisons, and crisis (pp. 5–6). Additional themes are repeated in each novel: "the alien world of the cell block, the animosity between the convict and his keepers, the macho inmate in a violent social environment, and the criticism of a country that treats humans this way" (Massey: 6).

The setting in fictional prison stories "is often pictured as a refuge from the trivial or prosaic" (Duncan, 1996: 13). As a refuge, its importance lies in the "prison as the quintessential academy and prison as a catalyst of intense friendship" (Duncan, 1996: 13). Given that the reading public is much smaller than the mass media, it is difficult to measure the importance of this influence.

Documentaries

A growing number of documentaries and docudramas have attempted to present the reality of prisons. Some of these have been made for television news shows such as "48 Hours" and "Primetime" or on cable TV stations such as Court TV. To accomplish their goals, these productions often trace the history of different correctional institutions, cite statistics (including the number of cells and cost to house prisoners), and use archival photographs, newsreel footage, reenactments, and interviews with current or ex-prisoners, COs, chaplains, and others. They often also incorporate copious footage of the prison (including its graveyard and cellblocks), dramatic language to describe individuals and incidents, and haunting music as a backdrop. Some are narrated by news personalities like Ted Koppel, Bill Kurtis, Hedrick Smith, Mike Wallace, and Tom Wicker or actors like Andre Braugher, Tim Robbins, or Paul Servino. Other documentaries mainly consist of a series of "talking heads," including convicts, COs, prison wardens, reformers, and judges.

Regardless of who produces and distributes these documentaries, they routinely feature stereotypical images of prisoners who are tattoo-laden, muscle-bound, and intimidating. Although students may enjoy these videos more than the class lecturer, these films often serve to reinforce the myth of convicts as violent predators.

Television

For the average viewer, television is easily accessible and relatively pervasive (e.g., airports, bars, and doctor's offices). Anyone who has access receives its message. Many people watch hours of television each day, and viewers do not have to be literate or even speak English to understand the content of a program. Television is also a powerful disseminator of style, which has a predominant visual component.

Two basic types of programs relevant to corrections have been produced for television broadcast: so-called infomercials and the series. First, during the 1980s, a number of criminal justice "reality TV" shows such as *America's Most Wanted*, *Cops*, *Top Cops*, and *Stories of the Highway Patrol* became popular. "Following the format of information commercials [infomercials] . . . television crime programs began to blend entertainment and government-sponsored messages" (Kappeler, Blumberg, and Potter: 11). These programs depended on the access and statement of "government officials, well-known relatives of crime victims, and law enforcement officers to inform the public about crime" (Kappeler, Blumberg, and Potter: 11). Although most focused on police work, only a few were done on prisons. It is unclear whether there was minimal or no public demand for correctional themes using this format.

Very few prison series have been produced for the American television market. Yet, there are a few exceptions: In 1997, the Home Box Office (HBO) cable station introduced *Oz*, which lasted six seasons. Created by Tom Fontana and produced by both Fontana and Barry Levinson (known for his critically acclaimed police series *Homicide: Life on the Streets*), the program, acknowledged as being HBO's first and longest series, looked at the lives of convicts and correctional workers in an urban correctional facility. This series somewhat resembled a soap opera with secretive relationships amongst the staff and inmates and frequently portrayed prisoners as predatory homosexuals or psychopathic killers who suffered from severe psychological problems. Only six to eight shows were aired each season.

Seemingly, both the viewing public and many criminal justice practitioners—particularly COs—thought the show was an accurate reflection of reality. On the other hand, many convicts found the series to be a gross distortion of prison reality. They did not accept this program as an honest representation of prison life. In fact, in the spring of 2000, the popular television comedy series *Saturday Night Live* did an episode poking fun at and parodying *Oz* (see Exhibit 2.1).

In the fall of 2005, the FOX Broadcasting Company debuted a new series called *Prison Break*. Directed by Paul Scheuring, the show focuses on the exploits of character Michael Scofield, played by actor Wentworth Miller. The protagonist's brother has been sentenced to death (naturally, for a crime he did not commit) and is awaiting his execution at the fictitious Fox River State Penitentiary. Scofield, who just happens to be a structural engineer with plans to the prison, commits a crime and is fortuitously

---

EXHIBIT 2.1

Oz

Between 1997 and 2003, HBO, a cable television station, aired *Oz*, a one-hour drama that was set at a fictional maximum-security prison called Oswald State Correctional Facility. Developed by Tom Fontana and Barry Levinson, it portrays the lives and struggles of inmates, correctional workers, and administrators in an experimental part of the prison called Emerald City. Here the emphasis was on rehabilitation and learning responsibility while inmates were behind bars. The characters, however, appeared some what stereo-typical and the cell blocks and tiers appeared to be made up of the "requisite" number of races and ethnic groups.

What explains the longevity of the series? In order for a series to air each season the producers (i.e., Fontana and Levinson), enter into negotiations with the network, in this case HBO, and determine how many shows they would do. The producers have to understand their relative competition and competing demands on the time for their personnel. For example, many are involved in other movies and projects. Producers and directors do not want to subcontract too much because then they give up control. There are definite start-up costs. It takes a while for directors to get in the groove with respect to having the appropriate personnel (actors, writers, etc.). Then after a while viewer fatigue sets in. The search for new issues to build a story around is more difficult. Steven Bochco, who produced *L.A. Law and NYPD Blues*, negotiated ten or more episodes, with Bochco as the last step in quality control.

---

sentenced to the same prison as his brother. Scofield's objective is to help his brother escape and, until this is accomplished, survive the prison experience.

Motion Pictures

Our attitudes and beliefs about jails and prisons are also shaped by movies (Crowther, 1989; Parish, 1991; Rafter, 2000: Chapter 5). Many of the images we have about prisons come from movies (Jones and Schmid, 2000). Whether these Hollywood films are screened in movie houses, transferred to videotape or DVDs and sold to televi-sion networks, or sold on the video/DVD market,[9] they present us with many of our definitive images of prison life. Indeed, movies that deal at some level with corrections could probably be placed on a continuum that ranks the film on the amount it deals with a correctional theme. For example, the Hollywood movie *Shawshank Redemption* (with actors Tim Robbins and Morgan Freeman) contrasts with *The Rock* (with actors Sean Connery and Nicholas Cage). "The prison film, a claustrophobic offshoot of the gangster film, was by 1933 a thriving sub-genre in its own right" (Shadoian, 1979: 169). "Public attitudes toward criminals in general, the types of people who are or should be incarcerated, and prison conditions that should be tolerated become evident through the treatment of criminal characters in film" (Munro-Bjorklund, 1991: 56–57).

EXHIBIT 2.2

Selected Hollywood movies on jails, prisons, or dealing with correctional themes

American Me

Birdsong

Birdman of Alcatraz

Brubaker

Chattahoochee

CB40

Con Air

The Green Mile

Iceman

The Longest Yard (1974 and 2005 versions)

One Flew over the Cuckoo's Nest

Shawshank Redemption

Since the 1930s, there have been more than 100 movies on adult male prisons alone (Cheatwood, 1998). Like television, this form of communication is accessible to most people. One need not be literate in order to understand the motion picture industry's basic message.

Few people have systematically investigated films about prisons. Although Munro-Bjorklund (1991: 56–61) examines the motion pictures made in the aftermath of the Attica riot (1971), it was not until Cheatwood that we had a more comprehensive treatment of all Hollywood movies on incarceration. As Cheatwood notes, "[M]uch of the research that does exist is highly impressionistic or treats only one film, one national event, or one limited time period." According to Travisino, "Hollywood and the television writers continue to portray the vilest aspects of prison life, and the public is led to believe that nothing can be accomplished because that's 'the way it is' with the system" (1980: 1, as quoted by Cheatwood: 21).

A handful of scholars have written about motion pictures that depict prisons. Rafter (2000), for example, suggests that prison movies serve four purposes: "to identify with the perfect man; . . . to participate in perfect friendships; . . . to fantasize about sex and rebellion; and . . . to acquire insider information about the apparent realities of prison life" (p. 123). According to her, "Traditional prison films invite us to identify with heroes, even superheroes" (p. 123). Prison films contain an abundant supply of "ideal companions, buddies more loyal and true than any on the outside" (p. 124). She adds, "[P]rison films with male inmates often have a homosexual subtext in which the buddy gets both a perfect friend and a lover" (p. 125). Finally, prison movies "offer the inside scoop, a window onto the inaccessible but riveting world of the prison" (p. 127).

Cheatwood analyzed fictional movies about adult male civilian prisons produced between 1929 and 1995. He classified the films into four categories based on different eras: Depression, 1929–1942; Rehabilitation, 1943–1962; Confinement, 1963–1980; and the Administrative Era, 1981–1995. He claims that "[p]rison era films . . . revolve around the themes of confinement, justice, authority and release. These components, . . . enable us to see how our theories and public positions are translated and presented to the public" (p. 210).

Cheatwood believes that Hollywood movies on prison have a "subtle" rather "than an immediate" impact on the viewing public (p. 211). He states, "People see pictures that support their established and currently held views of the world, and films can only gradually reshape or crystallize amorphous visions, perceptions, or ideas that the viewing public holds" (p. 211).

In covering films about prisons, Cheatwood states, "These have varied from military prison escape films to musicals about maximum security institutions" (p. 211). He limits his sample to "films whose predominant subject was incarceration in male, adult, civilian correctional facility. There are several pragmatic reasons for this limitation. In the public, the 'prison problem' tends to be identified with adult, male, civilian facilities. So few 'probation and parole' films exist that they do not constitute a genre at all. Although there are quite a few films about women's prisons, many are sexploitation films" (p. 211).

Cheatwood argues, "Within each of these eras, the treatment of distinct elements and the manner of their combination has been relatively consistent through the films produced. Further, the nature of these films displays a relationship both to the academic theories of corrections predominant in the era and to changes and events in the pragmatic operations of corrections in the nation" (p. 215).

Many of these movies have become very predictable. Rafter (2000: 117–123) suggests that stock characters, plots, and themes are prevalent in all prison movies. With respect to characters, we have "convict buddies, a paternalistic warden, a cruel guard, a craven snitch, a bloodthirsty convict and the young hero" (p. 118). In terms of repeated plots, we see riots, escapes, or the planning that goes into these events (p. 120). A particularly redundant theme is "rebellion against injustice. Innocents, . . . are being punished by diabolical officers and nasty fellow convicts. . . . To restore justice, the prisoners sometimes take matters into their own hands. . . . At others, someone comes to their rescue" (pp. 121–122).[10]

Finally, one of the biggest misrepresentations embedded in motion pictures is that of female prisoners (Morey, 1995; Faith, 1997). Few Hollywood films give accurate accounts of incarcerated women. Those that are available are generally pornographic in nature (often referred to as *B movies*) and include buxom blondes and "butch" guards. These films emphasize themes of domination, lesbianism, lust, and voyeurism.

News Media

Americans receive their news from a variety of sources: television, radio, magazines, newspapers, and, increasingly, the Internet. In fact, according to Cheatwood, "[m]ost people in the general public have formed their images of what prison life is 'actually' like from the mass media" (1998: 210).

In the twentieth century, because of advances in communications technology, the mass media has gained enormous influence over the kinds of messages communicated, heard, and seen, as well as the interpretation of important events. The mass media is probably the most important vehicle for conveying and shaping the cultural construction of crime and criminals. The media operates under the myth of objectivity—that reporting is balanced and fair. However, on closer examination we will find that most outlets have ideological and political agendas. News media outlets, in particular, are in a perfect position to communicate these misrepresentations.

By the same token, members of the news media serve a variety of functions including, but not limited to, and in increasing order of importance, providing information, educating the public, sharing opinions, stimulating debate, reinforcing dominant stereotypes, and most of all making a profit for their owners (Lichter, Rothman, and Lichter, 1986; Barak, 1995; Brownstein, 1995; Parenti, 1995).

At any news organization, the staff consists of a variety of reporters. The variability is largely a function of an organization's resources, and this in turn is fuelled by revenues and perceptions of audience demands (Ross, 1998a; 2000c: Chapter 2). Larger newspapers typically employ a crime or police reporter. Some, like *The New York Times*, can have upward of ten police or crime reporters. Unfortunately, few journalists are assigned to cover the prisons or jails on a full- or part-time basis. According to Chermack, "News media do not have a corrections beat that fulfils the same function as a police or court beat" (1998: 97).

One must also recognize that, in most news organizations, crime reporting is often an entry-level position. As part of a natural career path, most reporters may begin with this beat and then graduate to covering city hall, state politics, and eventually—if they are lucky or so inclined—federal politics. "Prompted by the nature of the media industry, television and newspaper reporters focus on 'hot topics' of entertainment value. In the early stages of myth development, media frenzy develops which allows for expanded coverage of isolated and unique events. Typically, the appearance of an uncritical newspaper or magazine article exploring a unique social problem starts the chain of events" (Kappeler, Blumberg, and Potter: 6). The journalist has "uncovered a 'new' social evil. Other journalists, not wanting to be left out, jump on the band wagon" (Kappeler, Blumberg, and Potter: 6).

Few content analyses of newspaper coverage of corrections have been performed (Jacobs and Brooks, 1983; Freeman, 1996; 1998; Ross, 1999). First, Jacobs and Brooks (1983) examined newspapers, periodicals, and television news broadcasts about prison that appeared in 1976. Second, Freeman (1996/1998) examined "the content of 1,546 newspaper articles concerning corrections that appeared through the United States between September 8, 1994 and November 24, 1995" (1998: 203).[11] Finally, Ross (1999), in an attempt to understand the issues focused on in corrections reporting, the prominence of the stories, the reporters who are covering this topic, and the sources of the stories, performed a content analysis of a year's worth (i.e., 1999) of criminal justice reporting appearing in *The Baltimore Sun*. Unfortunately, these studies are mere snapshots in the overall picture of corrections reporting. Moreover, the last two stud-ies might depict regional patterns of corrections reporting better than they do national content.

Members of the news media have been accused of a whole host of sins including, but not limited to, sensationalism, bias (selectivity), censorship, lack of interest in "serious and complicated questions," and superficiality. Needless to say, the reporters encounter several obstacles when trying to research articles or stories on correctional facilities.

According to Davis, "Much has been written about the emergence of the correctional 'boom' in America, yet for all the media attention, prisons remain a largely unchecked arm of American governance. In many states, corrections is among the largest budget items, yet coverage of correctional facilities and the convicts incarcerated in them is scarce" (1998).

Despite the United States having the highest incarceration rate and a so-called prison crisis, in the main, corrections is not a hot topic in the news. Why is this crim-inal justice agency avoided by the news media? There are probably two major reasons: lack of access by reporters and lack of interest by the public.

The amount of access reporters have to jails and prisons varies according to the type of facility and jurisdiction (Talbott, 1988; 1989; Anonymous, 1989; 1998a; 1998b; Hincle, 1996; Kindel, 1998). Most prisons rarely allow prisoners to be interviewed by reporters. Much of what *is* reported often comes from limited or biased sources, such as prison pub-lic information officers. In most cases, members of the news media are not allowed ac-cess to correctional facilities or to the convicts housed within. For example, jails and prisons generally do not share or announce news concerning the murders or assaults of prisoners with the news media. Each correctional facility has its own policies and procedures and some are more strict than others. The Supreme Court has derived "three major principles concerning prison access": The First Amendment "does not guarantee the public or the press a right to obtain information from prisons." Second, "[j]ournalists have no greater rights of access than [does] the general public." Third, "[t]he public's need for access to information will be balanced against other societal needs, such as law enforcement interests and personal privacy" (*Pell v. Procunier*, 1974; *Saxbe v. Washington Post*, 1974).

Another reason for the lack of coverage may have to do with a "self-fulfilling prophecy" of sorts. In other words, the news media does not report on corrections; thus, the public is not interested. Since a wider audience is not interested, neither is the news media. This is somewhat ironic given the "if it bleeds it leads" mentality of the media. Why do they or how can they focus so much time especially on TV, to murders, shoot-ings, and other things, but not turn to the inevitable result—prisons and corrections?

SOLUTIONS

How can we change this state of affairs? The following seven solutions, listed from least to most important, could possibly minimize or counterbalance the production and dissemination of myths produced by cultural industries.

First, building on Sir John Fielding's (a British magistrate) original desire that prisons need to be more open to inspection and investigation, correctional facilities must better facilitate interviews of prisoners by the media and academic researchers. Hopefully, these reports will document how problems with jails and prisons and of COs are commonplace.

Second, correctional facilities need to submit to periodic open houses through which the public is allowed a relatively comprehensive look at what happens within jail and prison walls. Admittedly, not all parts of correctional institutions will or should be open to the public. And it must be conducted in such a fashion as to not encourage a zoo-like atmosphere. Facilitating the public to see as much as possible about what goes on behind the razor wire will help them get a better picture of the concerns of convicts and COs.

Third, the mass media and especially Hollywood need to make a better effort to produce films with more accurate and less sensational portrayals of convicts, COs, and the criminal justice system. Criminology and criminal justice instructors should endeavor to use realistic accounts of life in prisons in their classroom instructional material (e.g., documentaries, autobiographies, and the like).

Fourth, we also should help journalists gain access to prisons. The reporters also need to be better educated about the conditions of prisoners and the powers of correctional officers and administrators. Journalism schools could be advantageous in this respect; perhaps some sort of partnership with J schools and academics might be beneficial.

Fifth, guest lecturers who have done time or who work in correctional facilities should be used more often and more effectively to talk about the reality of prisons. Ex-cons and correctional employees and administrators should be invited to speak to news organizations and to groups of students. They can offer a needed dose of realism to the classroom, more so than can many of the academic texts we currently use. We should caution our speakers against the overuse of sensationalism and counsel them to avoid a succession of "war stories."

Sixth, we might also depend more heavily on autobiographical books written by convicts and ex-cons (e.g., Jackson, 1970; Abbott, 1981; Abu-Jamal, 1996; Baca, 2001; Ross and Richards, 2003). These texts, although often biased or sensationalized for effect, can sometimes bring to light issues that are overlooked by other experts.

Seventh, a public relations or awareness campaign could bring to people's attention the powerful effects of our cultural institutions in shaping what we know about jails and prisons. Building on the success of the Adbusters campaign, documented in books like *No Logo* (Klein, 2000), this should hold these entities more accountable.

We live in a time when more is demanded of the public because the issues are so numerous, complex, and interrelated. Some people "tune out," but a modern representative democracy demands a public that is alert, well informed, and engaged (Ross, 2000a: Chapter 7). The ability to critically analyze controversial evidence is demanded. Finally, the misrepresentation of corrections, the misinformation, and the outright lies propagated by the government and media needs to be regularly challenged (Herman and Chomsky, 1988).

Unfortunately, there is a tendency amongst the general public to believe popular conceptions and myths about correctional facilities and convicts, especially their entitlements in U.S. jails and prisons, and adopt popular misconceptions. Most are in fact sweeping generalizations that contradict empirical reality.

KEY TERMS

American Correctional Association (ACA)   mass media
commodification of culture   myth
content analysis   news media
cultural industry   style
documentary
importation/exportation hypothesis

REVIEW QUESTIONS

PART 1: MULTIPLE-CHOICE QUESTIONS

1. Which of the following is NOT an effect of crime myths?

    a. the organization of our views of crime
    b. a conceptual framework from which to identify certain social issues as crime related
    c. the development of our personal opinions on issues of justice
    d. the prevailing views of crime are supported and maintained
    e. the complication of our understanding of crime

2. What is the name of the thesis that "suggests that it is difficult to track the sources of fashion, subcultures, etc. that exist in prison. Some are simply taken from the streets and intensified in prison. Others are actually created in prison" and make their way back to the street

    a. importation/exportation
    b. commodification of culture
    c. John Irwin
    d. regulation/free market
    e. cultural criminology

3. The majority of fictional writing on prison life is done by

    a. women
    b. inmates
    c. ex-cons
    d. males
    e. journalists

4. Cheatwood limits his analysis to Hollywood movies on

    a. all prisons in America
    b. adult civilian facilities
    c. adult male civilian facilities
    d. female civilian facilities
    e. prisons and mental institutions

5. Which of the following is probably the most important factor in the creation and sustainment of myths about crime and corrections?

   a. university professors
   b. mass media
   c. government
   d. prisoners
   e. all of the above

6. According to Cheatwood, about how many American films on prisons and incarceration have been produced between 1929 and 1995?

   a. 25
   b. 33
   c. 50
   d. 75
   e. 100

7. What did Depression-Era corrections films focus on?

   a. authority
   b. confinement
   c. escape
   d. justice
   e. release

8. A typical big-city newspaper would most likely not have which of the following types of reporters?

   a. court reporter
   b. crime reporter
   c. police reporter
   d. corrections reporter
   e. legislative reporter

PART 2: SHORT-ANSWER QUESTIONS

1. List the four issues, identified by Cheatwood, that are addressed in all prison movies.
2. What is meant by the expression "Commodification of Culture"?
3. What are the four eras (time periods) in which Cheatwood classifies prison movies?
4. What is a myth?
5. List five myths of corrections.
6. What are four solutions to reduce the myths of prisons?
7. List three reasons why Hollywood films on prisons should be critically examined.

8. What is a cultural industry?
9. What is the importation/exportation hypothesis?

PART 3: ESSAY QUESTIONS

1. Why do you think there have been few fictionalized television series on prisons?
2. Which organization/s is/are the most powerful in their attempts to mythologize prisons?
3. Which of the previously outlined suggestions will best minimize the number of myths about corrections?
4. Choose three primary cultural industries that create myths and describe how these industries create myths.
5. Who creates myths about the correctional system and how are the myths created?
6. Why are myths about corrections so successful?
7. Why is it in the best interests of certain groups to continue promoting myths about corrections?

NOTES

1. This chapter uses the words *myths*, *misconceptions*, *misrepresentations*, and *stereotypes* interchangeably.
2. This chapter's interpretation is mainly confined to the United States; however, the findings can easily be generalized to many of the advanced industrialized democracies.
3. For a more detailed examination of these myths, see for example my book *We Are Not in Oz Anymore: Exploring Myths about Prisons* (New York University Press, forthcoming).
4. Although Surette (1998: xvii) suggests that there are actually three "dominant social construction of reality engines," a discussion of this issue is beyond the scope of this chapter. Additionally, secondary sources may or may not be accurate.
5. Cultural industries are often analyzed through the academic prism of cultural studies or research on popular culture. Radio and sports are not covered in this chapter.
6. For example, it is difficult to separate the origins of the messages conveyed in a movie set in a prison and say the book upon which the film was based (e.g., *Dead Man Walking*).
7. This has probably evolved from or interwoven with what might be referred to as *gang style* (e.g., Miller, 1995).
8. Some outsiders have criticized these professional writers "as writing primarily for profit, . . . Needless to say, those profits, even for the most famous novelists . . . have been meagre" (Massey, 1989: 2).
9. The video/DVD market, an offshoot of the Hollywood movie industry, helps to shape teenagers' thinking. They are impressionable, and may lack, but desire, many of the entertainment venues available to adults. Bored by family TV shows, they look for excitement at the video store. Video stores rent numerous bad movies, often X or R rated, about prisons that were aired on television, public or commercial (cable).
10. Not only have academics commented on the stereotypical images presented by Hollywood films, but so has the correctional industry (e.g., Zaner, 1989).
11. Once again, a more complete review of these is available in Ross (2003).

PART II

Problems for Convicts and Correctional Facilities

Chapter 3

Misuse of Jails

INTRODUCTION

Almost all towns, cities, municipalities, and counties have a jail. They can be very small facilities or large institutions like Rikers Island in New York City or Los Angeles County Jail that resemble minicities in their own right (Irwin, 1985; Thompson and Mays, 1991).

Most of the public fail to distinguish between jails and prisons. People who are sent to jail are typically either pretrial detainees or individuals convicted of relatively minor crimes (known as misdemeanors). Pretrial detainees are determined by a judge, magistrate, or commissioner not able to make bail; cannot be released on their own recognizance; or have been accused of committing a serious felony and perceived to be a flight risk (i.e., they will not voluntarily return to court), and thus they await further processing by the criminal justice system.

Individuals who cannot make bail are typically poor, powerless, and come from the lower socioeconomic classes in society. Thus it should come as no surprise that most jails and correctional facilities in the United States predominantly house African Americans, Hispanics, Native Americans, and poor whites. They are often young, uneducated or poorly educated, and unemployed. This phenomenon has been pejoratively called warehousing (Miller, 1996; Welch, 1996: 172; Irwin, 2005). Very few of these pretrial detainees will have the nerve and financial resources to fight their cases. Instead they often plead guilty and then are released to the street for "time served." Regardless, they are saddled with a

Special thanks to Burk Foster for comments on this chapter.

EXHIBIT 3.1

Classics in Corrections

Jerome G. Miller's *Search and Destroy*

Longtime prison activist and researcher Jerome Miller (1996) reviewed his experience and research conducted by his organization, the National Center on Institutions and Alternatives, that explains what happens to the average inmate in several big city jails in America. He noticed that a disproportionate number of individuals (mainly poor African-American and Hispanic youths) who are confined in jails cannot be released on their own recognizance and are thus forced to remain locked up for long periods of times before their release can be secured by a public defender. They often plead guilty to a lesser charge and are released on time served. The later part of Miller's book consists of his interpretation of how criminological theory is decidedly racist.

---

criminal record that haunts them the rest of their lives (Miller, 1996). Despite their legitimate uses, holding cells and jails are routinely used as makeshift "drunk tanks, truant halls, and shelters for the homeless and mentally ill" (Welch: 167).

FUNCTIONS OF JAILS

Jails have approximately ten interrelated functions:

1. "receive individuals pending arraignment and hold them awaiting trial, conviction, or sentencing";

2. "readmit probation, parole, and bail-bond violators and absconders";

3. "temporarily detain juveniles pending transfer to juvenile authorities";

4. "hold mentally-ill persons pending their movement to appropriate health facilities";

5. "hold individuals for the military, for protective custody, for contempt, and for the courts as witnesses";

6. "release convicted inmates to the community upon completion of their sentence";

7. "transfer inmates to Federal, State, or other authorities";

8. "house inmates for Federal, State, or other authorities because of crowding of their facilities";

9. "relinquish custody of temporary detainees to juvenile and medical authorities"; and

10. "hold inmates sentenced to short terms (generally under 1 year)" (Gilliard, 1999).

EXPERIENCING JAIL

Introduction/Holding Cells

Shortly after being arrested, individuals soon learn if they are charged with a misdemeanor or felony. The first typically carries a maximum sentence of less than a year in jail,[1] and is considered by the criminal justice system to be a relatively minor crime. If the person is charged with a felony that carries a sentence of one year to life or death, then, in the eyes of the law, the individual has committed a serious offense.

After being handcuffed, patted down (searched for weapons and contraband), and forced into a police car or van, arrestees will arrive at the local lockup. Depending upon which law enforcement agency made the arrest, arrestees can be transported to the nearby district or division police station, "central booking" located in or near the municipal courthouse, the federal courthouse, or taken directly to the county jail. Alternatively, individuals may spend a couple of hours at the local police station in a holding cell, then be transported to central booking, where they will wait an hour or two before picture and print time.

The facilities vary in layout, smell, and color, usually with no bed and only a bench to sit on. Sometimes the newly arrested are held in their own cell, with another person, or placed in a "bullpen" or "drunk tank" with 50 or 100 other men. They can be dark or bright, have graffiti on their walls, and can smell of urine, excrement, sweat, and vomit.

No matter where the police take the accused, the routine is basically the same. Arrestees will be booked, which means being fingerprinted and photographed (also known as having one's mug shot taken). Any shoelaces, belts, and neckties will be confiscated, because the jailers do not want the person to use them to attempt suicide, or use them to hurt other detainees. Then arrestees are placed in a holding cell. Those staying longer will be strip-searched and typically given an orange jumpsuit.

All trips to prison begin with some jail time. This is usually, if computed properly, later deducted from a person's sentence as "credit for time served." Most prisoners (and COs) consider city and county jails to be worse than prison, especially facilities in large cities and in the Deep South (Ross and Richards, 2002). Regardless of their location, jails have few, if any, medical, recreational, or educational services.

Jails have five primary drawbacks. In general, they are, from least to most important, lack of privacy, poorly trained and paid personnel, overcrowded and unsanitary conditions, bad food and living conditions, and substandard or nonexistent medical treatment (Zupan, 2002).[2]

Lack of Privacy

There is little privacy in jail. Although it might seem like an invasion of privacy, in the case of high-profile defendants, every incriminating word said, phone call made, or letter written will be used in court to make a case against an arrestee or to drum up additional indictments against them or others. Jailhouse holding tanks are usually "bugged" with hidden microphones and video cameras.

This technology is rarely used for the convicts' protection. Instead, it provides the judicial system another opportunity to gather more incriminating evidence. The jailers are taping everything. Yet the facility need not rely on sophisticated electronic surveillance, as cellmates may be more than happy to inform law enforcement of anything their cellmates say. These "jailhouse snitches" will convey details of conversations entered into or overheard to law enforcement as a means (or so they hope), to extract special benefits and/or reduce their own sentences or jail time. And, if it is an important case, like homicide, rape, or large-scale drug conspiracy, sometimes there will be a police officer in the suspect's cell posing as his new best friend.

Access to phones is limited. Those who are in custody may have to wait a day or two to place calls.[3] Toilets are usually made out of stainless steel and do not have lids, door stalls—if they exist—are removed, and rarely is toilet paper found on the rollers.

Poorly Trained and Paid Personnel

Many lockup and jail facilities are staffed by "turnkey" officers, who are paid close to minimum wage, and who appear nearly as economically desperate as the prisoners. They are also typically less well educated and have less on-the-job training than their CO counterparts that work in state and federal prisons. There are constant staff shortages at jails. This is largely due to the turnover of employees. There are also few chances for higher advancement and the personnel have low opinions of the work they do (Welch, 1996: 184; Kiekbusch, Price, and Theis, 2003).

Overcrowded, Unsafe, and Unsanitary Conditions

Generally, jails have only holding cells, cellblocks with dayrooms, dormitory-style rooms, and solitary confinement. Cells are usually crowded with bunk beds stacked two or three high, with a dozen or more men in each cage. These facilities are also jammed with men sleeping in the dayrooms, gymnasiums, and on mattresses along the hallway floors. Some institutions do not have smoke and CO_2 detectors, fire alarms, fire extinguishers, or sprinkler systems, or if they do, they are faulty or inoperable.

Heating systems are typically poor. Little or no air conditioning or proper ventilation may be available, broken or missing. Medical equipment may be nonexistent, expired, or unsanitary. Likewise, basic electrical and plumbing systems may be inadequate, broken, unsafe, and unsanitary.[4] The facilities may be filthy and infested with different types of vermin (i.e., bedbugs, cockroaches, fleas, lice, mice, rats, etc.), with toilets that don't function properly, walls and ceilings that are dirty, plaster that is cracked and falling, paint that is peeling off the walls, and broken windows.

Inedible Food

Jails have a reputation for serving horrible food. If prisoners have money, they might buy food through a commissary or canteen.[5] In some facilities, COs feel sorry for the prisoners because they appear to be starving—but more likely because they could make some money on the side—make their rounds late at night with a cart to sell snack food.

In other lockup facilities, particularly when the individual is transported or arraigned, they are given bologna or cheese sandwiches and orange Kool-Aid that has a diuretic effect.[6] It must be understood that not all inmates can afford commissary, nor the benefits derived from being able to pay for their own food.

Poor Medical Care

Medical care is almost nonexistent in jail. Drug addicts, prisoners in a methadone program, and alcoholics frequently enter jail. They will undoubtedly suffer withdrawal symptoms and rarely is something given to the detainee to ease the transition. In the process, these individuals may have seizures or delirium tremors. If health care is given, it is typically slow and inadequate and medical equipment is often primitive and unsanitary. The care is often dangerous, inhumane, and unconstitutional. Part of the reason is that the medical and psychiatric care may be administered by private health companies like Prison Health Services that predictably and continuously focus on the bottom line (Von Zielbauer, 2005a; 2005b).

Conclusion

Jails often fall short of the provisions of the Eighth Amendment, which prevents cruel and unusual punishment. "Conditions are unconstitutional if they amount to unquestioned and serious deprivation of basic human needs" or of the "minimal civilized measure of life's necessities" (*Rhodes v. Chapman*, 1981). Additionally, "prison authorities may not ignore a condition of confinement that is sure or very likely to cause serious illness and needless suffering the next week or month or year merely because no harm has yet occurred" (*Rhodes v. Chapman*, 1981) (see Exhibit 3.2).

EXHIBIT 3.2

Documentary

The Second City: Inside the World's Largest Jail

This documentary, originally produced for Bill Kurtis's Investigative Reports (1999), takes the viewer on a tour of Los Angeles county jail, the largest facility of its kind in the United States and the world. People are admitted 24 hours a day and are charged with all kinds of criminal offenses. The jail is administered by the Los Angeles County Sheriff's Department. The documentary focuses on the challenges and fears of convicts, COs, and correctional administrators. It shows jail conditions such as overcrowding, what appears to be inedible food, weapons, and the violence and frustration of inmates. The documentary depicts how rival gangs, the Crips and the Bloods, are in separate holding cells, how they earn points for good behavior and may eventually return to general population, and an inmate demonstrating to correctional officers how to make a shank or knife from a tooth brush. The film also tracks the trials and tribulations of a young African-American male who was sent to the jail, or so he claims, for failure to pay traffic and speeding tickets.

SOLVING THE PROBLEM

Four primary approaches have been used to reduce the misuse of jails. One strategy has been to improve the physical structure or problems with the jail itself; the second has been to seek accreditation; the third tactic is to file legal suits against jail or prison systems; and a final method is preventing those charged or convicted of a relatively minor criminal offense from either stepping foot inside the jail or expediting their removal from this kind of correctional institution.

Improving the Physical Structure

There is considerable variability in the design of jails. In some settings large rooms are set up dormitory style with countless rows of cots and bunk beds, while in others there is a traditional design with separate cells that contain one to six bunk beds. As part of the desire to improve the physical structure of jails, there has been the design and construction of what has been termed the *new generation jails* (and prisons). "These buildings are intended to maximize security and efficiency by means of easy observation and electronic surveillance of inmates. Such patterns utilize advancements in electronic communications and shatterproof glass materials to replace steel bars and stone blocks, creating a lighter, more comfortable environment that is also very secure" (Roots, 2005: 628). The first structures of this kind were the metropolitan transition centers used by the FBOP and Oak Park (Supermax) Correctional Facility in Minnesota opened in 1982.

In the 1970s a new design and accompanying management philosophy has been introduced in many jails across the country. Through podular/unit architecture and direct supervision, podular/direct supervision (PDS) jails have been created. Often built in a system of "pods," or modular self-contained housing areas linked to one another, direct supervision jails helped eliminate the old physical barriers that separated staff and inmates. It is hoped that these new designs will prevent many of the blind corners where prisoner and staff assaults occur, and that a more "participative" and "proactive management philosophy" will increase communication at all levels. In this design, bars and other traditional aspects of secure facilities are eliminated, including "bars and the isolated, secure observation areas for officers" (Bayens, Williams, and Smykla, 1997). Instead, there is a more "open environment in which inmates and correctional personnel could mingle with relative freedom. In a number of such 'new-generation' jails, large reinforced Plexiglas panels supplanted walls and served to separate activity areas, such as classrooms and dining halls, from one another. Soft furniture is the rule throughout such correctional facilities, and individual rooms take the place of cells, allowing inmates a modicum of personal privacy" (Schmalleger, 2006: 376).

> Direct supervision jails have been touted for their tendency to reduce inmate dissatisfaction and for their ability to deter rape and violence among the inmate population. . . . A number of studies have demonstrated the success of such jails at reducing the likelihood of inmate victimization. One such study published in 1994 also found that staff morale

in direct-supervision jails was far higher than in traditional institutions, that inmates reported reduced stress levels, and that fewer inmate-on-inmate and inmate on staff assaults occurred. Similarly, sexual assault, jail rape, suicide and escape have all found to occur less frequently in direct supervision facilities than in traditional institutions. (Schmalleger, 2006: 377)

Direct supervision facilities are not without their criticisms. First, changing the architecture is not enough. "[N]ew generation jails are too frequently run by 'old-style' managers and correctional personnel sometimes lack the training needed to make the transition to the new style of supervision." Other problems include that fact that midlevel managers in these kinds of facilities "could benefit from clearer job descriptions and additional training." Finally, it has been argued that "better screening needs to be done of officers for direct supervision facilities" (Zupan and Menke, 1988; Schmalleger, 2006: 377).

Accreditation

Over the past three-and-a-half decades, jails and prisons have engaged in the accreditation process (e.g., Freeman, 2000: 332–335; Levinson, Stinchcomb, and Greene, 2001). "Accreditation is a comprehensive process, incorporating numerous measures and embraces virtually every facet of the organization being assessed." (Champion, 2004: 529). Sponsored by membership organizations such as the ACA, these entities send representatives out to facilities to investigate if they are adhering to strict standards and guidelines.[7] Other organizations have entered the scene. In 1978, the Commission on Accreditation for Corrections (CAC), a private, nonprofit organization was established. "Presently, it administers a national program for accrediting all components of adult and juvenile corrections. In 2001 there were 1,185 institutions and programs throughout the United States that earned CAC accreditation." Although approximately half of the country's prisons are accredited by the ACA, only 120 of the 3,365 jails have passed this standard (National Commission on Safety and Abuse in Prison, 2006: 16, 88). According to the National Prison Commission, "Every prison and jail should be accredited and the ACA should raise some standards-pushing institutions to excel beyond acceptable practice to good practice-and continue to strengthen the accreditation process" (p. 16). While ACA accreditation is important, keen observers have noted that it is lacking in important standards dealing with the offering of substance abuse counseling and exercise time to prisoners (National Commission on Safety and Abuse in Prison: 91).

Legal Suits

In recent times, on account of prisoner litigation and the efforts of several nonprofit organizations—including the American Civil Liberties Union (through their National Prison Project) and Human Rights Watch—have attempted to reform jails

(Welsh, 1992; 1995; Feeley and Swearingen, 2004). During the late 1980s, almost 33 percent of all jails in the United States were under court order to improve their conditions (Welsh, 1992). In almost each major city in the United States, local organizations advocate on behalf of jail inmates. In Baltimore, for example, the "Public Justice Centers" are at the forefront of bringing to citizen attention the abuses that have occurred in the Baltimore Diagnostic and Transition Center (i.e., the city jail). In New York City, the Prisoner Rights Project of the Legal Aid Society of the City of New York has filed papers against the NYC Department of Corrections. Numerous inmates have also submitted class action suits claiming inhumane and unconstitutional conditions and treatment, including overcrowding, delays in medical services, medical neglect, unsanitary food conditions, and a lack of access to religious amenities. In several cases, the federal government has threatened to issue or have implemented consent decrees against jails. This practice allows state and local correctional facilities to be taken over and administered by the FBOP unless specified changes are made. No self-respecting warden, commissioner of corrections, or governor likes this situation, so they are under extreme pressure to reform their correctional facilities in accordance with federal guidelines. In 2006, for example, because of court orders the State of California ceded control of the health care of its prisoners to a federal judge.

In an effort to legitimize the numerous lawsuits the prisoners and advocates have brought against correctional facilities, the federal government passed the *Civil Rights of Institutionalized Person's Act* (1980). This encouraged prisons to deal on an individual basis, with the complaints of prisoners. It ensured that inmates were protected against unconstitutional conditions. It also minimized external interference in the running of prisons and jails.

In the spring of 1996, however, Congress passed the *Prison Litigation Reform Act* (PLRA). "It places limitations on population caps and limits the time periods of injunctions and consent degrees placed on institutions, forces solvent inmates to pay part of the filing fee, and requires judges to screen prison claims to eliminate frivolous law suits" (Bartollas, 2002: 220). This made it almost impossible for the courts to initiate any actions against correctional facilities that were perceived to be overly broad. There is, however, some momentum now, particularly in legal circles to reform the PLRA and lift the narrow conditions under which prisoners can challenge their conditions of confinement (National Commission on Safety and Abuse in Prison, 2006: 85–87).

Preventing Those Charged from Spending Time in Jail

A considerable number of remedies exist that are supposed to prevent those who are charged and/or convicted of a relatively minor criminal offense from ever entering a jail. These measures typically include economic sanctions or a plethora of community-based corrections programs such as economic sanctions, diversion, pretrial release, and probation (McShane and Krause, 1993; McCarthy and McCarthy, 1997; Champion, 2002). The following section will discuss these options.

Economic Sanctions

Introduction   There are three basic types of economic sanctions: fines, restitution, and community service. Each is applied to individuals who have broken the law, depending on their different circumstances. Their use also varies from jurisdiction to jurisdiction.

Fines   In the United States, fines are predominantly used as sanctions for minor infractions or crimes, calibrated to the seriousness of the offense, and with individuals the criminal justice system believes have the ability to pay. Two of the biggest difficulties with fines are the establishment of the appropriate amount and collection.

As a response to these problems, day fines and enhanced collection procedures have been introduced and, in many respects, are reasonably more effective measures (McCarthy and McCarthy: 140). A day fine is tied to a person's daily salary. This sanction makes "it is possible to achieve the same relative economic impact on a rich offender as a poor one by taking the same proportion of income and wealth from each individual" (McCarthy and McCarthy, 1997: 142).

There are five basic difficulties with collecting fines:

1. role orientation;
2. dispersion of responsibility;
3. disincentives;
4. multiple tasks; and
5. enforcement dependence (McCarthy and McCarthy, 1997: 150).

Role orientation refers to the fact that the different components of the criminal justice system dislike acting as a collection agency. Dispersion of responsibility concerns the problem that too many branches of the criminal justice system are responsible for administering fees, including money collection and prosecution for nonpayment. With respect to disincentives, the organizational entity that collects rarely benefits from the money. Multiple tasks involves the fact that the diverse branches of the criminal justice system are probably already overtaxed with the work they have, and fine collection is perceived as one more burden. Finally, with respect to enforcement dependence, it has been recognized that many criminal justice agencies, once they have become accustomed to receiving funding through fines, tend to reorient their mission so that they can continue to secure this money (Miller and Selva, 1994).

In order to address the previously reviewed problems, many experts (e.g., Morris and Tonry, 1990) advocate the privatization of debt collection. According to these scholars, when it appears that the fines are finally uncollectible, they can simply be written off.

Restitution and community service   An increasingly popular alternative to fines is the use of restitution, where the person convicted of a crime pays money or provides a service directly to the victim. On the other hand, with community service, the individual convicted of the crime performs some sort of work that will benefit the neighborhood, town, or city where the crime was committed. Restitution is typically provided through money, and community service is usually given through menial labor—such as raking leaves, painting buildings, maintaining parks, picking up trash, low-skill construction work, washing government vehicles, or cleaning roads or highways—responsibilities that in most locales a public works department would normally handle.

The amount of restitution is usually based on the amount of loss (i.e., money stolen, replacement value or repair cost of damaged property, medical expenses, income lost, etc.). With this kind of sanction, victims may be involved in determining the appropriate response by the offender. Community service is issued when a specific victim cannot be identified and/or a person is found guilty of so-called victimless crimes.[8] Some individuals sentenced to community service voluntarily fulfill the order; others must report to a community service officer and are supervised while they comply with their obligation.

The kinds of things individuals have been required to do are limited only by the creativity of the judge. In some jurisdictions, there have been some unusual methods of community service. In California, five years before he was accused of killing his ex-wife, former Buffalo Bills running back O. J. Simpson was allowed to serve as the master of ceremonies for a community organization after he was convicted of assaulting his wife.

Those in favor of restitution and community service think that they have the potential to help rehabilitate offenders. Sometimes, advocates argue, particularly if victim offender reconciliation is used, the perpetrator can see firsthand the suffering they have caused the victims. Advocates also recognize that this is perhaps a rare chance for the criminal justice system to move beyond retributive sanctions toward ones that encourage social justice (Pepinsky and Quinney, 1991; Arrigo, 1998).

Others believe that most kinds of community service job details are not going to give those convicted of less serious crimes any valuable skills and simply treat the sanction as some form of bureaucratic ritualism.

Diversion

Introduction   Diversion minimizes or prevents those accused of a relatively minor crime from being formally charged and/or processed by the criminal justice system. This is also an opportunity for the accused to obtain necessary help or assistance in terms of alcohol, drug, or employment counseling and/or training (McCarthy and McCarthy, 1997: 37). The benefits of diversion to the convicted person includes avoiding the stigma of a criminal sanction and reducing the workload and expenditures of the criminal justice system. Over the years, diversion programs have increased, been improved upon, and been institutionalized by many jurisdictions. In big cities, diversion is most needed because jails and other programs of the local criminal justice system are most likely to be at or over capacity.

Forms of diversion   During the 1960s and 1970s a number of formal diversion programs were established. Today two types exist: unconditional and conditional. The former are "programs that remove the offender from the criminal justice process and place no conditions on his or her post diversion behavior . . . [The latter are] those that restrict the offender's post diversion behavior, monitor his progress in the community, and provide for reinstallment of prosecution if the conditions of diversion are not met" (McCarthy and McCarthy, 1997: 42).

The latter type of programs often require offenders to participate in some kind of treatment. They stipulate that, if the person does not complete the therapy successfully, they may then be formally processed by the criminal justice system (i.e., sent to jail).

Unfortunately, some research on diversion suggests that this approach has minimal benefits and can simply add to the cost of corrections. This criticism has a lot to do with how offenders are selected for diversion rather than the actual programs (McCarthy and McCarthy: 44).[9]

Drug courts   First started in 1990 in Dade County Florida, drug courts have spread rapidly across the United States. Although they began with individuals who did not have a history of violent crime, over the past decade the kinds of people that drug courts serve have become increasingly specialized. In short, if the arrestee completes a drug rehabilitation program and remains drug free for a year, the charges against them are dropped. Some focus on treatment, while others channel their resources into speedy disposition of cases (McCarthy and McCarthy: 89). There may also be special components. Typically, the judge, with the assistance of their staff, regularly and closely monitors almost every life change the participant makes. The main goals are reducing recidivism and substance abuse and then rehabilitation. This specialization has the added benefit of freeing up the criminal justice system so it can ostensibly focus on other kinds of cases (Brown, 2002; Rempel, 2003; Roman, Townsend, and Bhati, 2003).

Although drug courts have increased overall efficiency, one of the largest problems has been the difficulties involved with recommendations for some drug treatment programs. There are typically long waiting lists for these. Thus the arrestee goes to court, and then has a lot of downtime (thus opportunities to relapse and reoffend) while waiting to be admitted to the drug treatment programs.

It bears mentioning that recidivism is operationalized and measured differently by many researchers. Some see it as the person coming back to jail or prison, others interpret it as a measure of being charged with a crime, and for others it means a court appearance.

Alternatives to diversion   Instead of diverting individuals from the criminal justice system, some states have considered decriminalization of certain acts. There are many victimless crimes on the books that could be eliminated (i.e., possession of marijuana, prostitution, gambling, etc.) or sanctions for these actions reduced. Decisions to reduce the penalties are typically decided in a political context with political parties and well-funded special interest groups often taking opposing positions.

Problems with diversion   There are several difficulties with diversion including the facts that effectiveness is rarely or poorly measured and that individuals who are innocent but not yet convicted are often compelled or feel pressured to comply with diversion to avoid the trouble and expense of a prosecution (McCarthy and McCarthy: 61). Another aspect is that in some jurisdictions with zero tolerance policing or unconditional diversion, the practice of diversion may actually be declining.

Pretrial Release

In general, there are three major types of pretrial release: bail, prebooking alternatives, and post booking releases. Pretrial release is intended to accomplish several
purposes:

1. increased release rates;
2. speedy operations of the criminal justice system;
3. equal justice;
4. low failure to appear rates;
5. protection of the community; and
6. minimum economic costs with maximum benefits (National Center for State
   Courts, 1975).

Bail

Introduction   Shortly after being arrested, defendants appear in front of a judge
who determines if they can be released on their own recognizance or if they should
be granted bail. Posting bail requires the accused to give the court money, a bond,
or title to property (to be held in trust) to ensure that the defendant returns to court
on the proscribed date. The money does not have to be theirs. For example, in the
late 1990s, John Gotti Jr., the head of the notorious Gambino, organized crime
family managed to have his neighbors post their houses as bail for him. The
Eighth Amendment of the U.S. Constitution, however, prohibits courts requiring
excessive bail.

Despite the emergence of bail guidelines, judges exercise a considerable
amount of discretion in the amounts and conditions they establish in the granting
of bail.

Judges and magistrates take a number of factors into consideration when they
determine whether bail is granted and the amount that it is set at including

- the seriousness of the crime;
- previous criminal history of the defendant;
- the ties the defendant has with the community;
- the need to protect the victim and the community; and
- the presentations and perceptions made by the prosecutor and the defendant's
  lawyer.

If the defendant on bail fails to show at court, they forfeit the surety and the judge
then issues a bench warrant for the individual's arrest.

Regardless, the constitution does not prescribe a definitive amount for release on
bail. This is why many judges, acting out of an abundance of caution, set high bails
with defendants (McCarthy and McCarthy: 77).

Bail bondsmen   In order to keep bail functioning in a cost-effective manner, the criminal justice system depends on bail agents, more popularly known as bail bondsmen. There are more than 5,000 professional bondsmen in the United States (Toberg, 1983; McCarthy and McCarthy, 1997: 77). Despite their swagger and overzealous reputation, they provide a needed service for those who cannot afford bail. Bail bond offices are typically located close to the main courthouse and city jails. Many are open 24 hours a day, seven days a week, and are noticeable by their large red and sometimes flashing neon signs.

> Using their own assets or those of an insurance company, bondsmen will provide the surety required for a fee of between 10 and 15 percent. They are licensed by the state, choose their own clients, [and] may set their own collateral requirements. In addition, they may track down and return bail jumpers without extradition and by force if necessary. (Cole, 1994: 405)

To increase the possibility that their clients will show up in court, bail bondsmen—like good criminal defense lawyers—try to maintain regular contact with defendants and try to persuade their family and friends (if known) how important this process is. They may also psychologically prepare their clients for the possible outcome (i.e., incarceration). If the defendant fails to appear in court, the bondsman will try to return the person; otherwise, they will forfeit their bond.

Problems with bail   Just like fines, the bail system favors the wealthy and discriminates against the poor; the rich are less likely to feel the deterrent effect of bail. Many people believe that, despite the criteria, getting bail appears arbitrary. Take for example financier and billionaire Marc David Rich, who in 1983 was charged with tax evasion, fraud, and "dealing with the enemy." He was indicted, he posted bail, and in 1983 fled to Switzerland. During the Bill Clinton presidency (1993–2001), Rich's ex-wife Denise gave the Democratic Party several respectable financial contributions, and in the remaining days of the Clinton presidency money to establish the President's future library.[10] In January 2001, in the last few days that Clinton was in office, Rich was pardoned by Clinton.[11]

Bail reform   Bail has been modified through reform acts and guidelines. One of the most profound pieces of legislation was the *Bail Reform Act of 1966*, which "created a presumption in favor of release and the imposition of the least restrictive form of pretrial release that would ensure appearance at trial." The *Federal Bail Reform Act of 1984* expanded the criteria to be used for the release decision to *include protection of the community*. "This allowed judicial officials, following a hearing, to detain individuals on the basis of the perceived threat they posed to the community" (McCarthy and McCarthy: 74). This option, known as preventive detention, is used: If defendants committed a drug felony where there is a possibility of a ten-year sentence, if they used a firearm during the offense, or if they were convicted of a serious crime while on pretrial release in the five years preceding the current charge, they can be denied bail (McCarthy and McCarthy: 74).

Another way that bail has been reformed is through the use of guidelines. States use these to ensure a degree of uniformity or consistency in the way they secure the reappearance of defendants. "Bail guidelines were modeled after sentencing guidelines, in an attempt to achieve a more equitable system of determining bail . . . bail guidelines create a more visible system of decision making and hence one that is less subject to abuse" (McCarthy and McCarthy: 77).

Deposit bail   Initiated in 1964, deposit bail programs allow defendants to post between 5 and 10 percent of the total amount of bail that is owed. When the defendant returns to court, the amount is returned to the defendant for those who posted the deposit. "Most jurisdictions require that a small sum (usually 1 percent of the total bail amount) be retained by the court to cover the cost of administering the deposit bail system; in other jurisdictions a fee is retained only when a defendant is found guilty" (McCarthy and McCarthy: 79).

What happens to these federal statutes in the states? Shortly after the federal government makes a legislative change the states follow suit. The federal government often gives the states economic incentives to adjust their criminal codes and sentencing practices to resemble the federal one, for example, through block grants.

Nonfinancial pretrial-release program models

Introduction   Instead of sending defendants to jail or releasing them on bond, they may be granted a prebooking alternative such as a summons or a citation. Postbooking alternatives, on the other hand, may include "recognizance releases or conditional, supervised releases" (McCarthy and McCarthy: 79).

Prebooking releases   Summons and citations are notifications defendants are given and/or receive that order them to either pay a fine (thereby pleading guilty) or appear at a later time in court to answer the charge. In some jurisdictions, the defendant must sign the notification; in others this step is not necessary. In the United States, most people who are issued a citation generally show up to court.

Citations and summons are used with increasing frequency in some states for victimless crimes (e.g., the possession of small amounts of marijuana). Prebooking releases have lots of advantages. They save the court's and jail's resources. Generally speaking, the accused person can be released almost immediately after contact with the police.

Postbooking release   Postbooking release, also known as *on-recognizance releases* and *personal recognizance*, "provide for the release of a defendant [from custody] prior to trial based on his signed promise to appear for all scheduled court proceedings. No restrictions are placed on the defendants pretrial conduct and no financial payments are required" (McCarthy and McCarthy: 80).

There are two basic postbooking releases: *"promise to appear"* (PTA) and *"release on recognizance"* (ROR). Both are virtually indistinguishable. In the 1960s, the Vera Institute of Justice in New York City pioneered the ROR method that "is based on the assumption that judges will grant releases if they are given verified information about defendants' reliability and roots in the community. Court personnel talk to defendants soon after their arrest about job, family, prior criminal record, and associations and then determine whether release should be recommended" (Cole, 1994: 409).

Conditional and supervised pretrial release   Among the most used nonfinancial means of securing individuals return to court is the ROR. In order to qualify for this kind of community-based program, defendants must adhere to a number of conditions: reporting on a regular basis to a pretrial service agency, not committing another crime, and, in the case of a violence-related charge, not having contact with the actual or alleged victim.

In order to coordinate the provision of pretrial release, most jurisdictions have established pretrial service agencies. In some locales these are part of the court system, and in other places they part of probation and parole. These organizations supervise those on probation, parole, bail, or ROR. They can also help monitor the individuals and assist them in getting drug and alcohol treatment services, education, training, employment, and other forms of counseling. Pretrial service agencies may also be responsible for maintaining contact with those people who are on electronic monitoring equipment.

Probation

Introduction   If an individual is convicted of a misdemeanor (and in the cases of some felonies), judges have the discretion to grant the person probation. In short, the person convicted of the crime is given a jail sentence, but it is suspended if they comply with certain conditions while out in the community. This often means calling in on a regular basis to the probation officer, submitting to random drug (i.e., urinalysis) tests, attending some sort of alcohol or drug therapy, participating in job training, holding down a job, making restitution, etc. (Many of the difficulties with these community corrections programs will be discussed in Chapter 8.) "Almost two-thirds of all convicted offenders serve their sentences on probation . . . [it] is designed to keep the offenders in their home community while carrying out the sanctions imposed by the court" (McCarthy and McCarthy: 96). The number of people subjected to probation has rapidly increased.

Objectives of probation

There are five basic objectives of probation:

> to protect the community;
> to carry out the court-ordered sanctions imposed by the court;
> to assist offenders to change;
> to support crime victims; and
> to coordinate and promote the use of community resources in an efficient and effective manner.

Historical basis of probation   Some of the early practices that predated the modern use of probation included releasing those convicted of crimes to members of the clergy, judicial reprieve, and pardon. Over the years, probation has evolved into a rather complicated and bureaucratic sanction. Needless to say, probation, like many other community corrections programs, have a number of difficulties: role conflict for the probation/parole officer; the location of community corrections offices; rigid, bureau-cratic, or inflexible supervisors; the failure to make a meaningful reduction in recidi-vism; high levels of work-related stress; violence by probationers and parolees against their officers/agents; overcrowded/overburdened probation and parole officers/agents; and lack of adequate funding. (For a detailed discussion see Chapter 9.)

Starting in the 1980s, the number of people being sentenced to probation increased astronomically. However, the number of probation officers employed to deal with this onslaught did not match the amount. Predictably, we now have a probation crowding problem, with not enough personnel to supervise those on this kind of sanction (McCarthy and McCarthy: 101).

Because probation and parole officers act as both law enforcement officers and social workers, they may suffer from role confusion/conflict. They are often caught between the demands of supervising a large caseload, brokering resources that would help their probationers and parolees live a crime-free existence, and making sure they adhere to other numerous conditions of release (McCarthy and McCarthy: 133–134).

Sentencing guidelines and probation   Several factors affect who is allowed on pro-bation. These vary from state to state based on the prevailing legislation (McCarthy and McCarthy: 108). These variables include

> "the availability of probation services and the judges perception of the
> quality of those services can also influence judicial decisions"
> (McCarthy and McCarthy: 110);
> "the offenders' willingness to accept probation" (McCarthy and McCarthy:
> 110); and
> "the judge's perception of the appropriateness of probation for a particular
> offender" (McCarthy and McCarthy: 111).

Whether or not the judge feels that probation is appropriate, the recommendations of a presentence investigation (PSI) are prepared by a probation officer or agent (McCarthy and McCarthy: 111).

Boot camps   Over two-and-a-half decades ago, in the midst of a tough-on-crime era encouraged by conservative Republicans, various states set up military-style boot camps designed to deliver a mental and physical wake-up call to troubled lawbreakers. Having started in Georgia in 1983 and spread to 39 states over the next 15 years, the camps targeted adults, juveniles, and women.

These programs, which are separate from larger state correctional facilities, are designed to house inmates from 90 to 180 days. They involve a military or paramili-tary regimen, including physical exercise and academic courses to obtain their GED.

The original idea seemed to make sense: Put these people in an intense, military training type of situation, in which their every move is vetted by a drill instructor and a get-tough staff. Shock them out of their complacency and moral indifference. Reach them before it's too late. Just as the military once practiced psychological "teardowns" of young trainees, boot camp staffs were responsible for working on inmates' psyches, not to mention their behavior and attitudes.

Some individuals who were arrested for less serious misdemeanors and felonies, or those currently serving a sentence behind bars, would be ordered by a judge to spend a brief period of time in the boot camp. If they successfully passed this program, then they would be released on to probation or parole. Gung-ho politicians and many correctional administrators championed boot camps as a solution to overcrowding, recidivism, and, in the end, a method of achieving a rehabilitative effect.

Scholarly research proved otherwise. It was found that the program had marginal results. During the mid-1990s, a handful of rigorous evaluations sponsored by the Department of Justice's National Institute of Justice (NIJ) and the Office of Juvenile Justice and Delinquency Prevention (OJJDP) were conducted to determine the success of this correctional innovation. Unfortunately, these evaluations determined that inductees do no better in terms of recidivism (no matter how you measure it) in the boot camp environment than do those inmates who are sent to traditional correctional institutions. Moreover, it does not appear that benefits are accrued in the reduction in prison overcrowding. These conclusions and others led a number of states, including Georgia, to scale back their boot camp experiments.

One key factor that drove this overall scaling back was the discovery that boot camps, particularly those that served juveniles, were breeding grounds for the abuse of inmates. In Maryland, in particular, drill instructors were charged and convicted of assault. In December 1999, the state closed its juvenile boot camp (originally opened less than five years earlier) following routine allegations of physical abuse and broken bones and the dismissal and criminal convictions of a handful of drill sergeants. This and other problems prompted other states like Colorado and North Dakota to either scale back their boot camp program or close them altogether.

In 2005, in a South Dakota juvenile boot camp for girls, an overweight inmate who had been convicted of stealing $25 from a friend died after a forced run. The investigation determined that camp personnel thought she was simply malingering and failed to offer appropriate medical assistance. In January 2006, Martin Lee Anderson in the Bay County (Florida) Sheriff's Office Boot Camp was repeatedly beaten by his COs and he died shortly thereafter. Many other instances of this kind of maltreatment have been recorded, usually the result of a dynamic between inmate and CO that borders on the extreme.

As of 2006 there were 53 boot camps still in operation in the United States. State DOCs, juvenile justice advocates, even the families of boot camp inmates must take bold steps to end an experiment that has proved to be a failure. State-run boot camp facilities, like chain gangs and so many other debilitating methods of delivering punishment to the wrongdoer, must be closed.

CONCLUSION

Problems and solutions to jails abound. Many of the recommendations, however, have unintended consequences or are simply tinkering in the criminal justice system. Although many well-intentioned entities have tried to litigate against the conditions in many correctional institutions, it appears that the judicial system has dug in its heals and strengthened the power of DOCs to house inmates in poor living conditions. For inmates, although it is nicer to be housed in a newly constructed facility, like a new generation jail, changing the design of jails is not radical enough.

Most arrestees awaiting trial or sentencing would rather spend their time out of jail and in the community. But not all individuals released on their own recognizance or out on bail are model citizens. Moreover, certain parts of the criminal justice system are reluctant to vigorously enforce fines and community-based sanctions.

Failure of payment may mean several things including difficulties that the person may have in paying or the systems' lack of adequate means to collect. Sometimes inability to cover a fine may simply be a way that an ex-convict "works" or "plays" the criminal justice system in a passive aggressive way.

Solutions like intensive probation, electronic monitoring, and increased accountability of community corrections personnel, combined with criminal and civil sanctions for parents and guardians, may be more useful. Undoubtedly, most of these are fraught with problems too.

Another difficulty with many of the more recent community corrections programs is a concern with net widening (e.g., Austin and Krisberg, 1981; Cohen, 1985). Although the numerous types of diversion and community-based corrections programs may on the surface appear to be benign, they can also have the negative effect of placing more people under the watchful eye of the criminal justice system, leaving them with the lifelong stigma that a criminal sanction (e.g., charge and conviction) produces, which can dissuade employers from hiring them and some educational institutions from allowing them entrance.

Needless to say, federal and state governments, including private foundations such as the Soros Foundation, should increase their grant funding to organizations and individuals who investigate jail conditions and work to change things.

KEY TERMS

bail	net widening
consent decree	presentence investigation (PSI)
contraband	*Prison Litigation Reform Act* (PLRA)
deposit bail	probation
diversion	release on recognizance (ROR)
Eighth Amendment	role orientation
jail house snitch	warehousing

REVIEW QUESTIONS

PART 1: MULTIPLE-CHOICE QUESTIONS

1. What are common misuses of holding cells?
   a. drunk tanks
   b. truant halls
   c. shelters for the homeless
   d. all of the above
   e. some of the above

2. What is Rikers Island?
   a. jail
   b. prison
   c. place where the United States is keeping the captured members of al-Qaeda and the Taliban
   d. the most violent correctional facility in the United States
   e. all of the above

3. What type of people do jails typically hold?
   a. individuals who have just been arrested by police but have not been arraigned by a judge or commissioner
   b. pretrial detainees
   c. those convicted of federal crimes
   d. those serving sentences of a year or less
   e. all of the above

4. What are the typical problems with jail personnel compared to their counterparts at the state and federal levels?
   a. less educated
   b. paid less
   c. constant staff shortages
   d. receive less training
   e. all the above

5. Why are sentencing guidelines used?
   a. because the federal crimes are more severe
   b. because judges are not that creative
   c. to reduce arbitrary decision making
   d. most PSIs are unhelpful
   e. to save time and money

6. Which of the following is NOT an objective of pretrial release?
   a. It allows the state to increase the release rates.
   b. It facilitates the speedy operation of the courts.

   c.   It equalizes justice (makes it more fair).
   d.   It tries to protect the community.
   e.   It is very costly to the state.

7.   Which are the functions of pretrial service agencies?
   a.   supervision of persons released by the courts
   b.   making recommendations for specific conditions of release
   c.   putting defendants in touch with rehabilitative services
   d.   all of the above
   e.   none of the above

8.   Which term is used to describe the process whereby a judge imposes a prison term, but then suspends the execution of it for a period of time as long as the offender adheres to certain conditions?
   a.   diversion
   b.   parole
   c.   probation
   d.   intermediate sanction
   e.   some of the above

9.   What are drug courts designed to do?
   a.   reduce time to disposition
   b.   reduce pressure on nondrug caseloads
   c.   increase overall trial capacity
   d.   all of the above
   e.   none of the above

10.   What factor/s is/are taken into consideration when imposing day fines?
   a.   offender's income
   b.   offender's responsibility to a family
   c.   offender's ability to pay
   d.   both a and c
   e.   both a and b

11.   Which amendment prevents excessive bail?
   a.   First
   b.   Fourth
   c.   Fifth
   d.   none of the above
   e.   all of the above

12.   Which of the following is NOT a type of sanction?
   a.   probation
   b.   parole
   c.   community programs

    d. reincarnation

    e. none of the above

13. What is the most common assumption underlying bail?

    a. Defendants who face serious charges are not more likely to abscond.

    b. The fear of financial loss is the most powerful deterrent to individuals who would flee.

    c. The strongest showing of good faith is being drug free.

    d. All of the above.

    e. None of the above.

14. What is the name of the report that has the most influence to determine who will or will not receive probation?

    a. victim impact statement

    b. presentence investigation

    c. drug/Alcohol Anonymous counselor's report

    d. juvenile records

    e. clerk to judge

15. First-time offenders who have committed nonviolent crimes are usually given

    a. jail

    b. maximum security

    c. parole

    d. probation

    e. prison

16. Which of the following is an example of an intermediate sanction?

    a. intensive supervision

    b. drug testing

    c. probation

    d. parole

    e. attendance at Alcohol Anonymous

17. During a detention hearing, upon which criterion/a is/are the judges' decision made?

    a. whether there is a serious risk that the person will flee

    b. whether the person will obstruct justice or threaten, injure, or intimidate a prospective witness or juror

    c. if the offense was violent or punishable by life in prison or death

    d. all of the above

    e. a and b only

18. Which of the following is/are the objective/s of community-based corrections?

    a. community protection

    b. continuum of sanctions

    c. rehabilitation and reintegration

    d. cost-effectiveness

    e. all of the above

19. Which of the following is an assumption of community corrections?

    a. incarceration is destructive to individuals and their families
    b. cheaper than institutionalizing individuals
    c. prisons do not rehabilitate inmates
    d. community corrections is more effective than prisons in rehabilitating offenders
    e. all of the above

20. What is the name of the method of releasing convicts from prison prior to the expiration of their sentence?

    a. probation
    b. diversion
    c. parole
    d. community service
    e. pretrial release

21. What is the biggest problem with the use of bail?

    a. it costs too much to administer
    b. all persons are not equally able to make financial commitments
    c. too complicated to explain to pretrial detainees
    d. too much regulation
    e. none of the above

22. What are two basic forms of diversion?

    a. conditional and unconditional
    b. misdemeanor and felony
    c. determinant and indeterminate
    d. pretrial and posttrial
    e. simple and complicated

23. Which of the following is NOT a problem with diversion?

    a. no real way to test it
    b. may be a way to cover up poor police procedures
    c. person pressured into diversion may be innocent
    d. it is more costly than prison
    e. persons forced into programs even if it is of minimal utility

24. Which of the following are prebooking alternatives?

    a. fines
    b. citations and summons
    c. recognizance releases
    d. bail
    e. all the above

25. Which of the following is NOT a problem with debt collection?

    a. multiple tasks
    b. disincentives

    c. lack of personnel
    d. dispersion of responsibility
    e. role orientation

26. What is the name of the process that refers to formally acknowledged efforts to utilize alternatives to the justice system?
    a. plea bargaining
    b. diversion
    c. pretrial motions
    d. unconditional diversion
    e. discovery

PART 2: SHORT-ANSWER QUESTIONS

1. List four problems specifically facing jails (and not prisons).
2. What is the difference between restitution, community service, and fines?
3. Which amendment of the U.S. Constitution prevents excessive bail?
4. List three categories of approaches to address the misuse of jails.
5. Why does bail discriminate against the poor?
6. What happens if a defendant on bail fails to show at court?
7. List five uses for jail.
8. Who is the typical type of person held in jail?
9. What is a consent decree?

PART 3: ESSAY QUESTIONS

1. What is the biggest problem with the use of bail and how might it be fixed?
2. Many critical criminologists and community corrections practitioners say that alternatives to prison act as a form of net widening? Do you agree or disagree with this statement and why?
3. Which type of community correction is the most promising and why?

NOTES

    1. In some states this can be as long as 18 months.
    2. For early research on the jail experiences see, for example, Irwin (1985). He outlined four stages a person will go through: disintegration, disorientation, degradation, and preparation.
    3. It may take even longer in a prison. Many correctional facilities have only a few phones available to convicts, and their use sometimes is regulated by a sign-up sheet. It is not uncommon for a prisoner

to have to wait a week to make a call, and even then, only when his name appears on the time sheet. Immates are limited to short calls, usually collect calls or those paid for with commissary cards. Convicts are required to give up the phone after only a short time (5–15 minutes); if they linger on past their time and into the next time slot, the next man in line will typically become quite agitated.

4. There are numerous newspaper articles about and civil suits that have been brought against jail facilities in the United States.

5. The commissary will be discussed in greater detail in Chapter 5 of this book.

6. See the extended discussion on prison food in Chapter 5 of this book.

7. The AJA does not offer an accreditation program. Repeated e-mail and telephone inquiries (December 2005) with this organization failed to provide an answer as to why this was the case.

8. The expression *so-called* in connection with victimless crimes is used because the victims of these kinds of offenses are often hidden (e.g., the family that suffers loss of income or displacement because of the individual's actions).

9. Some of the diversion models include Alcohol Detoxification Centers, Family Crisis Intervention Units, Mediation and Counseling Following Arrest, Statutory Diversion, Treatment Alternatives to Street Crime (TASC), and Drug Courts.

10. A typical thing American presidents do when they leave office is help build a legacy, and ensure a modest income in revenues from the visitors as it becomes a tourist attraction.

11. When an individual is granted a pardon, this means that they are forgiven for the crime that they were convicted of and the sanction that they were administered. Pardons are occasionally granted to individuals who have been wrongfully convicted of a crime. Clemency, also known as a reprieve, lessens the penalty for the crime, but the person is still guilty of the crime. Commutations involve a reduction in sentence; however, it does not wipe out the charge the individual was convicted of (See extended discussion in Chapter 10.)

Chapter 4

Underfunding

INTRODUCTION

It costs American taxpayers approximately $34.5 billion each year to incarcerate convicts. More specifically, in 2006, the Federal Bureau of Prisons (FBOP) had a budget close to $5 million (www.usdoj.gov/jmd/2007summary/pdf/39_127_135_fps.pdf). And in 2001 (the latest figures available), "[s]tates spent $29.5 billion for prisons . . . about a $5½ billion increase from 1996, after adjusting for inflation" (Stephan, 2004). Moreover, "[s]tate correctional expenditures increased 145% in 2001 constant dollars from $15.6 billion in FY 1986 to $38.2 billion in FY 2001; prison expenditures increased 150% from $11.7 billion to $29.5 billion" (Stephan, 2004).

Although figures vary between the states and the federal system, on average it costs $22,600 a year to house and maintain state prisoners and $22,632 to provide the same function to inmates in the FBOP (Stephan, 2004). Still, prisoners, correctional officers (COs), wardens, and other correctional professionals are quick to admit that their field is seriously underfunded, and the effects are significant: overcrowding; prematurely releasing prisoners unsuitable for the community; continuously retrofitting old institutions; failing to hire appropriate people to work in the facilities; neglecting to properly train recruits; and scrambling to find money to pay for the renovation of old facilities, the construction of new prisons, and a patchwork of rehabilitative programs.

In the late 1990s, as a result of the passage of the *Violent Crime Control and Law Enforcement Act of 1994* (hereafter *Crime Act*), American jails and prisons got

Special thanks to Brad Chilton for comments on this chapter.

a temporary increase in funding in the form of grants from the federal government "to construct, develop, expand, modify, operate, or improve correctional facilities, including boot camp facilities and other alternative correctional facilities that can free conventional prison space for the confinement of violent offenders, to ensure that prison cell space is available for the confinement of violent offenders and to implement truth in sentencing laws for sentencing violent offenders."

However, starting with the George W. Bush presidency (January 2001), tax revenues from local, state, and the federal government have been spent on other pressing items. Especially in the wake of 9/11, governments have directed a disproportionate amount of their public safety budgets to law enforcement and cut back on courts and corrections. Moreover, politicians not wanting to appear soft on crime refrain from increasing the budget for corrections.

The familiar refrain of "corrections must do more with less" is frequently repeated in the legislatures and on the cellblocks and tiers. This policy, called *fiscal conservatism*, is "to be achieved through the development and implementation of cost-minimization strategies (cost containment, controlling building costs, land revenue enhancement) designed to reduce the public tax burden. The increasingly important component of fiscal conservatism is the privatization of correctional services traditionally provided by government" (Freeman, 2000: 106).

Regardless, although the purchase of land and spending money to maintain the physical plant of correctional facilities is high, the biggest expenditure, as with all businesses, is personnel.

GROWTH IN CORRECTIONAL SPENDING

Introduction

Over the past two decades expenditures for corrections have increased. This is largely due to a greater number of prisoners, occasioned by changes in previously mentioned sentencing laws and practices (i.e., three strikes you're out, truth in sentencing, and the abolishment of parole in several states and the federal system). Other increased costs have been caused by building out or by the construction of new facilities. Finally, the number of convicts with special needs is growing. This includes older inmates (people with longer sentences are aging inside prison), female inmates who have more special needs than their male counterparts, drug-dependent inmates who need special programming, gang members who need more secure housing, and inmates with medical (i.e., AIDS, TB, hepatitis) and mental health issues who may need expensive medical and/or psychological treatment (see Chapter 7).

Jails Become the Leaders in Expenditures

Between 1960 and 1985 spending by state and local governments on corrections were triple the amount they spent on law enforcement (Ford and Moore, 1992: 2). The increases in correctional budgets have taken place particularly with jails. "[B]etween 1986 and 1990, the annual median operating budget for jails across the nation rose by more than $1 million, from more than $2.2 million to $3.4 million" (Ford and Moore, 1992: 2).

Available Options

In order to deal with crowding and its economic costs, departments of corrections (DOCs) and the FBOP have taken three approaches: front-end, back-end, or increasing the capacity of facilities (Freeman, 2000: 5). The first strategy usually consists of reducing the number of prisoners entering jails and prisons. The second option involves letting inmates out of correctional institutions much earlier than their proscribed sentence or the use of legislative caps on prisoner populations in facilities. Lastly, DOCs have increased the size of their facilities or found ways to house more prisoners into the correctional facilities they currently run by being creative with the space they already utilize (Freeman, 2000: 5).

Front-End Measures

Significant savings can be achieved by preventing suspects or those convicted of crimes from entering the criminal justice system in the first place. Short of teaching people not to commit crimes or training them to take better precautions against being detected or caught, these processes, reviewed in detail in Chapter 3, can include different penalty structures and community-based corrections programs.

Back-End Options

The second strategy typically includes the enhanced use of early release including parole and other community corrections programs (e.g., furloughs). Often this is done through grants of time for good behavior while inside, inmates who have failing health, or incapacitated by age, or through enhanced transitioning into community corrections programs such as halfway houses. A vast network of residential treatment centers run by private (for profit) and nonprofit entities exist in America. "A related mechanism is legislative caps on inmate populations, which are tied to emergency release powers. The caps require release of inmates when the facility population reaches a certain proportion of capacity, typically 95 percent or higher" (Freeman, 2000: 5).

Many prisons now have geriatric cellblocks filled with elderly prisoners, many of them in wheelchairs, on respirators, or in beds hooked up to machines or intravenous tubes that provide fluids and medicine. The inmate population continues to gray, with more convicts serving life sentences and expiring behind the wall. Some prison systems allow elderly prisoners or younger convicts who have been diagnosed to die in a few months to apply for "compassionate release." This may allow a prisoner to go home to die in the company of their loved ones. The problem is that few convicts ever make it out the door before they pass away, as the application process may take many months to receive official approval.

Also, it goes without saying that correctional facilities must ensure that their count systems, records, and procedures are properly functioning in order to release inmates when they have completed the time mandated in their sentences. For example, in January 2006 a federal judge granted a $12 million settlement to former inmates of the D.C. jail that "had been needlessly strip-searched after their ordered releases" and in one case an inmate was held for almost two years more than his sentence permitted. Overdetention is not simply an "inevitabil[ity] due to adminis-trative needs." Solutions that have been proffered include processing the paperwork in the courthouse rather than in a holding area, "paper orders for each defendant explicitly giving their status," and officers making sure that "they do not take anyone into their custody without the appropriate paperwork" (Cherkis, 2007).

Capacity Expansion

Capacity expansion options are cheaper and the most timely option, but are not suitable for all jurisdictions. There are other cost minimization techniques including the use of detailed budgets and requests for proposals (RFPs). A budget carefully outlines the kinds of revenues expected/earned and expenses that will be incurred and the categories for those elements. This also means that expenditures be accounted for on a regular basis. A complementary method is the judicious use of RFPs. This is a formalized way through which government entities can get contractors to submit bids to do work or perform a service (Freeman, 2000: 109–110). Through this process a more rational approach to contracting for products and services can be achieved, thus minimizing expenses and ensuring compliance with agency directives.

Cost Minimization Strategies while Increasing the Number of Correctional Facilities

In some jurisdictions, legal mandates have forced DOCs to build new facilities, renovate existing ones, or modify other buildings for correctional purposes (Ford and Moore: 6).

Wardens and correctional administrators have four options, each with its advantages and disadvantages:

1. Purchase or lease new land, then build a new facility.
2. Acquire or lease land with an already existing structure, then assume the costs of renovating it.
3. Buy or lease land nearby.
4. Build an addition to an already existing facility.

Correctional administrators have managed to increase the capacity of jails through the use of makeshift jails and jail barges.

Constructing an addition to an already existing facility may save money that would otherwise be spent on purchasing or leasing land. Alternatively, locating a nearby satel-lite or annex jail or prison nearby may alleviate some of the costs associated with trans-porting staff and inmates (Welch, 1996: 186–187).

Building new structures is risky and very resource intensive (in terms of the time and money required). One alternative is to convert already existing structures—like mothballed government-owned buildings (e.g., public schools)—into correctional facilities. Similarly, during the 1980s and 1990s, New York City began to rely on jail barges—reconditioned boats that housed prisoners. These vessels, moored around the island of Manhattan, upset many middle- and upper-class residents, who feared a negative impact on community safety and a decline in their property values.

Unfortunately, both the back-end and capacity expansion responses also have problems. Since both these measures are reactive (the projects cannot be immediately utilized), it takes a considerable amount of time to have them implemented. For example, it can take a year or more for proposals to be vetted, and construction companies to submit bids, before a new correctional facility starts to be built. Reactive measures also do not force criminal justice planners to reanalyze sentencing practices and/or implement more effective community corrections programs (Ford and Moore: 6).

Development of Cost Minimization Strategies

There are three basic areas where the costs of jails and prisons can be reduced: "cost containment, controlling the cost of new prison construction, and revenue enhancement" (Freeman, 2000: 110).[1]

Some wardens, in an effort to generate additional revenue or offset potential financial setbacks, have recycling programs. Correctional facilities, as one can well imagine, generate a considerable amount of waste, and some of it can be used to generate income.

Other cost-saving mechanisms include

- reducing the number of inmates;
- decreasing the daily cost of incarceration; and
- controlling the cost of new prison construction.

When facilities are built or renovated, some DOCs have had contractors install more energy (and cost) efficient technology (insulation, thermostats, lighting, etc.). Some facilities are capitalizing on solar, wind, and geothermal energy to reduce electricity costs.

> Revenue enhancement attempts to develop nontaxpayer revenue sources through the implementation of three strategies: (1) inmate reimbursement, (2) surcharging the inmate use of technology, and (3) the construction of beds for leasing out. All three strategies can involve the use of inmate labor and varying amounts of interaction with the private sector. (Freeman, 2000: 110)

Classification is another way that cost savings can be accrued. In particular, inmates may be sent to a less secure facility; thus, it would cost less to house and supervise them. Alternatively, convicts may demonstrate significant change (including being "rehabilitated") and thus be amenable to be placed on parole (Ford and Moore: 8–9).

The lion's share of a facilities budget is primarily personnel. In particular, administrators eat up a considerable amount of money by relying too much on overtime. A correctional manager can address this problem through judicious use of scheduling, properly timed hiring efforts, and inducements to reduce staff sick time, including buying back unused sick time (Ford and Moore: 12). This also means making tough choices between mandatory and optimum staffing levels.

Some entrepreneurial sheriffs in small towns have been able to recoup costs, if not provide additional income for their agencies by leasing out space in their jail facilities to the Immigration and Naturalization Service (INS) (Welch, 2002).

Despite this problem, many states have not cut back on jail and prison spending. The reason behind this counterintuitive response is that most governors and state politicians do not want to appear to be soft on crime; thus, building a new correctional facility is often seen as being a supporter of law and order (Broder, 2003). Moreover, one must be careful about revenue enhancement programs because in the past we have had such deplorable experiments like the convict lease program. In Georgia, starting in 1868, for example, inmates were leased for $11.00 per year, with the only limitation being to avoid "unseemly cruelty" (a common-law limitation on the treatment of cattle, slaves, and other chattel). The price didn't go up for all the decades of the convict lease system (and many inmates were never returned).[2]

LEGAL CHALLENGES

There have been numerous legal challenges to the problem of overcrowding. Some of the landmark cases have included *Bell v. Woolfish* (1979). This supreme court case stems from a prison in upper New York State, where the administration was forced to place two or more inmates awaiting trial in the same cell. The prisoners argued that this was a form of punishment that was meted out even though they had not been convicted of a crime, thus violating their protections as guaranteed by the Fifth Amendment (i.e., due process clause) of the U.S. Constitution. The court argued that the short-term nature of the detention did not violate the law. In 1981, prisoners at a correctional facility in Ohio argued that the long-term nature of double bunking in their facility was unconstitutional. In this case, however, prisoners were arguing that it was cruel and unusual punishment guaranteed by the Eighth Amendment of the U.S. Constitution. Although supported by the federal district court, it was overturned by the Supreme Court that argued that the overcrowding did not inflict "wanton and unnecessary infliction of pain" that must be present for cruel and unusual punishment to have occurred.

THE PRIVATIZATION OF PRISONS AS A SOLUTION

Over the history of corrections the possibility that selected aspects of jails and prisons should be run by organizations other than the state has frequently been proposed and utilized. This practice dates back at least to 1348 when prisoners would be used as galley slaves, and 1598 when ship captains and merchants agreed to take inmates out of state facilities and transport them to America and other British colonies, where they would be forced into indentured servitude (Feeley, 2002).

Perhaps as a result of the conservative swing at the federal level and many state governments, correctional services have increased their reliance on private enterprise to build, operate, and provide services to jails and prisons. This includes such functions as educational, food, medical, security, and transportation services (Austin and Irwin: 69–70). There is currently a huge correctional industry in the United States. Companies such as the Corrections Corporation of America (CCA) and The Geo Group (which recently changed its name from Wackenhut Corrections Corporation) "account for over three fourths of the entire world wide market" and derive significant incomes from providing local, state, and federal prison services. Moreover, "The total amount of revenues now allocated to private prisons and jails is estimated at $1 billion" (Austin and Irwin: 65).

Approximately 7 percent of convicts are housed in private prisons and jails. Of that total about 5 percent are in prisons alone (Austin and Irwin: 65). Nevertheless, "there are some indications that growth in the use of privatization may be losing its steam and has reached a plateau. . . . The stock prices for most of the major firms have dropped substantially in the past year, and there have been a number of highly publicized management problems with several privately operated facilities in Texas, Ohio, and New Mexico" (p. 65). In the beginning, privatization creates competition that can drive the prices down as companies compete with each other; however, as fewer companies enter the market, the private companies start increasing their costs to purchasers.

In 1984, the first private prison opened in Tennessee. Since then roughly 150 of these kinds of facilities exist in the United States.[3] A number of entities own these businesses; however, the most prominent is the Corrections Corporation of American (CCA). It is a publicly traded company (under the symbol CXW) that sells its shares on the New York Stock Exchange. At one point in time the stock value soared 1,000 times its price, making its owners and investors "very rich people" (Hallinan, 2003: xvii). Other corporations such as Aramark and Canteen food services have done quite well supplying correctional services with food. Other items provided by private contractors include linen, medical, educational, and transportation services.

Private prisons are amenable to state correctional planners. They alleviate the stress connected with construction costs, financing, and maintenance. "In 1986, there were just twenty-six hundred privately managed prison beds in the United States. By 1995, there were over sixty-three thousand. States like Tennessee considered privatizing their entire prison system" (Hallinan, 2003: 145). In 2007 CCA "has approximately 72,500 beds in 65 facilities, including 40 owned facilities, under contract for management in 19 tates and the District of Columbia" (www.correctionscorporation.com).

Privatization calls into question several ethical issues. Given that society is responsible for arresting and adjudicating individuals, is it right for a corporation to profit from the misery of others? In private corrections, the staff often do not have the appropriate training to do their jobs. Privatization also makes it harder for the government to control what goes on in corporate-run prisons. Another problem concerns the fact that often after receiving a lucrative contract the provider will "sham" by providing less services or lower quality items to further enhance their profit margin.

Finally, numerous convicts have suffered under private-run medical care providers. Some (e.g., Prison Health Services [PHS]) have continuously run afoul of state inspectors, regulators, and DOCs. Nevertheless, DOCs have continuously renewed their contracts, and often take the position that something is better than nothing. The prison health industry is one area, among others, in the contemporary history of jails and prisons where privatization has failed, and where the function of providing health care must be resumed by the state. In short, the reality of prisons these days is that one cannot really talk about a system that is either public or private. We in fact have a hybrid system where selective aspects of the prison are contracted out to the private sector.

In an irony of sorts is that private prisons resocialize the costs when they can no longer achieve their goals. For example, in 1997, Ed Bradley, Associate Producer of the award-winning CBS television news magazine "60 Minutes," did an exposé of the private prison in Youngstown, OH—after six inmates had escaped—undetected for eight hours. The manual at this CCA facility simply instructed the staff at the prison to "call the local sheriff" if and when the inmates escaped. They simply dumped the problem back onto the state. This prompted the state of Ohio to pass laws attempting (unsuccessfully) to put the burden back onto private prisons to collect their escapees.

> Privatization in itself tends to focus so exclusively on profit that the increases in privatization seems due to corporate profit motives, rather than increasing crime waves, state difficulties in building and running their own prisons, and so forth. Thus, privatization of prisons seem only to promote an insatiable profit-motive of corporations in an unusual market (market-failure?) where more and more dollars seem to always be produced by state legislators.[4]

REVENUE ENHANCEMENT

One means through which prisons have tried to increase their revenues is by contracting with companies (e.g., phone) that provide services to prisoners for a fee, but then charge above market rates, and give the correctional facility a percentage of their income (i.e., a kickback). Others seek out private-sector companies and provide the labor for them. One of the more dubious practices in the history of corrections in America previously mentioned is the "convict leasing" procedure. The revenues then either fund prison programs or are placed back into the correctional facility's general fund. Meanwhile, the jails and/or prisons and the facilities' administration have discretion on how to allocate this money.

In 1947, the *Taft–Hartley Act* was passed. This prevented prisons from unfairly competing with local industries and labor markets. "Nearly ever since, it has been a violation of federal law for state prisons to sell their products in interstate commerce— unless, like the programs in South Carolina and Oregon, they are certified by a federal program known as Prison Industry Enhancement (PIE). This program was created in 1979, and until recently has been all but dormant. In 1998, for instance, thirty-five states were certified to participate in the program, but, all told, they employed just twenty-six hundred inmates, or about two tenths of 1 percent of the nation's state prison population" (Hallinan, 2003: 149).

"Under the provisions of PIE, inmates must be paid the same wages as free workers engaged in similar work. They must also be allowed to keep at least 20 percent of what they earn. The rest of their wages can be withheld to pay income taxes, child support obligations, room and board charges, and payments due to victim assistance funds" (Hallinan, 2003: 149). Obviously, this kind of program has received ample criticism from organized labor.

CONCLUSION

Short of abolishing jails and prisons (e.g., Mathiesen, 1974), there are several means of eliminating underfunding through a combined effort among activists, professionals, and administrators who can educate and lobby elected officials to spend more on corrections and pass laws that benefit the field. Wardens or senior command staff could apply for state and federal money to improve programs, for example. We should also encourage jail and prison administrators to use their funding more efficiently.

Additional efforts include supporting the election of those individuals who would make increased funding for jails and prisons their priority. At the state and federal levels, we can work to sanction, dismiss, or better educate and train correctional personnel and management. Correctional administrators should aggressively pursue dishonest or lazy staff. Sanctioning workers when they fail to comply with departmental policies is not easy particularly because of the blue wall of silence and the strength of CO unions.

At the institutional level, solutions include eliminating overtime and ensuring that there are enough trained and qualified staff on which supervisors can rely if someone is sick, on leave, or on vacation,[5] and improving communication between workers and administrators. We need to put an end to business as usual among elected politicians and government workers who approach their job in a casual and laissez-faire way.

If more money could be funneled to corrections, then we could implement more liberal approaches (e.g., rehabilitation) and refrain from poorly thought-out conservative ones (e.g., building more prisons, increasing the length of sentences, etc.). All told, this approach would in the very least alleviate the overcrowding problem. Sufficient space in prisons would prevent the diversion of suspects out of the system to probation when they really should be incarcerated. Also, more money funneled into the system means higher-quality and happier staff.

KEY TERMS

back-end measures
classification
compassionate release
front-end measures
jail barge

Prison Industry Enhancement (PIE)
privatization
revenue enhancement
sham/shamming

REVIEW QUESTIONS

PART 1: MULTIPLE-CHOICE QUESTIONS

1. What is the name of the relatively recent federal bill/act that provided funds for the building of regional jails?

    a. The *Civil Rights Act of 1964*
    b. The *Americans with Disabilities Act of 1990*
    c. *Violence against Woman Act of 1994*
    d. 1994 Crime Bill
    e. none of the above

2. What is the lion's share of a prisons budget used for?

    a. building new facilities
    b. food
    c. medical care
    d. inmates' education
    e. personnel

3. Which of the following are revenue enhancement strategies?

    a. inmate reimbursement
    b. surcharging inmates' use of technology
    c. leasing beds out
    d. all the above
    e. none of the above

4. What is a positive inducement offered by prison administrators to reduce sick time?

    a. only hiring healthy individuals
    b. buying back unused sick time
    c. building a gym
    d. providing healthy meals for free
    e. on-site doctor

5. During the 1980s and 1990s, when New York City experienced a shortage of cell space, with which method did the New York City Department of Corrections experiment?

    a. releasing a greater number of inmates out of custody
    b. greater reliance on bench warrants
    c. bail bonds
    d. jail barges
    e. housing inmates in cheap hotels

6. Over the past decade, at which level of government is the highest expenditure for prisons?

    a. federal
    b. state

    c. regional

    d. local

    e. none of the above

7. What is the function of PIE?

    a. to sell baked goods to prisons

    b. a prison industry

    c. a cost-accounting technique used by wardens

    d. to certify prisons to sell their products (made by convicts) through interstate commerce

    e. none of the above

8. What is a request for proposal?

    a. a method of soliciting bids for the provision of services or the purchase of articles

    b. a legal document used in transferring inmates from one facility to another

    c. a command issued by a warden to their subordinates

    d. all of the above

    e. none of the above

9. Which of the following is a front-end option?

    a. parole

    b. probation

    c. halfway house

    d. all of the above

    e. none of the above

10. Which of the following is the nation's biggest commercial operator of jails and prisons?

    a. Wackenhut

    b. Corrections Corporation of America

    c. Prisons Corporation of America

    d. Eagle Security

    e. none of the above

11. What is a jail barge?

    a. a method for transporting prisoners

    b. a type of weapon used by correctional officers to defend themselves

    c. a legal petition submitted by a pretrial detainee

    d. a method for housing inmates

    e. none of the above

12. What is the term given to the process whereby a terminally ill convict is allowed to go home and die in the company of their loved ones?

    a. sick leave

    b. medical leave

   c. release on own recognizance

   d. compassionate release

   e. none of the above

PART 2: SHORT-ANSWER QUESTIONS

1. What is a jail barge?

2. What is the name of the largest corporation operating private correctional facilities in the United States?

3. List the three typical options used to deal with underfunding.

4. What are five reasons why over the past two decades there has been such a huge growth in correctional spending?

PART 3: ESSAY QUESTIONS

1. Which is more useful—front-end, back-end, or capacity building—in order to deal with the financial problems of prisons?

2. What are three difficulties with privatization?

3. To what extent can private prisons help alleviate underfunding?

4. What are the advantages and disadvantages of privatization in corrections?

5. What do you think is the most effective way to reduce the costs of jails and prisons and why?

NOTES

1. As a result of wardens needing to reduce costs, a sector of the consulting industry now specializes in this sort of thing. In fact there is a monthly newsletter, *Corrections Cost Control & Revenue Report*, which specializes in helpful articles on this subject matter (Hallinan, 2003: 12).
2. Personal conversation with Bradley Chilton, February 21, 2007.
3. Private entities entered the correctional field about two decades earlier. One such example is in 1975 when RCA Services contracted with the state of Pennsylvania to run a training school for delinquents in Northampton, PA (Durham, 1993: 33). Since this is a juvenile facility and this book focuses on adults, it is mentioned here only parenthetically.
4. Personal correspondence with Bradley Chilton, February 21, 2007.
5. It is recognized that this will be difficult as many COs depend upon the overtime pay to supplement their income.

Chapter 5

Prison Conditions

INTRODUCTION

Conditions inside prisons vary among the federal system and the regional and state systems of corrections, between male and female prisons, and among different levels of security. Assessing the state of these environments is difficult as many firsthand descriptions seem like urban legends that are embellished to suit the personal goals of the storytellers. What this means is that not all prisons are filthy, have horrible food, and lack rehabilitative programs. Nevertheless, some of the most salient controversial prison conditions are unsanitary living conditions, the lack of reha- bilitative programs, the absence of adequate health and medical care, poor food, and violence, including sexual assault. These problems often lead to abuse, anger, depression, fear, frustration, and/or violence, not only among the prisoners, but the correctional officers (COs) too (see Chapter 11). Before continuing, however, it must be understood that these settings are affected by the powerful effects of the inmate social system and prison subculture (e.g., Sykes, 1958; Sykes and Messinger, 1960; Bowker, 1978). These underlying causes can exacerbate what on the outside might seem to be normal living and working relationships.

This chapter has benefited from the comments of Miguel Zaldivar.

HEALTH CONDITIONS

Introduction

When individuals are sent to prison, they must worry about catching serious and possibly life-threatening diseases. Correctional facilities are notoriously unhealthy places (McDonald, 1999; Speed Weed, 2001; Murphy, 2003). In the past, convicts routinely contracted cholera, yellow fever, and tuberculosis (TB) while doing time—which explains why TB used to be called *jail cough* or *prison fever*. Prisons are typically dirty, lack proper sanitary conditions, are overcrowded, and have poor ventilation. In situations like this, any communicable disease can quickly spread through the entire inmate population. Diseases are usually transmitted via air or through body fluids, such as semen, blood, and saliva.

Although the administrative corridors will be spotless, the cell house may be filthy. Generally, all the areas of the prison in which the public may enter or where the supervisors have offices are cleaned relentlessly. As one progresses to the interior of the prison, behind the security thresholds and into the cellblocks where the prisoners live, the hallways can be dim and dirty. The lighting and ventilation may also be poor (Ross and Richards, 2002).

Prisons also provide minimal health education. Information that could help convicts is rarely placed on bulletin boards or distributed in the form of memos or pamphlets about how to protect oneself from serious diseases. "The material provided is usually in the form of pamphlets, which are usually beyond the reading level of many inmates."[1] On the other hand, the prison staff typically receives better and more easily accessible information, annual training, and equipment to prevent themselves from getting sick. There are a number of health concerns listed from least to most important.[2]

Noise/Hearing Loss

Prisons are noisy places, with the slamming of cell doors, screaming and yelling, and a constant racket that reverberates off the cement and steel structures. The noise will remind an arrestee of a crowded transportation hub or shopping center, where the background drone of hundreds of voices may drown out one's own conversation. The noise is so bad that some prisoners suffer hearing damage (Jacobson, Jacobson, and Crowe, 1989; Ross and Richards, 2002). There is little that inmates can do to protect themselves from hearing loss, as there is no way to avoid the pandemonium except to cover their head with pillows when they are in their cell, sleep with earplugs, or take every opportunity available to be outside in the yard, where the sound dissipates. Hearing loss is especially a problem for older inmates.

Lung Cancer

Unsurprisingly, many prisoners smoke. In the past, convicts were allowed to smoke cigarettes or cigars and/or chew tobacco nearly everywhere. Jail and prison cellblocks were typically littered with cigarette butts and heavy smoke filled the air. Since the late 1990s, correctional administrators concerned with minimizing fires, environmental degradation, and most importantly avoiding lawsuits from prisoners (and COs) who may have developed respiratory illnesses or lung cancer from being forced to breathe secondhand smoke have banned cigarettes and cigars from the interior areas of jails and prisons or the complete correctional facility. Today, most institutions strictly forbid both staff and prisoners to smoke inside; all smokers are now required to take their habit outdoors. Some prisons may even have designated smoking areas in the yard (Patrick and Marsh, 2001).

Although nonsmokers and smokers attempting to quit may welcome these new institutional rules, many smokers are bitter about the change. For those individuals with a serious nicotine addiction, being locked in a smoke-free environment all day and night, except for the few hours they are allowed to be on the yard, can be very difficult.

Asbestos Poisoning

A considerable number of old buildings contain asbestos. It is a relatively inexpensive material that was used as a fire retardant, and to insulate heating and air-conditioning systems. In some structures using drop ceilings, the panels that were installed were also made out of asbestos. During the 1960s it was discovered that asbestos led to such life-threatening illnesses such as asbestosis, mesothelioma, and cancer. Since 1978, it has been illegal to use asbestos in residential and workplace construction. In the 1990s, at the East Oregon Correctional Institution, state inspectors noticed that the building had numerous pipes that were coated with highly toxic asbestos. An administrator had the prisoners remove it without any protective gear. Prisoners and COs became sick. When this occurred, they finally turned the task over to a professional asbestos abatement company.

Tuberculosis

Tuberculosis is a lung disease spread in places that are overcrowded with dirty, stale, and stagnant air. Although prisoners routinely (sometimes yearly) have TB tests, if a con has an adverse reaction (red marks on their skin), they are generally told by the medical staff that they should not worry. If, in fact, a con tests positive for a disease or illness, it is often kept secret, so the sick inmates will not be attacked by fearful prisoners (Bellin, Fletcher, and Safer, 1993).

Hepatitis

Hepatitis is a liver disease spread through blood, semen, bad water, or spoiled meat. Depending on its' strain, in the early stages, cons might not even know they have this ailment. As the illness progresses, the eyes and skin turn yellow (aka *jaundice*). It causes extreme fatigue, and, if it is not treated quickly, may lead to death of those afflicted. Many individuals from lesser developed countries, alcoholics, junkies, or other intravenous drug users suffer in varying degrees from this illness. There are several types of hepatitis. The three most common ones range from hepatitis A to hepatitis C (the most debilitating). In its worse case, hepatitis C affects sufferers the rest of their life. It is most damaging against your liver, which is needed to fight infections, get rid of toxins in your body, and store energy (Ruiz et al., 1999).

AIDS

Acquired Immunity Deficiency Syndrome (AIDS) suppresses the body's ability to fight ill-ness. Not only are homosexuals at risk, but so are intravenous drug users, including drug addicts, diabetics, and those who require frequent blood transfusions, like hemophiliacs. AIDS is one of the most highly concentrated diseases among the prison population. A 1994 survey, sponsored by NIJ, outlined how AIDS was nine times more prevalent in prisoners than in the general population (Hammett et al., 1995). According to a 2005 Bureau of Justice Statistics (BJS) report (Maruschak, 2005), based on a survey conducted in 2003, 1.8 and 2.6 percent of men respectively in federal and state correctional facilities were HIV positive.

The diagnosis of any of the previously reviewed diseases is confidential information. The prison medical staff may not take the time to do the appropriate tests to isolate the problem. They may figure that the minute they give prisoners the bad news, the cons will request medication, an extra expense incurred by the correctional system.

Solutions to Poor Health Conditions

In general, at both the state and federal levels, the provision of medical services in many American prisons is inhumane (Murphy, 2003). Both prisoners and correctional insti-tutions can minimize the health risks in jails and prisons. Some of these solutions are self-directed, while others involve the intervention of family members, the correctional facility, prison activists, or state or federal government. Each kind of disease requires its own sort of prevention. With respect to hepatitis, TB, and AIDS, convicts need to avoid coming into contact with other people's blood, saliva, sweat, and semen at all costs, as it could carry any number of infectious organisms. One method, prison regulations permitting, is for cons to take their personal utensils to the cafeteria. If inmates continue intravenous drug use behind bars, they need to take extra special caution to sterilize any drug paraphernalia and use condoms if they are engaging in homosexual contact. (Needless to say both these items are contraband.) Otherwise, a trip to the institution may be a good time to get clean.

The most common precaution used by prisoners to maintain or even improve their health is regular exercise—at least walking the yard, possibly jogging, weightlifting, or participating in sports like basketball, handball, or softball (Murphy, 2003). Exercise works off stress, helps a person lose weight, and improves prisoners' health. Some men overcome their addictions to alcohol and drugs, establish a daily routine of exercise, and leave prison in better health than when they arrived. Some minimum-security camps may have a tennis court, but cons will have to wait in a long line for the privilege of using this. Also important is educating oneself about food, including learning how to read food labels.

In addition, prisons should allow convicts condoms and bleach. Correctional facilities, however, do not like inmates to have condoms because they feel it will be used to smug-gle drugs and the realization that it condones an activity (sex—especially forced/non-consensual) that is prohibited. In 2001 only Mississippi and Vermont allowed inmates in their prisons to have condoms. Jails in New York City, San Francisco, Washington, D.C., and Philadelphia also allow condoms. Unfortunately, no follow-up research has been conducted to determine the effectiveness of condom use in correctional settings.

It is also important to make sure convicts are not issued the wrong medication or placebos by medical staff. In some facilities, occasionally inmates who may have previously held positions as pharmacists, nurses, dentists, or doctors before their convictions stand watch over the medication line every morning at sick call inspecting the prescribed medication provided to prisoners to make sure they are given the right pills.

When convicts do get sick, they hope it is nothing serious, as the medical services are typically limited and substandard. Prisoners who suffer from chronic or acute illnesses will find medical staff to be few, overburdened, and—even if they care to help—prevented from doing so by a prison health care system that is underfunded, bureaucratic, and severely limited in the services and medical procedures authorized. Prisoners who need surgery, expensive medication, or sophisticated medical protocols generally require family and friends to pressure prison administrators. A life-threatening illness—for example, cancer, a heart attack, or a stroke—will require outside intervention—possibly a lawsuit, or multiple letters, e-mails, or phone calls from a powerful politician—to get cons transported to a civilian hospital for treatment (Murphy, 2003).

Prisoners who have severe unattended medical problems (or more likely, the family or friends of those incarcerated, if they still maintain contact) need to enlist the aid of grassroots organizations and elected politicians who can contact or write their warden and appropriate members of the state departments of corrections (DOCs) to properly monitor the situation. DOCs should switch to public companies where the records would be more readily accessible to the scrutiny of the public, media, and other government oversight agencies. Finally, the federal government, with the assistance of the Centers for Disease Control and Prevention (CDC), should institute nationwide mandatory hepatitis (and other infectious disease) testing and treatment for all jail and prison inmates and those individuals under community corrections supervision.

Over the past eight years a number of telemedicine programs have been established in prisons. "Telemedicine (also referred to as 'telehealth' or 'e-health') allows health care professionals to use 'connected' medical devices in the evaluation, diagnosis and treatment of patients in other locations. These devices are enhanced through the use of telecommunications technology, network computing, video-conferencing systems and CODECs. Telemedicine customarily uses two methods to transmit images, data and sound—either 'live', real-time transmission where the consulting professional participates in the examination of the patient while diagnostic information is collected and transmitted, or 'store and forward' transmission, where the consulting professional reviews data asynchronous with its collection. Many programs employ both transmission capabilities, to maximize efficient use of resources appropriate to the medical services being provided" (www.amdtelemedicine.com). In Texas, through the University of Texas, Medical Branch in Galveston, inmate health care is about $8.00 per prisoner.[3] Indeed telemedicine is an improvement over the previous method of healthcare delivery in many correctional facilities, but it is no panacea. In prisons, some of the medical services are run by private Health Maintenance Organizations (HMOs), like Correctional Medical Services (CMS) (e.g., Hylton, 2003). Occasionally, we get a window into this world. For example, Hylton outlined how CMS "controls the health care of all prisoners in ten states and manages a portion of inmate health care in another seventeen." In general, the author provides a convincing portrait of how several important aspects of these businesses are beyond the scrutiny of the average member of the public. Most importantly, CMS uses a number of clever "accounting practices" to create the impression that their provision of health care is well intenioned, but in reality they do as much as possible to avoid using up its company resources. Private HMOs are often beyond the scrutiny of the average public. In order to improve this state of affairs, perhaps the DOCs should switch to public companies, where the records would be more accessible.

Governments can do a lot to improve health care behind bars. Some of this was mentioned, almost in passing, in the Commission on Safety and Abuse Report including "end[ing] co-payments for medical care" and extending Medicaid and Medicare to eligible prisoners (2006: 13). "To drive down the costs, legislators pressure corrections administrators to require prisoner to make co-payments for their medical care. While co-payments seem reasonable on the surface, they cost more in the long run by discouraging sick prisoners from seeking care early on, when treatment is less expensive and before disease spreads" (p. 14).

Another recommendation from the Commission on Safety and Abuse (2005–2006) was for DOCs to partner with their local public health commissions. According to the Report, "It is disappointing that public health departments have not taken a more active role in ensuring quality health care for prisoners and that county and state executives have not encouraged partnerships between jails and prisons and a broad range of community health-care providers—including public hospitals, local clinics, teaching institution, and doctors and nurses in private practice" (p. 39). The commission cited a number of jurisdictions where this takes place, but did not go into great detail. Nevertheless, they do add, "[p]artnerships with community and public health providers broaden the pool of qualified broaden the pool of qualified caregivers who are committed to working in a correctional environment by allowing them to remain connected with community clinics and hospitals, teaching universities, and public health agencies. The partnerships increase the chances that caregivers will have some sensitivity to the particular cultural and language barriers" of prisoners (p. 40). The commission pointed out a number of advantages to this recommendation including "increase[ing] the odds that people will have clear access to necessary heath services after release—sometimes from the very same doctors and nurses who treated them in jail" (p. 41).

Additionally, there have been calls for mandatory HIV/AIDS testing of prisoners. This measure has been opposed by many civil libertarians, prisoner rights groups, and AIDS activists in the United States and elsewhere (e.g., World Health Organization). These groups believe that mandatory testing will lead to prisoners being singled out by both correctional staff and other convicts for victimization in some shape or form (Young, 2006).

Lawyers and prison reform activists have also pressured DOCs to providing better health care. The most significant court case in this policy area is *Estelle v. Gamble* (1976). Here the Supreme Court stated that "deliberate indifference to the serious medical needs of prisoners constitutes the 'unnecessary and wanton infliction of pain' proscribed by the Eight Amendment."

POOR FOOD

A considerable amount of controversy surrounds the quality of food in prison. Why? Food holds enormous importance for convicts not just for its nutritional value, but for psychological purposes too (Valentine and Longstaff, 1998; Ross and Richards, 2002: Chapter 7). Nevertheless, inmates' perceptions and reality of food are often based on what the individual was used to eating on the outside. Indeed, some of the firsthand stories told by cons about meals sound like urban legends or myths. Moreover, like so many things in the field of corrections, the food differs from one institution to another.

Cafeteria Food

Convicts frequently refer to institutional meals as dog food, Ken-L Rations, or Alpo. It is typically served in large cafeterias, also called the canteen, chow, mess, or dining hall. In general, it is basic institutional food that one might receive at a public hospital, or served in the military.[4] On the extreme end of things, the best meals are often served on holidays or when "dignitaries" visit. On these occasions, the kitchen might prepare food of somewhat better quality.

Some facilities have special dietary food lines for those with medical conditions (e.g., diabetics), or those whose religion bans the eating of particular foods. For example, the "Common Fare" diet (a simple meal with no pork, no mixing of meat and milk products, and no utensils used in food preparation that have come into contact with pork—for all intents a kosher diet) is often requested for prisoners of the Jewish and/or Muslim faith. Rarely are there strictly vegetarian or vegan meals served in prison (Ogden and Paul, 2001). Some correctional facilities integrate the local cuisine into their menu; in the Deep South, they might serve catfish, fish heads, corn bread, and grits. And black beans might be more prevalent in Florida than in Texas.

Some days, however, the food is prepared, served, and thrown out, with only a small number of cons daring a taste. Occasionally, the fruit and vegetables appear to be bruised, overripe, rotten, or canned (Ross and Richards, 2002: Chapter 7). And the meat and chicken seem to be of lowest quality. Moreover, convicts routinely complain that COs place excrement, rodent parts, and insects in their food (Hassine, 2004). Whether this actually happens is hard to verify.

Prisoners who work in the cafeteria generally eat better and more, as they have greater access to food items. Many also use this job detail to go into an underground business. They may steal food (e.g., tomatoes, green peppers, chicken, and roast beef) and sell it to more financially well-off inmates. Or they may make simple meal items (e.g., grilled cheese sandwiches and hamburgers) and sell them in dormitories and cellblocks. Mess hall workers because of access to yeast, sugar, and fruit may also be either suppliers to or manufacturers of hooch, moonshine, pruno, or rotgut (i.e., alcohol).

The institutional food is often not only of poor quality, but it may also disappear and not even be served in the mess hall. In some correctional facilities, staff may eat or steal the better food, and take it home to feed their family, pets and farm animals, or sell it on the black market (Ross and Richards, 2002: Chapter 7).

Depending on the prison system, those who are in solitary confinement may receive "prison loafs," in which the food offered for the day is ground up, placed in a baking pan, and then reheated before being served to the inmates. In Federal Bureau of Prisons (FBOP) administrative segregation, prisoners eat the same food as those in general population.

Solutions to Poor Food

In many correctional facilities, the cons who have institutional jobs, a racket, or access to outside money mailed in either buy kitchen food or eat commissary items, which they store in their lockers. In some prisons, well-heeled and well-connected prisoners may purchase luxury food items like steaks and lobsters, or food from chain restaurants like Pizza Hut or Kentucky Fried Chicken that are smuggled in by correctional workers (Ross and Richards, 2002: Chapter 7).

Most prisons have a commissary, which sells basic items to general-population prisoners. These include food, stationery, toiletries, and clothing. In terms of food, the list will contain cheap brands of cookies, crackers, candies, and canned food like tuna, salmon, and sardines The commissary account is funded through convict labor when they work and earn a minimal amount of money to be placed in their account, and through individuals on the outside (e.g., family and friends) who deposit money into it.

Depending on the facility, the commissary is located in a hallway, open either once a week or once a month. Order forms are distributed or made available to the convicts. They list a limited selection of items for sale along with their prices. If prisoners can afford to buy food through the commissary, they avoid the dining hall. Prisoners buy food items from a commissary with some idea of how they are going to eat for the week or month.

The commissary is typically run by an officer who has a few prisoners working for him. Alternatively, it can be worked by an experienced convict whom the prison administration trusts. COs call cons down to the commissary by cellblock. In some correctional facilities, prisoners stand in a very long line leading up to a glass or metal screen window in front of a counter. Alternatively, after submitting the commissary slip, prisoners wait until their number is called.

Each prisoner fills out their commissary list, checks off what they want, adds everything up, puts their name and inmate number on the form, and then presents their ID or commissary card (which may be one and the same thing) at the window. The wait depends on several factors, but an inmate can complete their transactions within 45 minutes.

Unfortunately, the items at the commissary are generally overpriced, increasing inmate hostility toward the correctional system. In the FBOP the profits of the items sold are supposed to be placed in an inmate trust fund. This account is used for buying recreational items and sports equipment.

In some minimum-security state facilities, convicts who have enough money in their commissary account will purchase their meals out of vending machines, heating them up in a microwave oven (Elrod and Brooks, 2003). If vending machines are not present inside the facility, then they may be located in a visiting room—with food prices seriously inflated. Naturally, there are rumors that the vending service is owned by relatives or associates of the warden or retired COs (Ross and Richards, 2002: Chapter 7).

In order to prevent food poisoning many prisoners skip cafeteria meals that appear risky, and instead supplement their diet with commissary food, vitamins, and a lot of liquids to flush their system. Common precautions used by prisoners to protect themselves from bacterial infections are to wash their hands frequently and to eat liberal amounts of hot peppers and salsa, which can be purchased at the commissary. This also works to clear the nasal passages and sinuses, and may help with cold symptoms and allergies (Ross and Richards, 2002: Chapter 7).

PHYSICAL VIOLENCE

Introduction

Violence is endemic to most correctional facilities and has several dimensions. The most common types, psychological and physical violence abound in correctional settings (Fleisher, 1989; Bottoms, 1999). Psychological violence (or trauma) is often a precursor to and the effect of physical violence. The first affects the convicts' mental state and often leads to cynicism, anger, depression, and resistance to authority. Physical violence affects the prisoners' bodies and eventually their minds. The following section reviews the different kinds of violence experienced by convicts and briefly discusses gangs behind bars.

Violence by Convicts Against Themselves

The Problem

Occasionally, otherwise mentally stable cons will hurt themselves. This includes cutting themselves with sharp objects, pulling their hair out, banging their heads against walls or cell doors, or engaging in dirty protests (i.e., smearing feces all over their body). It is not uncommon to find an older prisoner who one day wakes up and decides he cannot "take it anymore." He shakes hands with his buddies and then, during yard time, he walks past the kill zone (i.e., prohibited area next to a wall or fence) and is shot to death by one of the COs in the towers. This is called *death by gun tower*.

Another form of suicide is the escape attempt. If convicts try to climb the wall, they will be electrocuted by high-voltage lines or cut by razor wire. More than likely, cons will die on the wall. If, by some small chance, they make it over, odds are they'll be shot down by their pursuers. Escaped convicts are usually wanted dead or alive. Or a prisoner may make a spectacular swan-dive leap from the fifth-floor tier down to the cement floor below. That's why, among other reasons, in most correctional facilities there is wire mesh extending up from the handrails to the ceilings of the tiers or there is netting between the floors, similar to those found under a circus trapeze.

Other forms of suicide include hanging, overdosing on drugs, slitting wrists, and neck, or having sex with an individual the inmate knows to be HIV positive. A prisoner committed to killing himself might one night drink a considerable amount of prison hooch (alcohol), or ingest whatever drugs he can get, then place a plastic bag over his head, go to bed, and suffocate in his sleep.

If prisoners attempt suicide, they must make a neat finish of themselves and not bungle the job. Otherwise, cons who have attempted suicide will be locked up in the hole or in the psychiatric unit. The COs typically want prisoners to live, if only because if cons die, there will be an investigation with a lot of questions to answer and copious paperwork to complete.

The prison infirmary has few medical personnel, and rarely are prisoners taken outside the gates to a civilian hospital; otherwise, there would be an epidemic of cons faking suicide attempts as a ploy to go to a civilian hospital, facilitate an escape attempt, or even just break the monotony. Cons rarely speak to a psychologist or counselor and will more than likely be sent back to the tier when it looks like they have calmed down. If they are in a minimum-security facility, convicts might be taken to a hospital. Here an ambulance can make it into and out of the facility relatively quickly, as compared to a penitentiary.

Solutions for Suicidal Prisoners

Inmates who are determined by the correctional staff to be suicidal are placed on suicide watch. Typically, the prisoner is removed from his regular cell and is placed in a cell or area where he can be regularly monitored not only by COs, but in some facilities by other convicts, and with the assistance of audio and video surveillance. Oftentimes, suicidal inmates' clothes are taken away from them and they are given a suicide gown or smock. In some correctional institutions this is called a banana suit, yellow suit, or dress (Bruton, 2004: 75–77). The construction of this garment varies from one institution to another. According to Bruton, retired Warden of the Minnesota Correctional Facility-Oak Park Heights, "This piece of clothing is made out of Kevlar with straps in the back that hold the gown on with heavy-duty Velcro. The outfit looks like a thick life jacket and is similar in appearance to a hospital gown without sleeves" (p. 76). In some prisons they have a program known as *suicide companions* wherein compassionate convicts receive suicide prevention training and are detailed to suicide-prone prisoners.

Violence by Convicts Against Other Prisoners and Correctional Personnel

Introduction

There are several kinds of physical violence that cons engage in including assaults, disturbances, rebellions, riots, and sexual assault (Cohen, Cole, and Bailey, 1976; Fleisher, 1989). Sometimes the distinctions among these types are difficult to discern because of the fluidity of the actions. The following section attempts to clarify the different kinds of violence and also elaborates on weapons and gangs.

Assaults

Prisoners are frequently beaten, stabbed, or killed in correctional facilities. Despite collection efforts by the U.S. Department of Justice's BJS, data on violence in prison is notoriously unreliable (National Commission on Safety and Abuse in Prison, 2006: 25). Nevertheless, the higher the security level, the more potential for violence. However, the most violent convicts are young men serving long sentences; older prisoners may be more dangerous, but more logical in their use of violence. That's why they have survived long enough to become older prisoners. Younger prisoners are more inclined than are grown men to have fistfights (Cooley, 1993; Ross and Richards, 2003).

Some of the physical violence is planned; cons might carefully plot out how they will attack or what they will do to a fellow prisoner or CO. Most violence, however, is spontaneous and is the result of some annoyance or irritation. This frustration may start when someone steps in front of a prisoner in a long line. It is more than a bother, it is a challenge. The line-jumper believes or wants to find out if the prisoner can be intimidated. If the line-jumper gets away with it, he'll be back another time, perhaps upping the ante.

What bothers many convicts, and is in fact one of their biggest fears, is that once they have decided that they can do "their own time," situations arise where they have to prove and/or defend themselves and this inevitably will put them in a position where they will engage in another crime, be convicted (aka *catch another case*), extend their time behind bars, and never go home (Hassine, 2004).

Correctional officers (and administrators) need to keep a close eye on all forms of violence in order to respond appropriately. If they overreact, they may have a riot on their hands. The correctional workers generally do not like it when cons fight because it generates onerous paperwork. But some COs have been known to instigate violence, for example, by putting two cons who hate each other together in the same cell and sitting back to watch the fireworks. Meanwhile, jails and prisons experience their share of disturbances, rebellions, and riots (Useem and Kimball, 1989).

Disturbances

Disturbances are low-intensity acts of resistance that have the potential to escalate. Usually, they begin with an altercation—someone tips over a table in the chow hall or damages institutional property in an outbreak of frustration and anger. If the food in the dining hall is particularly vile that day, the cons may fill up their trays and simultaneously throw them on the floor.

A disturbance may start with one con who damages a chair, and then, suddenly, 50 other prisoners are doing the same thing. Often, there may be no overt reason for the outburst, and there is no sanctity to the actions. Cons will equally destroy a dining hall, turn over a delivery truck that entered the prison, trash a chapel, or trample a bed of newly planted flowers. Some disturbances include inmates stopping up their toilets and having the water overflow into the corridors, making it a mess and unsafe to walk around cells and the hallways. These actions are signs of resistance, indications that inmates have not been totally beaten and still have some fight left in them, the result of collective frustration and boredom.

Some disturbances are caused by the annoyance of excessive noise. Sound reverberates in cellblocks, which are made primarily of cement and steel. As is often seen in Hollywood films, unhappy prisoners make noise by pounding on metal doors or banisters or screaming profanity at COs. Some cons aren't shy about throwing human waste products at the guards (known as *sliming*) (Ross and Richards, 2002).

With 200 convicts yelling profanities, officers are not going to put the whole cellblock in the hole—but they can take away privileges, like yard time, weekly movie, or commissary, which only enrages the cons that much more. Typically, however, the institution will go into lockdown mode. Few disturbances ever come to the attention of the public. Most DOCs try to avoid responding to media requests for information on such incidents because they fear publicity will create contagion, the spreading of rebellion to additional correctional facilities.

Rebellions

Rebellions include work and hunger strikes. A common form of protest in correctional facilities, especially for political prisoners, is the hunger strike. The situation (especially if the media gets involved) has the potential to embarrass the prison authorities.

A work strike is when convicts refuse to come out of their cells and/or go to the factory, cook, or clean. Without prison labor, administrators cannot effectively and efficiently run the correctional facility. COs usually try to identify the ringleaders (with the help of prison snitches), and will often throw the provocateurs in the hole. The administration then usually transfers the troublemakers to a higher security prison. Work strikes usually end because eventually the cons get hungry and run out of food stored in their lockers. So the prison, much like any other big corporation with striking workers, typically waits out the cons. Strikes do not usually last more than a week or two.

Riots

The American correctional enterprise has suffered notorious riots including those at the New York State Penitentiary at Attica in 1971, New Mexico State Prison at Santa Fe in 1980 (Useem, 1985; Colvin, 1992; Rolland, 1997), the Ohio Correctional Facility Lucasville Prison in 1993, and USP Atlanta in 1995 (Hamm, 1995). The Attica riot resulted in 39–43 dead,[5] including 11 prison employees. Santa Fe left 33 prisoners dead, most killed by other cons in an orgy of sadistic brutality that included murder by blowtorch, decapitation, and dismemberment, as well as beaten COs being gang-raped and then sodomized with nightsticks and lead pipes (Useem, 1985). The Lucasville riot resulted in 10 dead (Lynd, 2004). Each of these riots included serious injuries to hundreds of prisoners, additional time added to sentences, and tens of millions of dollars of damage to penal institutions. When all is said and done and the riot is put down, life becomes tougher for the surviving prisoners.

Sometimes riots begin when cliques or gangs decide to settle scores by attacking their rivals. Race or ethnic hatred and battles for prison dominance are another reason. Conditions of confinement may be so oppressive that the cons feel that they have no other choice than to retaliate. Long prison sentences, some with no parole and little opportunity for earning "good time" (a reduction in sentence), breed revolt. Riots are not just about COs or workers getting injured or killed; oftentimes, they involve prisoners' attempts to settle old debts.

When a riot is coming, convicts can almost literally feel it in their bones. Prisoners who have been through them before are more skilled at surviving the next one. If experienced cons do find themselves in the midst of a prison disturbance, rebellion, or riot, they try to keep a low profile and do not get caught up with the ensuing excitement. Some of the novices will stay in their cells to avoid the frenzy that runs through the corridors, modeling their behavior after the lifers.

When convicts riot, they typically begin by taking over a tier, cellblock, or part of the prison (e.g., cafeteria), with hopes of controlling the whole institution. Convicts know that even though they can take control of some or even all of the facility on any given day, they cannot hold it for long. The officers will eventually be supported by local law enforcement, state police, the National Guard, or other military reinforcements. The authorities will do whatever is needed to retake the prison, including using tear gas, shotguns, or automatic weapons.

Prisons are made from concrete and steel, but that hasn't stopped innovative cons from doing a good job of burning them down. They use cleaning fluid, bleach, and floor wax, and then pour it on their mattresses. There is a chemical reaction among these components, and eventually enough heat is produced for the paint on the concrete to start burning, finally causing the concrete to burn as well. Many roofs are constructed of wood and tar, which will easily go up in flames. Some prisoners will suffer the effects of smoke inhalation, others will be burned to death in the blaze. In most riots, more convicts than COs are killed.

Prison riots are doomed to fail. No matter how many COs are taken hostage, beaten, or killed, the uprising will inevitably be crushed by overwhelming force. COs and administrators who survive—or their replacements—will have months if not years to take revenge on those who have defied them. This includes pressing administrative and criminal charges against the rioters (Mahan and Lawrence, 1996).

Usually, the only time the news media reports on a prison riot is when convicts take hostages or set an institution on fire. In these situations the news gets out of the prison relatively rapidly and news organizations cannot ignore the situation as it develops.

Weapons

Many disputes are settled with shanks, homemade weapons made from toothbrushes, pencils, razor blades, broken glass and tape, or any metal, plastic, or wood that can be sharpened and fashioned into either a cutting or a stabbing device. An experienced convict can make a weapon out of nearly anything. For example, a newspaper rolled tight can be used like a knife to thrust at an opponent's vulnerable body parts. Harden this with toothpaste or plaster, and it can be made into a zip gun when it is filled with match heads and a projectile. Another common weapon is a pillowcase filled with soda cans, or a bar of soap hidden in a sock. Prison yard plants and cleaners can also be used as poison, fire accelerant, or explosives. And dental floss can be used to strangle a person (Ross and Richards, 2002: 122).

The Solutions

Avoiding fights   Generally, there are a number of rules for avoiding violence in prison. Much of this is referred to as the inmate code (e.g., Sykes and Messinger, 1960; Ross and Richards, 2002: 72). It mainly involves being overly polite, taking your turn, being aware of your surroundings and personal security, and not ratting out another prisoner (i.e., becoming a prison informer/snitch). This also means avoiding gambling, drugs, and alcohol.

Con bosses, trustees, and peacekeepers   In some DOCs the administration has experimented with the use of convicts policing other inmates. Unfortunately, in the more extreme versions the newly arrived convicts enter a system of indentured servitude where the power of the trustee is absolute. Encouraging inmate participation and input in the administration and management of correctional facilities is in principle a sound idea. However, the existence of con bosses, prison trustees, or what in California are known as prison *peacekeepers* is almost always doomed to fail (Marquez and Thompson, 2006). The history of American corrections has numerous examples of prisoners given the power to police other inmates, and in almost all cases this practice encourages corruption, intimidation, violence, and reinforces cruel and unusual punishment but at the hands of fellow inmates (Dilulio,1987). The California Department of Corrections, for example, has recently abolished the Prison "Peacekeeper" model and moved to a more impartial method of ensuring inmate compliance and mediation on the tiers, cellblocks, and yards of its prisons.

Separating known enemies or rival gang members   Correctional facilities are obligated to conduct some sort of check to make sure that inmates who have difficulties with each other are not in the same cell or cellblock. Oftentimes, this is done during classification (see Chapter 6). But scores are not always settled by individuals who know each other. Occasionally, there is a contract set up for the assault or murder of another inmate. If the facility knew this, then transporting one of the two individuals elsewhere would make sense.

Reducing the possibility of riots   Given the devastating effects of riots, it is understandable that experts have conducted research on how to best resolve them. Useem et al. (1995), for example, conducted an in-depth study concerning how major riots in U.S. prisons successfully ended. They place these into three stages: preriot, actual riot, and postriot. Before riots take place, prison administrators are advised to ensure that their prisons have a riot plan that includes "command structure with well-defined lines of authority," clear instructions on the use of force and weapons, interagency cooperation that specifies each agency's responsibilities, and proper training. In order to "prevent and deal with riots" the correctional facility must provide adequate supervision of staff in connection with "security practices," "ensure security of the physical plant and equipment," encourage staff to pay attention to "false clues" and to communicate this information to superiors, and use a combination of force and negotiations and "strategies that range from immediate use of force to waiting until inmate leaders are ready to negotiate. Unfortunately, similar research has not been conducted on the convict side of the equation. Finally, prison officials also have to provide opportunities for inmates to blow off steam, like yard time, a gym, or a library.

CORRECTIONAL OFFICER VIOLENCE

Introduction: The Problem

The prison staff periodically uses physical violence, or less than lethal force (e.g., pepper spray and TASER guns) against convicts (Pratt, Maahs, and Hemmens, 1999). COs are allowed by law to use force when life and property are in peril. Additionally, most correctional systems require their officers to be trained in and follow the "continuum of force" model where it is understood that there is a range of appropriate responses to inmates who are uncooperative and disobedient, including physical presence, verbal commands, and show of force by having several officers present. This means that violence should be the last resort rather the method of first choice.

When officers do beat convicts, it is often out of retaliation, because they have attacked the officer or have instigated work strikes, riots, or escape attempts. Occasionally, COs have been accused and convicted of torture (Kerness and Ehehosi, 2001). Also if staff violence occurs, then they try to do this discretely in ways to minimize witnesses. If force is necessary, it often takes place when the COs have power in numbers. In the FBOP, for example, each institution has a Special Operations Response Team (SORT) (pejoratively referred to by inmates as the *goon squad* or Ninja Turtles). This group typically consists of five officers and one lieutenant. They are used when inmates refuse to get out of their cells. This is typically called a cell extraction. The most important question with respect to violence by COs is, How frequently is it used and is it done in an indiscriminate manner? Unfortunately, empirical research on this behavior does not exist.

Correctional officers do not need to use violence to get convicts to follow orders, rules, procedures, and policies. They typically achieve their authority through five bases of power. Two most important ones are legitimate and informational (e.g., Hepburn, 1985). If cons complain about the COs or talk about their acts of deviance or crimes, prisoners may expect some sort of retribution by a CO.

Most often, COs will avoid using violence if they can. To begin with, most prisoners are in better physical condition than most COs. Additionally, there is a strong likelihood that other inmates will come to the assistance of the inmate being beaten. Moreover, it creates too much ill will that is remembered for a long time. Instead, COs will rely on threats and other nonphysical shows of power. Unlike the violence inflicted by the cons on each other, most CO violence is more subtle. If they dislike an inmate, COs either alone or in a group may engage in several disrespectful actions. These are as follows:

> *Confiscating their possessions.* COs will take correspondence and pictures of loved ones including children, girlfriends, or wives as well as sheets, clothing, food, and legal papers.
>
> *Destroying their belongings.* This may include tearing up their mail, artwork, books, and educational material (usually under the guise of a cell search).
>
> *Playing with the temperature.* Prisons can refuse to turn up the heat in the winter, or leave the air conditioners off in the summer.

Denying privileges. COs may refuse convicts telephone privileges, trips to the infirmary, or strictly control the amount of toilet paper they can use or when they can get a new roll.

Placing inmates who hate each other in the same cell. COs can move inmates who hate each other into the same tier, cellblock, or cell. Convicts are moved into cells with individuals that the COs know are sadistic or have a vendetta against. This situation may lead to an assault or homicide. Although the CO may have to account for this "error in judgment," there is always the possibility of plausible deniability.

Repeatedly tossing (searching) cells. Cells can be frequently searched and/or this can be done when it is most inconvenient for the prisoner. In the middle of the night, while prisoners are sleeping, COs may turn beds over, dumping prisoners on the floor. The COs might drag convicts to the floor, handcuff them, and go through all their personal effects while searching for weapons and contraband items (Kalinich, 1986).[6] And, in the process the con is hurt; his head or other parts of his body may hit the walls, doors or bars on cells.

Constantly strip-searching inmates. Strip searches, ostensibly used to detect drugs, weapons, and other forms of contraband, can be another form of intimidation. If they want, COs can order inmates to do this numerous times a day (Ross and Richards, 2002).

Frequently transferring inmates to different facilities. Often referred to as diesel therapy, some inmates frequently ride the prison bus or van for weeks on end from one institution to another. In these situations they do not eat or sleep well and their health often deteriorates.

Solutions

Increasingly over the years, DOCs have been sensitized to and trained their officers in the previously mentioned use of force continuum. This specifies when and how correctional force can be applied to inmates. In general, this method allows officers to use force only after all other methods have been exhausted. Also proper training of officers in use of force has had some effect on lessening excessive force against inmates. Having a use of force policy that is handled through a grievance procedure is a solution. A considerable amount of use of force by COs is a reflection that the senior management is not being appropriately attentive or simply looking the other way (Hemmens and Atherton, 2000).

Over the past three decades, as a partial solution to this problem, many DOCs are also using video surveillance technology not simply to monitor inmates, but prison officer violence too. This equipment is purported to be fail-safe. However, creative COs can find places to assault inmates where no cameras have been located. Additionally, if a cell extraction is about to be performed, COs will often videotape it in case a legal suit emerges and the procedures are called into question.

Regardless of the perpetrator or victim, we also need better mechanisms to capture the data on violence behind bars (Commission on Safety and Abuse in Prison, 2006: 13).

In fact, just like the practice in some daycare centers in the United States, it may act as some sort of deterrent if webcams were installed in selected parts of the prison and families allowed access to see what was going on.

Passive Aggressive Behavior

Prisoners have several creative ways to resist authority. Many of these methods, in prison slang called *slow playing,* are similar to what a child going through the "terrible twos" stage may do when they get stubborn. One way is to comply with direct orders, but do it very slowly or poorly. For example, when an officer tells a group of cons to paint a corridor, what under normal circumstances should take a day ends up requiring a week. In other words, convicts carry out the order in such a manner as to anger the officer. Alternatively, inmates might ignore the officer and pretend to be hard of hearing. This typically frustrates the officer (Lerner, 2002).

At other times convicts may refuse COs direct orders like getting out of their cells. In this case the COs can perform a cell extraction. Most cell extractions involve the participation of a number of COs wearing riot gear, and sometimes use less than lethal weapons like pepper spray. These procedures are also now done with someone video-ing the event, in case the inmate files a grievance or initiates a civil suit for damages incurred during this procedure.

Another more involved action is for prisoners to file writs, motions, lawsuits, and class action suits. Administrators and officers consider jailhouse lawyers to be some of the most dangerous people in prison because they know how to write legal motions and bring them before a court. At the very least, even if the convicts are denied satisfaction by the legal proceeding, they succeed in tying up the DOCs resources, and possibly embarrassing the prison authorities. It is also a form of communicating with the outside about the conditions of confinement, and it may intimidate the prison authorities (Thomas, 1988).

In most lockups and prisons, COs are quick to say that the majority of the inmates do not get into trouble because they follow the rules. The problem population comprises approximately 1 percent of the prisoners in an institution. When there is an incident, such as a stabbing on a tier, COs cannot place all of the suspects on administrative segregation (aka *the hole*). COs can try to investigate the incident, but rarely can they prove the identity of the culprit/s.

Gangs   Some jails, prisons, and penitentiaries are literally run by gangs (Stastny and Tyrnauer, 1982; Camp and Camp, 1985). Even if convicts want to "do their own time" and be left alone, there are strong pressures to join a gang for self and mutual protection. In situations like these, unaffiliated individuals are subject to routine victimization and they may not be able to defend themselves. Gang members may coerce, extort, or steal material possessions or services from convicts. Sometimes this is done when inmates conduct a cell invasion, by running on mass into the victims' cell and grabbing anything of value (Hassine, 2002).

Prison gangs typically coalesce around race, ethnicity, nationality, and neighborhood. One of the most common distinctions is among African-American, Hispanic and white gangs that dominate many correctional facilities. Gang members basically "hang together."

This means eating as a group in the cafeteria, walking the yard together, pumping iron (lifting weights), and sticking close to each other at work assignments or in housing units. The loners—the people without social skills or friends—and those who are physically weak are vulnerable to being physically attacked or preyed upon (ACA, 1993; Ross and Richards, 2002).

The Different Types

A number of ethnic and racially based prison gangs exist (ACA, 1993). In these milieus there is often considerable diversity. Amongst the African-American gangs, prisons have incarcerated members of the Black Guerrilla Family, the Vice Lords, the Crips, and the Bloods. Hispanic and Latino gangs have included the Neta and Latin Kings, which are predominantly Puerto Rican and Hispanic, and the Mexican Mafia and La Nuestra Familia, which are mainly Mexican American. White gangs include the Aryan Brotherhood, Dirty White Boys, Outlaws, and Hells Angels. Some, like the Colombians (many of whom are affiliated with the drug cartel), are multiracial, which makes trying to identify groups based solely on skin color difficult, but they share similar mannerisms, language, and style of dress.

Most of these organizations have long histories. Gang membership often evolves and spreads geographically. In the California institutions, some of the Blue Bird Gang and Hells Angels of San Quentin (motorcycle gangs) eventually became the white supremacist Aryan Brotherhood. The black gangs of the 1970s, like the Crips and Bloods, first started in Los Angeles. Soon they began started in other cities in California, then made their way across the Midwest to the East Coast, where they became established in New York City, Boston, and Philadelphia (Moore, 1978).

The public generally thinks that gang members are teenagers and young adults, but gangs, in fact, include all different age groups including junior gangsters, gang warriors (i.e., "gang bangers"), and older gang members (Klein, 1997). These groups also include "wannabes," associates (i.e., family or friends who are loosely connected to the members), and auxiliaries (i.e., lady friends). A few of the senior members may have established legitimate businesses that employ high-powered accountants and lawyers and have the resources to buy judges, politicians, and their way out of prison. Ultimately, gangs are a form of organized crime (Lavigne, 1989).

There are different kinds of gangs: Some exist primarily for economic gain (focusing on business activities like selling drugs, theft, and extortion), while others are formed for mutual self-protection, and some gangs are more violent than others. Gang culture is often an extension of street life into the penitentiary. Traditions learned in the ghetto or barrio are often "imported" into correctional facilities (Irwin and Cressey, 1962).

Gang affiliation will typically depend on the region of the country in which convicts have to do time. For example, in Illinois and New York, a disproportionate number of Hispanic gangs such as Latin Kings, or Vice Lords, or black gangs such as El Rukin or Black Gangster Disciples are part of the criminal element. In Florida you may see Puerto Rican gangs like the Nietas and 27s. In California and

Texas, correctional facilities house the Mexican Mafia, Texas Syndicate, Texas M, and Texas Family among other gangs. Much like political parties, gangs have different factions or divisions. In the Mexican organizations, for instance, there are both urban and rural components.

Joining a Gang

Gangs recruit new members on the street, in jail and prison and have colonized many state and federal pens (Hagedorn, 1988). A gang may serve as a surrogate family providing social and emotional needs for its members, both on the street and in prison. In fact, some members refer to the gang as their family.

Joining a gang carries many obligations and responsibilities including participating in feuds, revenge, and retaliation against rival factions. These conflicts may extend from the "hood" to the penitentiary and last for years. An important aspect of all gang affiliations is respect. Young men and women who grow up in inner-city neighborhoods want to be respected and not "dissed" (Anderson, 2000). And the way respect is usually displayed in the ghetto and barrios is often through style (e.g., Ferrell, 1993; Ferrell and Sanders, 1995; Miller, 1995)—by the clothes you wear, the money you spend, the car you drive, and the violence you engage in. In the institution, gang members are known by the ways in which they carry themselves, including altering their uniforms, sharing their food and contraband, and the individuals they hang out with in the chow hall and yard (Bourgois, 2002).

Gang members often expect to go to prison. When they go to a correctional facility, they try to make themselves comfortable. This means that they want new uniforms that are sharply pressed and a locker full of cigarettes and commissary food. Some want nothing more than to watch sports channels like ESPN every day all day.

How They Work

Gangs are organized to carry out business, not only on the street but also in prison. They are heavily involved in bringing contraband into the penitentiary. These items vary from institution to institution, state to state, and typically include alcohol, cell phones, cigarettes, condoms, currency, drugs (i.e., dope), tobacco, tattooing materials, and nicotine patches. These are components of the "inmate economy," used for exchange.

Gangs use many methods to get contraband into prisons. One way is to have visitors bring dope into the visiting room. Another method is to simply throw items over the wall or fence in a tennis ball or to use slingshots to propel the projectile. Another method is airdrops, in which drugs are released from small airplanes that fly over the institution at night (Ross and Richards, 2002).

Gang members may also recruit or coerce COs to bring contraband into prison. They may compromise the COs by threatening to report any deviant or illegal behavior they observe or hear about. This includes seeing them drinking alcohol on the job, appearing intoxicated, doing drugs, or having sex with a prisoner. Alternatively, a convict may successfully threaten an officer's family by finding out where they live. Still, some COs—because they are paid so little or want to make extra money—smuggle prohibited items into the institution.

In many prisons, it is not uncommon to find that some gangs focus a lot of their attention on sports betting. Since the standard currency in prison is a carton of cigarettes or postage stamps, this is usually the minimum bet placed. On the other hand, convicted dope dealers who are used to "living large" and having a lot of money may bet $10,000 to $20,000 on a game. The loser will need to have the money sent in from the outside. If he is lucky, his girlfriend, relative, or friend will arrange to have the money put on his commissary account. Then he needs to go to the commissary and purchase items on a regular basis to pay his gambling debt. Alternatively, if he owes $1,000, he may have a buddy on the street pay it to the gang on the outside (Ross and Richards, 2002).

Finally, a sophisticated gang may actually get new members or wannabes (who do not have a criminal record) to apply for a job as a CO with the state DOCs. Some jurisdictions appear so desperate to hire and have such low-qualification requirements that they will employ anyone who does not have a felony conviction. If hired, the person then acts as the go-between to smuggle drugs and other forms of contraband into the prison (Hagedorn, 1988).

Solutions

Many prison systems have tried to implement gang prevention programs. Most DOCs educate COs in how to identify gangs (Gaston, 1996; Valentine and Schober, 2000). During classification, DOCs try to determine membership and if possible separate gang members

---

EXHIBIT 5.1

Classics in Corrections

Film *American Me*

This Hollywood movie (released in 1992) portrayed the problems of contemporary Mexican-American prison gangs, in particular the Mexican Mafia (MM) also known as *La eMe or* (eMe for short), how they operated, their power struggles inside the group, and how they coped with drugs, family, and prison life. Based on a true story of a Mexican-American individual called Santana (played by actor James Edward Olmos) who rises from juvenile street criminal to respected leader of an East Los Angeles gang that had members both in well-known California prisons such as Folsom State and in the barrios of major urban centers in California. During his first incarceration in juvenile hall Santana kills a rapist and garners the respect of his fellow inmates. He starts La Clique (the gang) in early adulthood and quickly competes with other Mexican and Chicano gangs, Aryan Brotherhood, and African-American ones (like the Black Guerrilla Family) in the prisons where they were incarcerated. Members are recruited, sell drugs, and in some instances are obligated to kill traitors or liabilities. What becomes ever present is the loyalty to the gang, and how in all choices that it is stronger than family. A considerable amount of activity in the film takes place around the prison yard, in the cells, and outside of the watchful eyes of the COs. In some cases the characters overemphasized a tough guy image and this contributed to the stereotypical or cliché feel of the movie.

from the general population so that they do not threaten other inmates. "Texas has gone even further in its attempts to control gangs. In most DOCs correctional managers have designated gang intelligence officers in each prison who gather gang-related information and identify gang members and leadership. Active cooperation in the sharing of information with other criminal justice jurisdictions has prevented the recruitment . . . they try to put gang members in administrative segregation" (Fong, Vogel, and Buentello, 1992). Other options are to place gang leaders in Supermax prisons where they will have minimal or no contact with fellow inmates.

Gang treatment and rehabilitation is another option. Occasionally, DOCs institute these kinds of programs. For example, in 1993, the Hampden County Correctional Institution in Massachusetts tried the following. After segregating gang members, the DOC then gives them a cognitive training program (Toller and Tsagaris, 1996a; 1996b). In some prison systems like those in New York State, programs led by inmates are implemented. The Alternatives to Violence Program (AVP), which started in 1975, is run by lifers who hold workshops and teach younger inmates about the causes of violence, how it can escalate, and how to avoid it.

Sexual Assault

Most people who are sent to prison fear being raped (Lockwood, 1980; Rideau, 1992; Human Rights Watch, 2001). Undoubtedly, there is both consensual and coerced sex in prison. These practices are also complicated by male prostitution. Nevertheless, sexual assault is rarely about physical attraction or gratification; it is about violence, politics, power, and business. Some convicts routinely and habitually exploit others sexually.

When in prison, some convicts or groups of cons try to coerce fish (the new arrivals), using fear and/or violence to force them into sexual submission. To surrender will put a fish at the mercy of the violent thugs. If new cons resist, this stance may become a source of challenge for rapists, while victims may risk serious injury (and they might be raped regardless) or even be killed.

Solutions

Experienced prisoners suggest that, in the long run, for physical safety and psychological peace of mind, resistance is the best course of action. Cons must demonstrate with tough talk and threatening behavior that they are prepared to defend themselves and that anyone who assaults them will pay a price. Most sexual predators generally make cost–benefit calculations and will almost always go for the easy mark rather than the hard target.

One of the solutions for individuals who are raped or fear being sexually assaulted, especially if they are homosexuals, is to place them in administrative segregation. This action has a number of advantages and disadvantages. One of the drawbacks is the fact that once sent there they will get labeled, and if they want to return to a regular cellblock, they will have a difficult time not appearing like a pariah.

Some of the means through which prison systems deal with cons pent-up sexual frustration and alienation are the use of extended family visits/conjugal visits and furloughs (Lockwood, 1980). Another may be stiffer sanctions. These practices may not, however, stem the problem of prison rape. Again, these are token programs, available in few institutions and for only a handful of prisoners.

Conjugal visits   Few prison systems allow conjugal visits. If they are permitted, it is only for prisoners with no "shots" (i.e., disciplinary reports), who are living in minimum-security correctional facilities, and who are "getting short" (within a year of release) (Hensley, Koscheski, and Tewksbury, 2002; Hensley, Rutland, and Gray-Ray, 2002). Typically, a conjugal visit may last eight hours, one day, or a weekend if it involves family and children. Conjugal visits are allowed in nine states. The very first "program began in South Carolina in the late 1800s. In 1918, the Mississippi State Penitentiary at Parchman, initially an all-black penal farm, began allowing wives to visit. But for half a century, only those two states allowed conjugal visits. Then, in 1968, they were joined by California. Other states soon followed, and in 1980 Washington State, for the first time, allowed wives to spend the night in its prisons" (Hallinan, 2003: 133). In the Washington State program, "Twice a month they come for a visit, which takes place in one of six trailers on the reformatory grounds. The trailers are essentially fully furnished mobile homes intended, as much as possible, to mimic an apartment in the outside world. There are bedrooms, bathrooms—even a small kitchenette or family meals" (Hallinan, 2003: 135).

Hallinan adds, "There is little statistical evidence that family visitation programs work, largely because they have gone unstudied. . . . In the absence of statistics, the only way to judge the program is through anecdote and experience" (Hallinan, 2003: 134). The results of what little research has been done on the effect of conjugal visits are divided with respect to their impact on both homosexual behavior and sexual assaults in prison (Hensley, Koscheski, and Tewksbury, 2002; Hensley, Rutland, and Gray-Ray, 2002).

Furloughs   Some prisons allow furloughs through which prisoners are permitted to go home for a couple of days to be with their spouses and families. Convicts can be either accompanied by COs or unaccompanied. A furlough is a temporary release of an inmate from a facility. A few correctional facilities for women actually maintain a residence on the grounds so mothers can spend a weekend with their children, but no men are allowed. Still, most have discontinued conjugal visits, so the convicts must make do with what sexual relief they might get breaking visiting room rules. It is not unusual to see prisoners and wives on visiting day sneaking into the public restroom to have sexual relations (Ross and Richards, 2002).

Stiffer legislation and sanctions   Over the past few years, with the passage of the *Rape Elimination Act of 2003*, the federal government is taking the issue of male rape in prison more seriously. The $60 million that was earmarked for this bill was to enable the Department of Justice's BJS to conduct a two-year survey to be administered in state and federal prisons concerning the pervasiveness of the sexual assault.

One of the results of this initiative was a report produced by the Washington-based Urban Institute (Zweig et al., 2006) that involved a survey and analysis of state correctional administrators to determine what sorts of programs or changes they have implemented in the area of rape prevention in correctional facilities. The authors of the report found initiatives in the areas of developing policies, prevention, investigation and prosecution, victim services, staff training, documenting incidents, collaboration with other entities, and a search for additional funding.

Supermax prisons as a solution to prison violence   Over the past decade, correctional systems at the state and federal levels have introduced or expanded the use of Supermax prisons (Suedfeld, 1974; Rogers, 1993; King, 1999; Kurki and Morris, 2001; Toch, 2001). These facilities—also known as Special (or Security) Handling (or Housing) Units (SHUs) or Control Handling Units (CHUs)—are stand-alone correctional institutions, or wings or annexes inside an already existing prison. They are known for their strict lockdown policies, lack of amenities, and the use of prisoner isolation techniques. Escapes from Supermaxes are so rare that they are statistically inconsequential.

Research on Supermax prisons in the United States   The mass media and academia have been relatively silent with respect to Supermax prisons—and with good reason. It is difficult for reporters and scholars to gain access to prisoners, COs, and administrators. Correctional professionals are reluctant to talk with outsiders for fear that they may be unnecessarily subjected to public scrutiny.

History of Supermax prisons in the United States   Supermax prisons are a result of the recent growth in incarceration that has occurred throughout many of the world's advanced industrialized countries (Toch, 2001). In 1994, the federal government opened its first Supermax prison in Florence, CO, and the facility was dubbed the "Alcatraz of the Rockies." In the years that followed, many state DOCs built their own Supermax prisons. Part of the reason for the proliferation of this kind of correctional facility is the conservative political ideology that started during U.S. President Ronald Reagans administration (1981–1989). During the 1980s, as a response to an increase in the public's fear of crime, a progressively punitive agenda guided criminal justice and led to an increased number of people incarcerated in all types of prisons. This approach was continued by Reagan's Republican successor, George H. W. Bush (1989–1993).

Originally designed to house the most violent, hardened, and escape-prone criminals, today Supermaxes are increasingly used for persistent rule-breakers, convicted leaders of criminal organizations (e.g., the Mafia) and gangs, serial killers, and political criminals (e.g., spies and terrorists) (e.g., Suedfeld et al., 1982; Barak-Glantz, 1983; National Institute of Corrections, 1997; Riveland, 1998; Lovell et al., 2000; Neal, 2002; Bruton, 2004). In some states, the criteria for admission into a Supermax facility and the review of prisoners' time inside are very informal or even nonexistent.

Number of convicts in Supermax facilities   The number of convicts being sent to Supermax prisons is growing. The Supermaxes, maintained by the FBOP in Marion, IL, and Florence, CO, for example, "incarcerate approximately 1,500 people" (www.bop.gov/locations/weekly_report.jsp, July 20, 2007), including such notable criminals as "Unabomber" Ted Kaczynski and Oklahoma City bombing coconspirator Terry Nichols. Nevertheless, only a fraction of those incarcerated in state and federal prisons are sent to a Supermax facility. In 1998, approximately 20,000 inmates were locked up in this type of prison, representing less than 2 percent of all the men and women who are currently incarcerated across the country.

Conditions of confinement   One of the more notable features of all Supermax prisons is that prisoners are typically locked down 23 out of 24 hours a day. Other than supervision by COs, inmates have virtually no contact with other people (fellow convicts or visitors). Access to phones and mail is strictly and closely supervised or restricted. Supermax prisoners have very limited access to privileges such as watching television or listening to the radio.

Supermax prisons also generally do not allow inmates to either work or congregate during the day.[7] In addition, there is absolutely no personal privacy; everything the convicts do is monitored, usually through a surveillance camera that is continuously on. Communication with the COs usually takes place through a narrow window on the steel door of the cell, and/or via an intercom or microphone system.

Although cells vary in size and construction, in general, they are 12 by 7 feet in dimension. A cell light (called a nightlight) usually remains on all night long, and furnishings consist of a bed, a desk, a stool made out of poured concrete, and a stainless steel sink and toilet. Despite these simple facilities and the fact that prisoners' rehabilitation is not encouraged (and is next to impossible in these conditions), Supermax prisons are more expensive to build and run.

In Supermaxes, inmates rarely have access to educational or religious materials or services. Almost all toiletries (e.g., toothpaste, shaving cream, and razors) are strictly controlled (Hallinan, 2003). When an inmate is removed from his cell, he typically has to kneel down with his back to the door. Then he is required to place his hands through the slot a 1 foot by 8 inch hole in the door, then be handcuffed.

Effects of Supermax incarceration   All told, the isolation, lack of meaningful activity, and shortage of human contact take their toll on prisoner's psychological well-being. Supermax inmates often develop severe psychological disorders, including delusions and hallucinations, which may have long-term negative effects (Grassian, 1983; Grassian and Friedman, 1986; Haney, 1993; Haney and Lynch, 1997; Zinger, Wichmann, and Andrews, 2001; Briggs, Sundt, and Castellano, 2003; National Commission on Safety and Abuse in Prison, 2006: 54–56).

Unfortunately, we do not have comprehensive psychological data on individuals kept in these facilities. But numerous reports have documented the effects. The conditions inside Supermax prisons have led several corrections and human rights experts and organizations (i.e., Amnesty International and the American Civil Liberties Union) to question whether these prisons are a violation of (1) the Eighth Amendment of the U.S. Constitution, which prohibits the state from engaging in cruel and unusual punishment, and/or (2) the European Convention on Human Rights and the United Nations' Universal Declaration of Human Rights, which were established to protect not only the rights of people living in the free world but also those behind bars.

Supermax prisons have plenty of downsides, and not just for the inmates. Some people have suggested that Supermax facilities are all part of the correctional industrial complex (e.g., Christie, 1993). Most of the Supermaxes in the United States are brand new or nearly so. Others are simply freestanding prisons that were retrofitted. According to a study by the Urban Institute, the annual per-cell cost of a Supermax is about $75,000, compared to $25,000 for each cell in an ordinary state prison (Mears, 2006).

We have plenty of superexpensive Supermax facilities—two-thirds of the states now have them. But they were designed when crime was considered a growing problem, and now we have a lower violent crime rate that shows no real sign of a turn for the worse. However, as good as these prisons are at keeping our worst offenders in check, the purpose of the Supermax is in flux.

Cracks in the armor [8]   No self-respecting state director of corrections or correctional planner will admit that the Supermax concept was a mistake. And you would be wrong to think that these prisons can be replaced by something drastically less costly. But correctional experts are beginning to realize that just like a shrinking city that finds itself with too many schools or fire houses, the Supermax model must be made more flexible in order to justify its size and budget.

One solution is for these facilities to incarcerate different types of prisoners. In May 2006, Wisconsin Department of Corrections officials announced that over the past 16 years, the state's Supermax facility in Boscobel—built at a cost of $47.5 million (in 1990) and with a capacity of 500 inmates—has always stood at 100 cells less than its capacity. It will house maximum-security prisoners—serious offenders, but a step down from the worst of the worst. This shift in policy will increase the utility of the Supermax and perhaps justify its expense.

The Maryland Correctional Adjustment Center (aka *the Baltimore Supermax prison*) opened in 1989 at a cost of $21 million with room for 288 inmates. Like its cousin in Wisconsin, the structure has never been at capacity. In order to pick up the slack, not only does it hold the state's most dangerous prisoners, but it also houses 100 or so inmates who are working their way through the federal courts, and serves as the home for Maryland's ten death row convicts.

Converting cells is one approach, but not the only one. Other ideas include building more regional Supermaxes and filling them by shifting populations from other states. This would allow us to completely empty out a given Supermax, and then close it down or convert it to another use. There's also the possibility that some elements of the Supermax model could be combined with the approaches of traditional prisons, creating a hybrid that serves a wider population. But different types of prisoners would have to be kept well away from each other—a logistical problem of no small concern.

Prison litigation   Beginning in the 1960s, and throughout the last four decades, there has been an increase of lawsuits brought forth by/against correctional facilities and prison systems. Relying on different amendments to the U.S. Constitution, prisoners, activist lawyers, and judges have passed numerous important legal reforms concerning prison conditions and practices. Relying on notions of civil rights based in the First, Fourth, Fifth, Sixth, Eight, and Fourteenth Amendments, prisoners in state facilities won important victories. Several landmark cases have been passed including *Trop v. Dulles*, *Guthrie v. Evans*, and *Ruiz v. Estelle*. These success stories, however, do not mean that the practice of corrections is in step with judicial mandates. Why? Many policies and practices, which have been banned, are, for one reason or another, still in practice to varying degrees (Chilton, 1991: Chapter 8).

CONCLUSION

The brunt of prison conditions is felt by inmates. Most people do not willingly go to jail or prison because they fear having to live for an extended period of time in the terrible conditions inside. The general public believes that harsh prison conditions are appropriate to serve as deterrents and punishments for individuals predisposed to engage in crime. However, if anything reigns true about deterrence and prisons, it is that the findings are specious. Likewise, prison administrators are willing to allow the media access to correctional facilities to the extent they believe that they are doing a proper job and that their prisons may act as a deterrent to potential criminals or delinquent youth entering the system.

KEY TERMS

acquired immunity deficiency
  syndrome (AIDS)
cell extraction
commissary
conjugal visit
dirty protest
furlough

hepatitis
kill zone
slow playing
suicide by escape
Supermax prison
tuberculosis (TB)

REVIEW QUESTIONS

PART 1: MULTIPLE-CHOICE QUESTIONS

1. What is the acronym for the organization that runs the federal penitentiaries?

   a. BOP
   b. FBI
   c. NIJ
   d. OJP
   e. NIC

2. What is the disease referred to as *jail cough* or *prison fever*?

   a. AIDS
   b. cholera
   c. HIV
   d. tuberculosis
   e. yellow fever

3. What is the most common precaution used by prisoners to maintain or improve their health?

   a. reading
   b. exercise

   c. running marathons

   d. eating vitamins

   e. swimming

4. Which of the following names do some prisoners use to refer to their institutional meals?

   a. dog food

   b. Ken-L Rations

   c. Alpo

   d. all of the above

   e. none of the above

5. What is the name of the place at which a prisoner can buy a limited amount of food?

   a. commissary

   b. tuck shop

   c. prison store

   d. all the above

   e. none of the above

6. What type of convicts are NOT typically sent to Supermax prisons?

   a. violent

   b. hardened

   c. escape-prone

   d. gang leaders

   e. those awaiting trial

7. Which type of power does the CO use that gives them the right to exercise control over prisoners by virtue of the structural relationship between the position of the guard and the position of the prisoner?

   a. legitimate

   b. coercive

   c. reward

   d. expert

   e. referent

8. Who identified the five bases of guards' power?

   a. Goffman

   b. Hepburn

   c. Pung

   d. Ross

   e. Sykes

9. What is the name given to new prisoners?

   a. cats

   b. dogs

    c.   fish

    d.   frogs

    e.   Yankees

10. What are Supermax prisons also referred to?

    a.   special handling units

    b.   control handling units

    c.   detention centers

    d.   both a and b

    e.   none of the above

PART 2: SHORT-ANSWER QUESTIONS

1. What are three health concerns/diseases currently facing corrections?

2. List two of the most famous prison riots that have occurred over the past 40 years.

3. What is the standard medium of exchange in the prison economy?

4. What is the name for the inmate who helps others in lawsuits and challenges to the prison administration?

5. List three examples of self-inflicted violence that can occur in correctional institutions.

6. What is diesel therapy?

7. List two federal Supermax prisons.

8. List two alternative names for Supermax prisons.

9. What is the inmate code?

PART 3: ESSAY QUESTIONS

1. In your opinion, what is the worst prison condition and why?

2. What are the three most important ways that prisoners can deal with prison conditions?

3. How can correctional officials improve the delivery of health care to prisoners?

4. Why have Supermax prisons proliferated in the United States?

5. Are Supermax prisons a violation of the constitutional provision against cruel or unusual punishment? Justify your answer.

NOTES

1. Personal correspondence with Miguel Zaldivar, June 2007.

2. These problems are compounded when inmates are disabled and have special medical needs like wheelchair accessible ramps.

3. Personal communication with a representative of firm, June 2006.

4. Some will argue that the food in terms of nutritional value is better than what many of the people in the poorer countries eat.

5. Reports vary on the number of people dead.
6. Contraband typically includes cell phones, drugs, money, and weapons, but now in some prisons cigarettes, nicotine patches, and all tobacco products (including chewing tobacco) are banned.
7. There are notable exceptions. The Maryland Department of Corrections, for example, allows some Supermax inmates to congregate during yard time.
8. This section draws from Ross (2006a).

Chapter 6

Classification/Proper Assessment

INTRODUCTION

Officially, prison systems use classification systems (aka *designation*) as a means to assign prisoners to different security levels. Typically, the hard-core violent convicts serving long sentences are assigned to maximum-security prisons, the incorrigible prisoners serving medium-length sentences are housed in medium-security prisons, and the relatively light-weight men serving short sentences are sentenced to minimum-security camps, farms, or community facilities. In higher security correctional facilities inmates spend more time in cells, and there is more scrutiny over their activities. In lower security facilities, prisoners have more free time, privacy, recreational amenities, and longer visitation hours.

> Before 1980, most of the nations' prisons and jails used "subjective classification," which relies heavily on the judgment and hunches of line officers. Since then, every prison system has shifted, at least as a matter of policy to "objective classification." These standardized and automated classification criteria "place greater emphasis on fairness, consistency, and openness in the decision-making process" (NIC, 1992). (National Commission on Safety and Abuse in Prison, 2006: 29)

For some convicts, the decision where they will be sent is already made before they enter a correctional facility. In the federal system, judges may only make designation/security/programming recommendations—only the Federal Bureau of Prisons (FBOP) can

An earlier version of this chapter appeared as Richards and Ross (2003). This chapter has benefited from the comments of Jay Hurst.

make a designation or other correctional decision, under the constitutional separation of powers doctrine. Depending on sentencing guidelines and one's criminal history, a decision is made with respect to what security level would be most appropriate for them.

Where a convict is sent depends on a number of factors. Typically, the division of probation and parole prepares a presentence investigation (PSI) report, which is another data-gathering exercise by the criminal justice system to collect personal information. The probation or parole officer reviews a number of factors relevant to the convicted persons' circumstances including their criminal history. They prepare a report that makes a recommendation where the person should be sent. The document is given to the judge and shared with the defense attorney and prosecutor. The judge may or may not adopt the recommendation. In fact, they can completely ignore it. By the same token, some well-heeled and high-profile defendants (e.g., Martha Stewart) or their loved ones may employ the services of sentencing consultants. These professionals can be accessed through membership organizations like the National Alliance of Sentencing and Mitigation Specialists and the National Association of Sentencing Advocates. For a hefty fee, they prepare a report that recommends where a client should be sentenced. The defendants' attorney gives this to the prosecutor with the hope that the judge is influenced.

Classification of inmates serves many functions for the departments of corrections (DOCs) and the individual correctional institutions. In general, it determines which facility and security level the person will be sent to. This may facilitate the rehabilitation of the person, and protect convicts and correctional officers (COs) from being hurt by an inmate who should be at a higher security correctional institution (i.e., one doesn't want the wrong person in the facility). Classification also saves the taxpayer money because sending too many prisoners to higher security prisons, which are more costly to operate, drains the DOC's scarce resources.

THE PROCESS

Typically, classification occurs at intake, also called the fish bowl, reception center, and receiving and departure. "Correctional treatment is generally assumed to begin with the classification process. Classification procedures are conducted in reception units located within the prisons or a special reception and classification centers at another location. Classification committees, reception-diagnostic centers, or community classification teams sometimes perform these processes. The purpose of classification varies among institutions, but basically it is expected to help with inmate management or treatment planning efforts" (Allen and Simonsen, 2001: 245).

Classification officers and case managers are typically civilians, called noncustody personnel, who usually have a university degree. In the FBOP, classification is done by BOP case agents. Classification was formerly done by regional designators operating from each regional office. But this task has now been consolidated in the new central center in Grand Prairie, TX.

Although intake procedures differ, convicts typically arrive scared, hungry, worn, wearing handcuffs, belly chains, and dragging leg irons. Standing in line, they are ordered to strip, are searched, then sprayed or dusted with delousing chemical, issued clothes, then ordered to submit to a battery of token medical and psychological exams administered by COs who are easily confused as medical staff. Convicts call this *kicking the tires*. Rarely does it make a difference if the prisoner is HIV positive, ready to have another stroke, or near death. The line marches on.

The new prisoners may spend weeks or months at the reception center, housed in cells or dormitories. Eventually, they are ordered to a classification meeting where an officer announces their official security level and prison assignment. Sometime later they are transported to their new home—a penitentiary, prison, or camp.

In many systems classification is a two-part process. The first one selects which correctional facility inmates will be sent to. Once they are transferred, it is then determined which program best suits them (e.g., work, counseling, academic or vocational, or special treatment) (Allen and Simonsen: 288).

Depending on the correctional system, prisoner classification is typically reviewed one or more times a year. In the FBOP this is called a *team meeting*. A prisoner with a major disciplinary report may be reclassified very quickly, and transferred to administrative segregation (the hole) or cuffed and transported to a higher security prison. To no surprise, being reclassified to lower security takes more time, is rarely initiated by staff, and may require repeated requests by the inmate and/or his attorney.

FBOP PRISONER CLASSIFICATION

Classification Levels

The number of classification levels varies from one correctional system to another and is subject to change based on a number of factors including overcrowding, and new facilities coming on line (i.e., being built and completed). In order to get a sense of the complexities of classification, the FBOP classification levels are reviewed. The FBOP has five levels, compared to only four levels for the California Department of Corrections. The BOP uses an "inmate classification system" as a means to segregate, punish, and reward prisoners. This is a "classification ladder," with high security in the federal system at the top and minimum security at the bottom. As prisoners complete their sentences and get "short" (which means a year to release), they might be moved to minimum-security camps or community custody. Unfortunately, most men and women move up the ladder from minimum to medium, or medium to high, rather than down. Few medium- and high-security prisoners ever make it to the camps.

The classification designations have changed over the years to accommodate the growth in FBOP prisons and population. The old system had six security levels, with 6 to 5 being maximum, 4 to 2 being medium, and 1 being minimum. USP Marion (the first Supermax penitentiary) was the only level 5 institution. U.S. penitentiaries were level 5 (e.g., USP Atlanta, USP Leavenworth, USP Lewisburg, and USP Lompoc); the federal correctional institutions ranged from 4 to 2 (e.g., FCI Talladega, FCI Sandstone, and FCI Oxford), and the federal prison camps were 1. Security levels 2 to 6 are "in" custody, which means inside the fence or wall. Level 1 is "out" custody, which means federal camps that have penetrable security fences. Level 1 community custody refers to prisoners in camps who were eligible for community programs—work assignments or furloughs.

In the 1990s, the FBOP collapsed these six security designations into five: high, medium, low, minimum, and administrative (equivalent to high security, but reserved to detention centers, a mix of pretrial detainees and inmates and Federal Medical Centers [FMCs]). The BOP prisoner population is approximately 10 percent high (USP), 25 percent medium (FCI), 35 percent low (FCI), and 25 percent minimum (FPC), with the rest not assigned a security level; many of these men and women are in administrative facilities (medical or detention), transit, or held in local jails or private prisons. *Administrative* refers to Administrative Detention Max (ADX) Florence (CO) (the highest security prison in the country), FTC Oklahoma City (a medium-security transport prison), and the federal medical centers (which may be maximum, medium, or minimum security).

The Central Inmate Monitoring System

FBOP staff must check the Central Inmate Monitoring System (CIMS) before any prisoner is reassigned to a new cellblock, dormitory, or prison. CIMS is a computer system that tracks nine special categories of inmates:

1. "Witness Security" prisoners are government informers who have testified, are testifying, or will testify in court cases.

2. "Special Security" prisoners are prison snitches cooperating in internal investigations.

3. "Sophisticated Criminal Activity" prisoners are those inmates identified as being involved in large-scale criminal conspiracies, for example, organized crime, drugs, or white collar. They may be men or women who were targets of the federal Racketeer Influence and Corrupt Organization (RICO) or Continuing Criminal Enterprise (CCE) prosecution, which carry life sentences (Richards, 1998: 133). Many of these convicts are suspected of being connected to major drug-smuggling organizations or they refused to plead guilty, cooperate, and inform on other persons.

4. "Threats to Government Officials" prisoners have been convicted of writing letters, making phone calls, or issuing verbal remarks that convey the intent to do bodily harm to public officials.

5. "Broad Publicity" prisoners are those inmates involved in high-profile cases.

6. "State Prisoners" are inmates serving state sentences who were transferred into the federal system because they were "difficult."

7. "Separation" prisoners are those who have been moved to another institution because they are government witnesses, institutional snitches, gang leaders, or persons in danger of being killed or killing someone else.

8. "Special Supervision" prisoners are police, judges, and politicians who are provided protective privilege (Richards and Avey, 2000). These men and women are usually designated to camps (because they may be unnecessarily victimized or killed in a penitentiary).

9. "Disruptive Groups" prisoners may include members of organizations, such as street or prison gangs and political groups (i.e., Black Panthers and Communists).

Regardless of the sophistication of this listing, convicts may not know they have been singled out for such attention.[1]

THE PROBLEMS WITH CLASSIFICATION

There are several difficulties with classification: overcrowding prevents the timely transfer of inmates to suitable programs; correctional facility labor is prioritized; women prisoners are hampered by the lack of appropriate institutions; quantitative assessments are too narrow; inmate files are typically incomplete; participation in prison programs is a bad measure; disciplinary matters have a disproportionate effect on allocation; and classification may be used for unofficial purposes.

Overcrowding Frustrates the Process

Although in principle classification is a valuable tool, it is frustrated by correctional facility conditions. Unfortunately, the best-laid plans often fail. One of the most problematic is overcrowding. This prevents inmates from entering appropriate educational, counseling, and vocational programs and facilities that they would be best suited for (Allen and Simonsen: 246).

Institutional Job Details Take Precedence

The day-to-day demands of running an institution and "available vacancies" often take a backseat to classification decisions (Allen and Simonsen: 246, 288). It may be recognized that the convict needs more formal education so he is assigned remedial classes, but since the prisoner is a baker, and the kitchen is short qualified personnel for that day or week, he will be assigned to kitchen duty instead. Others examples include "an inmate may genuinely want to learn welding. If the welding class is filled, . . . but there is a vacancy in the furniture shop, the inmate may be assigned to the furniture shop; no effort would be made to offer additional welding instruction. Also, inmates will often be assigned to a maintenance operation, such as food service or janitorial work that is unlikely to conform to their own vocational ambitions" (Allen and Simonsen: 288).

What complicates matters is that "[i]nstitution personnel may genuinely wish to provide the recommended program for an inmate; however, the need to keep the institution going inevitably shapes decisions. Personnel may rationalize maintenance assignments on the basis that many inmates need the experience of accepting supervision, developing regular work habits, learning to relate to co-workers, and the like. All of that may be true, but the treatment staff members are no less frustrated than the inmates are when prescribed programs are ignored" (Allen and Simonsen: 289).

Women Prisoners Suffer the Most

Women make up less than 10 percent of the prison population (see Chapter 7). They are usually confined in one or a few correctional facilities in each state. These prisons may hold female prisoners classified for different security levels in various sections of the same institution. Exceptions include the large states and the FBOP where women with different security levels may be imprisoned in separate institutions. In any case, the steady increase in the incarceration of females may result in the further differentiation of women's prison.

Quantitative Measures Are Poor Indicators

There is an implicit belief that better data and statistical analysis will somehow improve things for prisoners and correctional staff alike. The problem is that convicts and COs are different constituencies with often competing concerns. The inmates want less restrictive classification (minimum or medium security), in which they might have better living conditions (i.e., more time out of cell, less restrictive family visits, better access to programs, and less violence). In comparison, prison staff may want prisoners to be housed in more restrictive environments (i.e., maximum security, control units, segregation) where they are "locked in" and have little freedom of movement, thus giving the COs more control and less exposure possibly to assault and injury.

Inmate Files Are Incomplete

"Inmate files" (which usually include PSI reports, criminal offenses, and institutional reports) should not be the sole determinate of classification decisions. Simply analyzing inmate files and observing classification hearings do not explore the full dimensions of the character of the individual convict. Ethnographic or qualitative research, on the other hand, can be used to get a better understanding of the real issues involved (Ross and Richards, 2002; 2003).

Participation in Prison Programs Is a Poor Indicator

Using prisoner participation in prison programs as a measure is problematic. Activities i.e., (work, vocational training, education) include custodial responsibilities i.e., (washing dishes, mopping floors, cleaning bathrooms), duties that masquerade as training i.e., (cooking, mowing lawns, hoeing fields, tending crops, painting and repair), and basic education programs (ABE, GED). Few of these activities elicit prisoner enthusiasm or are considered real opportunities to learn new skills or knowledge. *Positive program participation* is usually defined by prison staff as the convict showed up, did not refuse direct orders, and made a good show of pretending to work or study. In many institutions existing programs are very basic and do not serve many prisoners. They seem to exist mainly to silence external critics, fulfill state mandates, and occasionally provide public relations benefits to the news media. Of course, when push comes to shove and the correctional budgets are cut, what programs do exist are the first to be terminated.

A more important problem (Berk et al., 2003) is that the prison system may no longer expect prisoners to participate in programs, as they may no longer exist. Most U.S. prison systems do not pretend to provide vocational or educational programming. Prison administrators limit their responsibility to operating orderly institutions, trying to control contraband and violence and prevent escapes. The way many DOCs have solved this situation, although incredibly expensive and controversial, is by building high-security institutions (e.g., Supermax prisons) and filling them with reclassified prisoners.

Disciplinary Reports Are Often Circumspect

Classification consists of reviewing any "disciplinary actions" (aka *disciplinary reports*) and "demonstration of positive participation in an inmate program." COs routinely issue "write-ups," what are called *shots* or incident reports in the FBOP, *115s* in the California Department of Corrections, or simply *tickets* in many prison systems, every chance they get. Prisoners housed in overcrowded cellblocks or dormitories may collect minor "tickets" for petty infractions or major tickets for defending themselves against predatory or aggressive individuals. Many prisoners claim disciplinary committees rule against convicts without affording them due process rights. By writing a letter to a newspaper, or calling a congressional office to complain about staff or the lack of medical services, a convict may collect tickets, get dragged to the "hole," be reclassified, and eventually be shipped out to the penitentiary or Supermax.

Using disciplinary reports as the primary criterion for the reclassification of prisoners may lead to the construction of more maximum-security prisons. It costs more to house prisoners in high-security correctional facilities. As previously mentioned, prisoners who serve time in these institutions suffer more psychological problems and are less prepared for release.

Classification May Be Used for Unofficial Purposes

Classification may unnecessarily load up high-security prisons with underclass minorities, where tension and ultimately more violence occurs. African-American, Hispanic, Latino, and Chicano prisoners are more likely to be "young," gang affiliated, and to collect bad conduct "tickets." The FBOP and many states have struggled for years with schemes to "racially balance" institutions (Henderson et al., 2000). Like school busing programs, they transport prisoners from institution to correctional facility, trying to somehow racially integrate prisons as dictated by policy directives and Supreme Court decisions.

Depending on the prison system (including the budget, number of institutions, population counts, and level of disorder), prisoners are shuffled from one institution to another. These transfers may or may not reflect official classification schemes. When a given prison is bursting at the seams, with men sleeping in hallways, three to a one-man cell, or on bunk beds arranged in recreational areas or classrooms converted into makeshift dormitories, official policy is ignored, and busloads of prisoners are transferred to whichever facility has empty beds. This is commonly referred to as *population override*, and it is frequently used.

SOLUTIONS

As argued earlier, classification has numerous problems. Much of this is connected to a prison bureaucracy that is "resistant to change and partly to the poor environment for change provided in the prisons themselves" (Allen and Simonsen: 247). Moreover, "[s]everal states have abandoned classification reception-diagnostic centers as counterproductive because the centers raised inmate and staff expectations above the level of possible achievement. The treatment model has a place somewhere in corrections, but not, it seems, in high-security prisons" (p. 247).

Nevertheless, approximately five solutions can be marshaled in order to improve the classification process. First, *have prisoners actively participate in the classification decisions*. Convicts are rarely asked to comment on prison policy and procedure. If they do, they are typically subject to recrimination. While prisoners may not be considered stakeholders (Berk et al., 2003), convicts become more involved in the decision making.

Second, *hire more qualified personnel* to deal with the large number of cases. This also means that they should be better educated, trained and accommodations should be given by their respective organizations that enable them to obtain advanced training.

Third, *increase the number of correctional professionals* responsible for classification. This way decision making can be shared amongst more people. The idea here is that another set of hands and eyes should help improve the entire process.

Fourth, *provide enough time for the professionals to properly investigate each case*. This means that classification should be done more frequently and over a long enough period of time where the convicts can be observed and interviewed in different settings.

Finally, *increase the pay for classification officers*. That way it would make this job task more attractive to correctional professionals. Until these strategies are experimented with or implemented, classification will probably be a game of correctional personnel will simply be going through the motions.

CONCLUSION

In the United States massive numbers of people are incarcerated on a daily basis. And there is a belief that better classification procedures will minimize our problems with incarceration; at the very least they may save the taxpayer the increased costs of housing prisoners in more restrictive settings.

The point is that classification includes additional factors that may not be amendable to statistical number crunching. Some of these variables may not even be known to the research team or even the prisoner.

Nevertheless, as long as the classification of prisoners is based entirely on outdated measures of individual behavior (criminal offense, conduct inside correctional facility, gang affiliation), without reference to the bigger structural issues (poverty, racial discrimination, the war on drugs) that have created the boom in prison population, or prison programming that could lower the rate of disciplinary reports and predictable parole failure, very little will change.

Classification determines if an inmate fits any special needs categories including health, physical, or mental disabilities including addictions. Ideally, this process should lead to rehabilitation, which in turn should reduce recidivism. Classification should save the DOCs' money, and ultimately the taxpayer's. It will also protect correctional workers from being a victim of physical violence.

KEY TERMS

Central Inmate Monitoring System (CIMS)
classification
disciplinary reports
fish bowl
kicking the tires
population override
prison camp

Racketeer Influence and Corrupt
   Organization (RICO)
security level
shots
Supermax
team meeting

REVIEW QUESTIONS

PART 1: MULTIPLE-CHOICE QUESTIONS

1. What is an alternative name for the place where classification takes place?
   a. fish bowl
   b. salad bowl
   c. super bowl
   d. tidy bowl
   e. none of the above

2. What does the acronym CIMS stand for?
   a. Correctional Institute Management System
   b. Central Inmate Monitoring System
   c. Correctional Independent Motoring Seminar
   d. Cons Independent Microsoft System
   e. none of the above

3. What is the name of facility where most prisoners enter the state correctional system?
   a. central station
   b. reception center
   c. assessment center
   d. classification house
   e. halfway house

4. What problems arise that often hinder the proper classification of prisoners?
   a. institutional needs
   b. correctional officer dislike/hatred of prisoners
   c. overcrowding
   d. all the above
   e. none of the above

5. What is the name given to the highest security prisons?
   a. FBOP
   b. superclassification
   c. super institution
   d. Supermax
   e. The Colorado Pen

PART 2: SHORT-ANSWER QUESTIONS

1. What are five problems with the classification of prisoners?
2. What are five solutions that could improve the classification of convicts?
3. List four levels of security used by the FBOP.
4. How many Supermax prisons does the FBOP have?
5. What process may mitigate the need for classification?

PART 3: ESSAY QUESTIONS

1. How would you improve classification?
2. What are three functions of classification?
3. What do you suspect is the future of classification for both the state and federal correctional systems?

NOTE

1. CIMS is controlled by 28 C.F.R. § 524.72 and USDOJ–FBOP Program Statement (P.S.) 5180.04, *Central Inmate Monitoring System* (August 16, 1996).

Chapter 7

Special Populations

INTRODUCTION

Most correctional personnel and administrators recognize that certain kinds of inmates may need different facilities, policies, and programs. Often the departments of corrections (DOCs) and Federal Bureau of Prisons (FBOP) are viewed as lagging behind in their approach toward these groups, and only when there is some sort of crisis are they forced to change. This chapter identifies these special populations, outlines the problems they face in correctional institutions, and advances some solutions. In particular, the analysis focuses on problems connected to the mentally ill, those suffering from HIV/AIDS, the graying prison population, and women behind bars.

MENTALLY ILL

Problems

Given the number of inmates who are suffering from mental illness, some observers may legitimately question whether the mentally ill are a separate special population in correctional facilities. In particular, according to the most recent Bureau of Justice Statistics (BJS) report (James and Glaze, 2006), approximately 45 percent of federal prison convicts, 56 percent of all state prisoners, and 64 percent of jail inmates are suffering from some sort of "mental health problem." According to the study, "Mental health problems were defined by . . . a recent history or symptoms of a mental health problem" (p. 1). The primary diagnosis is depression and/or some sort of psychotic disorder (e.g., suffering from delusions or hallucinations).

Predictably, the symptoms are highest among jail prisoners, and less so when one moves to the state and federal systems. According to James and Glaze (2006), "The high rate of symptoms of mental disorder among jail inmates may reflect the role of local jails in the criminal justice system. . . . Among other functions, local jails hold mentally ill persons pending their movement to appropriate mental health facilities" (p. 3). More specifically, mental health problems are "more common among female, white and young inmates" (p. 5). In terms of care, some convicts with mental health problems receive 24-hour supervision in a special housing or psychiatric unit while others are only provided with either some sort of counseling or drug therapy (i.e., psychotropic medications).

Whether the number of prisoners who have some sort of mental health problem or illness is increasing is difficult to determine because comparable statistics have not been kept for a lengthy period of time. In 1998, for example, approximately 283,800 inmates were determined to be "mentally ill" (Ditton, 1999). As mentioned earlier, 1,264,300 of all federal, state, and local inmates suffered from some kind of mental health problem. Although the terminology for this affliction may not be exactly the same, it would seem that the number was 4.5 times greater in 2005 than it was in 1999.

Nevertheless, correctional workers, administrators, and prisoners will agree that there has been an increase in the number of people with mental health problems being sent to and living in American jails and prisons. This is often because the mentally ill are turned away from mental institutions or are too challenging for the traditional mental health facility (National Commission on Safety and Abuse, 2006: 46). Most DOCs and the FBOP are not equipped to "handle these inmates. Line-officers are not trained to deal with the idiosyncrasies of these individuals introduce[d] to the prison environment. Furthermore, the FBOP lacks the mental health professionals to treat these inmates."[1] The mentally ill end up making greater demands on staff time, are frequently manipulated and victimized by other convicts, and often end up in administrative segregation for their own protection and/or for the safety of staff and inmates.

In addition, there are not enough skilled staff who are responsible for these inmates' well-being. One only needs to take a look at the DOC's and FBOP's Websites to notice that there is a desperate need for psychologists and psychiatrists. Not only are correctional officers (COs) and administrators poorly equipped to deal with these individuals, but so are the inmates. They may not have the necessary patience to live and work with mentally ill individuals, and thus the latter inmates are in greater danger of being ridiculed or attacked.

Most of the time, the mentally ill are medicated—sometimes heavily—and they seem to walk the halls in a zombie-like state. It is acknowledged that "the presence of counseling personnel and services is often uneven, fragmented, or inadequate" (Arrigo, 2005: 595). "The majority of inmates receiving therapy/counseling and medications were housed in facilities without a mental health specialty" (Beck and Maruschak, 2001: 4). One of the problems is that many of the mentally ill are sent to solitary confinement—a punishment whose issues are outlined in Chapter 4. Arrigo reminds us that "[i]n those instances where treatment is uneven, absent, or otherwise ineffective, questions remain about whether the correctional milieu is itself responsible for breeding and sustaining long-term mental illness and dysfunctional behavior" (2005: 593).

Solutions

Finding appropriate solutions for housing, managing, and treating mentally ill prisoners depends on the onset of the mental illness, the individual's response to medication and/or therapy, the inmate's level of functionality, and the availability of housing alternatives. Indeed, there is a range of places in which mentally ill convicts can be detained. In the United States, however, there are only 12 facilities whose "primary function (identified by the largest number of inmates) was mental health confinement" (Beck and Maruschak, 2001: 4). As mentioned earlier, most inmates "receiving psychotropic medication were in general confinement or community-based facilities."

In short, those suffering some sort of mental illness should be shifted to secure facilities in which licensed and competent mental health professionals can properly assess, monitor, and provide them with appropriate therapy to stabilize and hopefully improve their conditions. Other suggestions include using better screening on intake and making sure that skilled mental health professionals and not simply COs are making the decisions about what kinds of facilities would best house these inmates (Commission on Safety and Abuse, 2006).

THE GRAYING PRISON POPULATION

Problems

Over the past three decades, the average age of prisoners has increased. By December 2005, there were 63,500 prisoners who were over the age of 55. Although not specifically considered elderly at this age, this statistic represents 0.027 percent of the total jail and prison population (Harrison and Beck, 2006). The higher average age of prisoners can be tied to longer and harsher sentences, as well as to the fact that Americans on the whole are living longer. The graying prison population means that they need special medical treatments, procedures, prescriptions, and supplies. "Elderly men in prison have a high incidence of respiratory and heart problems, diabetes, depression, poor circulation, arthritis, bladder problems, Alzheimer's, Parkinson's, and hypertension" (Crawley, 2005: 354). These kinds of inmates have "specific health and mobility needs" that require "significant financial, regime, and indeed, health and safety implications in the prison environment" (Crawley: 354). This easily becomes a financial burden to the correctional system. "Health-care costs comprise 10 to 20 percent of prison operating costs and are the fastest-growing item of corrections budgets, due in large part to an aging prison population that require greater and more expensive medical attention" (Welch, 2004: 457).

Solutions

A considerable debate exists regarding the proper procedure for dealing with an increasingly elderly inmate population. Solutions range from providing specialized facilities to early release (Soderstrom and Wheeler, 1999). In particular, "[o]lder inmates are less interested in GED classes and other educational programs and more interested in learning how to secure Social Security benefits upon their release. Preparing them to return to the community might be the most pressing problem facing the correctional system" (Welch, 2004: 458). Anything the jails and prisons can do to help them with this reality may be the best solution for the graying prison population.

Another solution is to encourage DOCs to utilize compassionate release. According to Price (2005) this practice "is appropriate when circumstances unforeseen at sentencing make continued incarceration unjust, and when no other adequate legal mechanisms exist to effect sentence reduction" (p. 150). In reality, the procedure, though publicly supported by many state and federal guidelines, is rarely used.

HIV/AIDS

Problems

Every few years, the Department of Justice, through the BJS, conducts two corrections related surveys (i.e., the "National Prisoner Statistics" and the "Deaths in Custody Reporting Program") that provide information on HIV-infected and AIDS prisoners (e.g., Maruschak, 2005). As of December 31, 2003, 2 percent (22,028) of state inmates and 1.1 percent (1,631) of federal convicts had HIV. Those with full-blown AIDS amount to 5,944 prisoners. Although the number with HIV was down from 23,864 to 23,659, compared to the previous year (2002), there were approximately 6 percent more cases of AIDS. This is about three times the rate found throughout the general population. The majority of HIV/AIDS cases are concentrated in New York, Florida, Texas, and Georgia, which have some of the country's largest prison populations. As a percentage, there are currently a greater number of females who have HIV/AIDS compared with men.

Solutions

A number of solutions to the identification, education, and treatment of HIV/AIDS patients in jails and prisons have been advanced (Hammett, Harmon, and Maruschak, 1999; Welch, 2004: 450–456). To begin with, and as previously mentioned in an earlier chapter, there are both arguments for and against mass screening of all inmates in correctional facilities. Advocates say that it will allow convicts who are HIV positive or have AIDS to get the treatment they so desperately need. Opponents point out that rarely can the information be kept secret and then the patients' confidentiality will be breached. It is generally understood that, once inmates are behind bars notions of privacy almost always take a backseat to institutional safety and mass screening may make better sense.

Clearly, better education and training of both correctional workers and inmates is fundamental to minimize the spread of AIDS and to reduce irrational fear connected to the disease. Proper medical care, especially the administration of AZT, a drug that curtails the development of the HIV/AIDS, is advocated. Also integrating those with AIDS into the general population rather than segregating them has been found to be helpful to minimize stigma and other forms of social isolation. Other suggestions are distributing condoms among consenting homosexuals in prison, and providing access to long-term hospitalization will help ease the pain and suffering related to this illness.

As mentioned earlier, one of the solutions offered by the National Commission on Safety and Abuse in Prison is to partner with local public health departments. The specifics here, however, are lacking. Additionally, there are a number of nonprofit organizations that provide free information and counseling to prisoners who have AIDS/HIV or suspect that they may have been infected. One of them, for example, is the Osborne Association, located in New York's Bronx neighborhood. Prisoners can call collect and receive information on the disease as well as on preventative measures (www.osborneny.org/aids_in_prison_project.htm).

WOMEN

Problems

As of 2005, there were 107,518 women prisoners in the United States. This represents 7 percent of all convicts (Harrison and Beck, 2006). Women are typically sentenced to jail or prison for crimes such as frequent convictions of petty crimes (e.g., shoplifting), possession of drugs, small-scale drug dealing, embezzlement, credit card fraud, writing bad checks, and homicide. Recent statistics suggest that the categories of crime for which women are serving time in state facilities indicate that 34.8 percent are violent, 29.1 percent connected to drugs, 30.0 percent property-related, and 5.3 percent public order offenses (Harrison and Beck, 2006: 9).

Over the past two decades, many women convicts are found to be typically single, between 25 and 34 years old, and struggling to survive poor economic circumstances. Most are minorities, have never finished high school, and have multiple children. In terms of racial breakdown, 50 percent are African American, 36 percent White, and 16 percent Hispanic. According to profiles that have been developed, the average female inmate may have dropped out of school somewhere around the ninth grade because she became pregnant and had no one to take care of her child. She never acquired a formal education that would allow anything more than a low-paying, service-sector job such as that of a hotel maid or kitchen staff. She periodically, if not totally, depends on public assistance. When the inmate was younger, she was most likely sexually abused; she has a history of being physically abused by men, dating back to her teenage years. She uses alcohol and/or drugs, and has been arrested many times (Ross and Richards, 2002: Chapter 11).

Because of the war on drugs, stiffer mandatory sentencing guidelines, and the widespread acceptance of females as legitimate criminals, a considerable number of women have entered the prison system in the past two decades. Since 1983, it's estimated that the number of women has grown by 344 percent, as compared to 207 percent for men.

Women are less likely to have a history of violent crime. When they do kill, however, the victims are usually their fathers, husbands, boyfriends, or children; rarely do they commit an act of violence against strangers. And despite the fact that today more women than ever before are being charged with serious drug felonies, they typically serve as accessories rather than principal actors. Over the past two centuries, conditions have improved for female prisoners. In the nineteenth century, most women prisoners in England and the United States were not separated from the men, inevitably leading to physical and sexual abuse. Even when they were confined in a separate wing of a coed facility, women were vulnerable to abuse by male administrators, correctional workers, and prisoners. A number of women reformers championed the cause of female inmates, and by the twentieth century, many states and the federal government had established prisons solely for women that were increasingly staffed by women.

Most states have numerous prisons for men and at least one facility for women. Nearly every state has at least one women's prison. However, some of the more sparsely populated states—which might have a total of only 50 female convicts—end up shipping them to a neighboring state or housing them in separate wings of county jails. Men do time in facilities with security levels ranging from minimum to Supermax. Because there is usually only one women's prison in an entire state, all the security levels are typically contained within the same institution. Therefore, most female prisons look like minimum-security camps. About a fifth of females are incarcerated at coed facilities where, although they live in separate units, the only contact with members of the opposite sex is in vocational, educational, and recreational settings (Pollock-Byrne, 1990; Owen, 1998).

There are no maximum-security or Supermax federal prisons for women in the United States. The highest security correctional facility for women at worst resembles a medium-security prison for men. For example, the Federal Prison Camp in Lexington, KY, houses 400 female prisoners, yet has no fence or gun towers. At the same time, there are women housed there who are serving life sentences. If more women in correctional custody attempted escapes, one can be sure that state and federal planners would install additional security features. Correctional systems don't erect sophisticated security because they don't expect these women to escape and commit additional crimes.

Although women's prisons typically have fences, they have less razor wire and detection facilities. Even though it would be relatively easy enough to break out of such a facility, escapes from women's prisons are rare events. This does not mean that life behind bars for women is easy. Five of the most important problems that face women prisoners that are qualitatively different than those that face men include sexism, violence by COs against women inmates, child custody while behind bars, pregnancy, and release.

Sexism

The criminal justice system (and jails, prisons and community corrections, by extension) is disproportionately sexist. Typically, this means that if there is some sort of vocational training, it tends to be sex-role-based. For example, women convicts might be trained as office assistants, cosmetologists, seamstresses, and domestic servants. According to Welch, "[S]ome of these programs are self-defeating. For instance, some states require a license to work in cosmetology, and such licensing is denied to ex-inmates. Moreover, cosmetology and clerical work are 'pink-collar' jobs, which are generally low-paying and often considered dead-end employment" (2004: 178). According to Owen (2005), "rehabilitative programs for women offenders are typically based on generic programs that make few gender distinctions. . . . For example, women's prisons are deficient relative to men's prisons in educational and vocational programs they offer. Men's prisons typically provide a greater variety of such programs and training for more skilled (and better compensated) occupations" (p. 1054).

Violence

Historically, the sexual abuse of female prisoners by male staff members is common (Human Rights Watch, 1996). These incidents include "sexual abuse, sexual assault, sexual harassment, physical contact of a sexual nature, sexual obscenity, invasion of privacy, and conversations or correspondence of a romantic or intimate nature" (Owen, 2005: 1052). Indeed, there have been numerous reports made by women prisoners that they've been raped by male officers in jails and prisons. In most states, any sexual relations between prison staff and inmates is considered by law to be sexual assault. In short, there is no such thing as consensual sex between prisoners and COs. Hundreds of correctional workers have been fired and/or indicted and convicted of sexual assault charges resulting from their coercion of female prisoners. "Conservative estimates for the rate of sexual victimization of women in prison indicate that nearly 30% will experience some form of unwanted sex while confined" (Arrigo, 2005: 595).

Some state prison systems, like that of Georgia, have implemented tough "no touch, no contact" policies. In these settings, men are not allowed to supervise women convicts. If a male is to enter the unit, an announcement, almost like a warning, of "man or male on range" can be heard. At some federal prisons for women, hotlines allow female prisoners to make complaints if they've been sexually abused. This is sometimes a public relations exercise simply designed to garner support from the wider public and to tell them that something is being done about this problem. It's been said that when incidents of such abuse come to the public's attention, state correctional systems will have their public relations department representative cover for the bureaucracies' intransigence. Even today there are a number of states that have not outlawed staff–inmate sex.

Maintaining Custody of Children

Many women prisoners are mothers who may feel that their children have been abandoned to the makeshift care of relatives or social service agencies. When mothers serve time, their children are often relegated to a relative or social service agency, foster home, or put up for adoption. A lot of women lose legal custody of their children when they are adjudicated as "bad mothers."

Some women prisoners were great mothers before they went to prison, but because of their crimes, their children have been legally removed from their custody. Incarcerated mothers must worry about worst-case scenarios; for example, her spouse divorces her while she is in prison, remarries, moves to another state with the children and disappears. Most female convicts who have had their children taken away are often consumed with remorse about their criminal behavior.

The situation is made worse by laws such as the *Adoption and Safe Families Act* passed in 1997. Originally designed to "to keep abused or neglected children from languishing in foster care while their biological parents, often drug-addicted, tried to kick their habit," the law has become a tautology of sorts. In short, the simple fact that the mother was incarcerated for a specific period of time is interpreted as grounds for determining abuse (Cohen, 2006a). Additionally, "[i]nmates often can't attend a hearing on whether their parental rights should be terminated. In some cases they aren't even informed about those hearings, which may be held hundreds or thousands of miles away" (Cohen, 2006a). The United States is "the only nation that routinely moves to terminate the parental rights of incarcerated parents whose children are in foster care" (Cohen, 2006b).

Giving Birth Behind Bars

Many women enter prison while pregnant and give birth to their children while serving time. According to BJS data, as many as 6 percent of the women entering state and federal prisons are pregnant. There are no reliable statistics on the number of pregnancies that result in termination, miscarriage, or birth. Worse, some women prisoners have been raped by COs while incarcerated and were forced to give birth to the offspring. When a prisoner goes through childbirth, she'll be handcuffed and transferred to a civilian hospital. The cuffs are not taken off during either labor or delivery. With luck, the baby will be taken in by a relative. More likely, the baby is turned over to foster care or put up for adoption (Amnesty International, 2001).

A very small number of correctional facilities may allow a mother to care for her newborn in the prison for a short time. For example, larger jails like Rikers Island in New York City have neonatal centers. But this usually only happens if the female prisoners will be released shortly, perhaps within a few weeks, so neither they nor their babies will be a burden for the system.

Some people mistakenly believe that a pregnant woman can be absolved from a prison sentence. Contrary to what may have taken place during an earlier time in American history, when it comes to sentencing a woman, the courts no longer care if she is pregnant. Carrying a child does not provide any protection from being sent to prison, nor does it serve as an excuse for immediate release.

Reintegration of Women

After their release from jail or prison, many women prisoners who are also mothers immediately begin searching for their children. Like their male counterparts, they leave prison with little money, no place of their own to live, and no job. They usually stay with relatives or complete their sentence in halfway houses. Some of these facilities are fairly depressing and are usually located in underprivileged neighborhoods. Pass by one of these on a hot summer day and you'll see women parolees congregating on the front steps while cars filled with leering men cruise by looking for a new girlfriend. Other female prisoners remain isolated inside the house, frightened of the pimps and dope dealers who frequent these neighborhoods. Most of these women will return to a life of dependency that includes social service agency handouts or the games of the street.

Solutions

Correctional officers, administrators, and planners must develop an awareness of the role that sexism can have in the way we treat women behind bars. It is hoped that the additional number of women correctional officers and administrators will have an impact on this problem, but reliable empirical research here does not exist. This would go a long way in introducing appropriate vocational programs. Also the DOCs need more funding for facilities and programs where women inmates can not only give birth but raise their infants. Additional mechanisms that would encourage conjugal visits by family members may lessen the pain and suffering women may feel when they are cut off from their loved ones.

CONCLUSION

Many of the solutions to special problems rely on letting public health and community service agencies take a larger role in providing services to inmates. Increasing prisoner and correctional awareness and training can go a long way in improving the lives of prisoners. This is easier said than done as correctional agencies' budgets are typically relatively small and their ability to do outreach is often hampered.

KEY TERMS

Adoption and Safe Families Act   graying of prison population
AZT   psychotic disorder
compassionate release

REVIEW QUESTIONS

PART 1: MULTIPLE-CHOICE QUESTIONS

1. What is the primary diagnosis for prisoners suffering a mental illness?
    a. low self-esteem
    b. gender identity disorder
    c. depression

   d. psychotic disorder

   e. both c and d

2. In which correctional facility would you see the highest incidence of mental illness?

   a. jail

   b. state prisons

   c. federal penitentiaries

   d. all the above

   e. none of the above

3. What are the biggest causes of the graying of the prison population?

   a. stiffer penalties

   b. the tendency for people to live longer

   c. old people are committing more crime

   d. both a and b

   e. none of the above

4. Which is the most typical category of crime that a woman serving time in state facilities most likely would have committed?

   a. violent

   b. connected to drugs

   c. property-related

   d. public order offenses

   e. none of the above

PART 2: SHORT-ANSWER QUESTIONS

1. List four solutions to HIV/AIDS in correctional facilities.

2. Why might the mentally ill not be considered a special population?

3. Why has the American prison system been accused of being sexist?

PART 3: ESSAY QUESTIONS

1. How does the *Adoption and Safe Families Act* passed in 1997 affect women inmates?

2. How can public health and community service agencies take a larger role in providing services to special populations behind bars?

NOTE

   1. Personal correspondence with Miguel Zaldivar, June 2007.

Chapter 8

Rehabilitation

INTRODUCTION

Prisoner rehabilitation has both philosophical/ideological and programmatic implications. With respect to the first dimension, analysts have delineated the context of rehabilitation into three areas: changing how prisoners respond to their environment, altering their motivations, and changing their lifestyles (Alleman, 2002: 25–37). The second perspective, however, deals with the practical aspects of rehabilitation in correctional facilities, which typically means job training, education, and counseling. Unfortunately, most jails and prisons devote scant resources toward this goal. Thus, we are left with human warehouses, where little attention is paid to rehabilitation, treatment, or providing prisoners with the opportunity to better prepare themselves for a law-abiding life.

Rehabilitation of prisoners is not a new concept or a recent process. In fact, one of the first prisons, the Walnut Street Jail in Philadelphia, established by the Quakers (aka *the Society of Friends*) in 1790, was an attempt to change the ways of criminals. This facility originated the *silent and separate* system that the rest of the Pennsylvania correctional facilities such as Western Penitentiary (built in 1818) and Eastern State Penitentiary (built in 1829) adopted. Walnut Jail administrators believed that if prisoners were kept separate in a cell with a bible, they would have time to reflect on their sins and transgressions and, when they were eventually released, be morally upstanding citizens.

This chapter has benefited from the comments of Francis Cullen and Miguel Zaldivar.

The rehabilitation movement also had adherents in the reformatory movement, which can be traced back to the first juvenile reformatory established by Zebulon Brockaway in New Jersey in 1876. At that time, correctional planners also introduced the so-called medical model into corrections. Here prisoners were considered to be sick and thus afforded a number of treatments to make them healthy. "Taking a genuine medical approach to corrections, prison officials began reorganizing programs and introducing a therapeutic staff" (Welch, 1996: 96).

Not only does rehabilitation have a historical context, but it also has ideological origins and implications. Liberals and radicals generally favor rehabilitation, whereas conservatives place more emphasis on punishment and community safety. This is probably why in American political history, Democratic regimes prefer correctional innovations and programs to help convicts and ex-cons, whereas Republicans scale back these kinds of initiatives and disproportionately focus on punishment and public safety. If there is a problem with recidivism rates, it has typically been under a corrections regime that has turned decidedly punitive. Most of the slip in public support for rehabilitation tended to occur in the late 1960s and early 1970s. It has remained fairly stable since then (Cullen, 2006).

Experts and opinion leaders from both ideological camps have been critical of rehabilitation for different reasons. "[M]any liberals pointed to the problems that the programs were unwittingly causing. [They] . . . cautioned against the proliferation of correctional programs because they were actually adding to the crime problem, especially juvenile delinquency. That is, the more programs and interventions that are available, the more likely it is that a person who is arrested will be dragged further into the system" (Welch, 1996: 103). This process is typically referred to as *net widening*. This has a disproportionate effect on juveniles who are brought under the watchful eye of the criminal justice system.

Rehabilitation, whether as part of institutional corrections or as an option under the community-based part of corrections (e.g., probation and parole), is complicated and in many respects almost impossible. In order to ensure rehabilitation, the correctional system needs to closely evaluate each inmate and program them accordingly. This typically occurs at classification and thus can have an important impact on rehabilitation.

THE CURRENT STATE OF REHABILITATION

Today's jails and prisons are typically about punishing individuals convicted of criminal charges and attempting to increase public safety, not rehabilitation. A generation ago, part of the correctional focus was on attempting to somehow change convicts' attitudes, behaviors, and employability in anticipation of their eventual release. A quarter-century of experiencing the high rate of recidivism (caused primarily by technical violations) has put this approach in disfavor. Today's emphasis is on protecting the public by locking up criminals and ensuring that they serve most, if not all, of their sentences.

Largely motivated by the Attica riot (1971), a considerable amount of scholarly attention has been focused on figuring out how to improve corrections. One of the most noticeable pieces of research was a report popularly credited to Robert Martinson titled "What Works?—Questions and Answers about Prison Reform." It was the product of a long-term study under the directorship of Douglas S. Lipton, established by the New York State Division of Criminal Justice, to determine how to best rehabilitate offenders. The document was a synthesis of 231 English-language studies, published between 1945 and 1967, on attempts to rehabilitate prisoners. The report, which weighed in at 1,484 pages, was originally blocked from publication. After some legal maneuvering, Martinson managed to get a summary printed in the spring 1974 edition of the journal *Public Interest* (Hallinan, 2003: 33–36). In short, he concluded that "with few and isolated exceptions," the rehabilitative programs "had no appreciable effect" on recidivism. If you closely look at the longer study, he was really saying that across categories of intervention (e.g., counseling and probation) no modality seemed to work reliably (more often than not). Nevertheless, most people have interpreted this to mean that absolutely nothing worked to rehabilitate convicts to prevent them from recidivating. Although scholars like Ted Palmer (1975) criticized Martinson when he pointed out that 48 percent of the studies that had recidivism data in Martinson's study showed positive treatment effects, Martinson's findings were welcomed by conservatives at the time who finally found a semirespectable scholar to support their claims and efforts. For the historical record, Martinson later recanted his position in a 1979 article published in the *Hofstra Law Review*. In this later piece he stated, "But whether they work—and how well they work—depends on the conditions under which they are applied" (Hallinan, 2003: 36). However, "[b]y 1979, though, few people wanted to listen. The movement away from rehabilitation and toward punishment was well on its way-propelled, in large measure, by Martinson's original article. Conservative politicians and academics had seized upon the article and used it to bolster arguments for longer and more punitive sentences" (Hallinan, 2003: 36)—this despite the accumulation of good science on rehabilitation (e.g., Cullen and Gendreau, 2000; Andrews and Bonta, 2006). Finally, to support the conservative approach toward prison confinement, in 2001, Congress (under Representative Dick Zimmer) passed *The No Frills Prison Act*, barring such amenities as televisions and coffee pots in Federal Bureau of Prisons (FBOP) cells.

Nevertheless, most Americans and selected correctional practitioners support rehabilitation (Flanagan and Caulfield, 1984; Cullen, Cullen, and Wozniak, 1988; Cullen and Gendreau, 1989; 2000; Cullen, Fisher, and Applegate, 2000; Kifer, Hemmens, and Stohr, 2003). More specifically, advocating rehabilitation is strongest for juveniles and less so for violent inmates. In general, Americans support both treatment and punishment—they do not see them as irreconcilable approaches. Finally, we now have a growing body of knowledge on what works with convicts (mainly cognitive-behavioral programs with high-risk convicts, preferably delivered in the community and followed up with aftercare and employment). How one implements these programs is, of course, another story. Regardless of how we tinker with the programs, correctional settings are typically suboptimal environments for rehabilitation of inmates.

VOCATIONAL TRAINING

There are several kinds of vocational training that convicts receive; however, these are bounded by job availability, work assignments, their pay, and types of jobs available (Gerber and Fritsch, 2001). The following section reviews these issues.

Job Availability

In jails and prisons the distinction between vocational training and working a job is often blurred. Good jobs in prison (such as they are) are in short supply. Getting a decent assignment and avoiding bad work details is important for maintaining prisoners' morale and earning some meager wages to place in their commissary account. When meaningful jobs are not present, there are often make-work duties; these are typically boring cleaning and gardening jobs. Working makes it easier for convicts to do their time. Nevertheless, prisoners do more than make license plates, street signs, and mailbags. Prison industries where convicts can work both in state prisons and at the federal level are a vital part of our national economy, producing thousands of different products and providing services marketed all over the country. These include office furniture, clothing, textiles, electronic parts, and vehicle services. Convicts may also work for private contractors doing telemarketing, providing banking and credit card services, airline and hotel reservations, and managing state lotteries.

Work Assignments

Not everybody in prison has a job. There are never enough work assignments for the whole population. Some inmates spend the whole day in their cells, venturing forth only to go to meals, the library, or participate in some sort of recreation, like working out with weights or playing handball. In an institution of about 2,000 prisoners, 400 (20 percent) of the convicts will be working in the prison industries (factory), 100 (5 percent) will be in the kitchen, another 100 will be mopping floors, another 100 doing maintenance work (plumbing, carpentry, air-conditioning repair, painting) and groundskeeping (cutting grass, planting flowers, shoveling snow), 200 (10 percent) will be in GED classes, 50 (2.5 percent) will be in drug treatment class, 200 will be in the hole (usually 10 percent of the prison population can be found in the hole at any one time), and 200 (10 percent) will be on medical leave, laid up in their cells or the infirmary with diabetes, heart problems, bad backs, or other problems. The rest of them, over 30 percent of the prison population, are confined to their housing units, bored out of their minds (Ross and Richards, 2002).

In order for the facility to function at all, convicts must do almost all the menial labor. They may work in the kitchen preparing meals, or spend years sweeping, mopping, and waxing corridor floors, or in the laundry cleaning massive amounts of clothing.

Inmate Pay

Just because the inmates have a work assignment does not mean they will be paid. The institution is under no obligation to compensate prisoners for their labor. In fact, many prisons in the country do not pay the convicts anything. Departments of corrections (DOCs) will budget very little funds for inmate pay. The reason why they pay cons is so prisoners can buy small things from commissary or pay for telephone use. If no one has money in their commissary account, inmates often feel desperate.

There is usually a waiting list a couple of years long to get a position in prison industries, because that's the best way for convicts to make money. In any event, inmate pay for general labor is very low, a few dollars a week. Mopping floors pays about 12 cents an hour, and working in the factory ranges from about 40 cents to $1.10. To the authorities, work for convicts is a privilege, not a right. In prison, even bad jobs are hard to get.

Types of Available Jobs

Vocational training generally means kitchen duty, maintenance work, or groundskeeping, which is supervised by correctional officers (COs) who provide little instruction to the inmates. Although these are officially called vocational programs, the convicts know it as work assignments. Unless convicts are "physically or mentally challenged" (i.e., mentally ill, or suffering from a mental disability), washing dishes 12 hours a day, seven days a week can hardly be called vocational training; it will not lead to a better job on the outside.

Although the FBOP runs UNICOR, which exists to simultaneously train inmates and produce needed products for the federal government, there may be a two- to three-year wait for jobs. Nevertheless, some prison systems have incorporated the private sector into their job training. Selected businesses believe that it is in their economic self-interest to establish a premise in a correctional facility. Selected inmates are then allowed and paid the prevailing wage, and a portion of their salaries are deducted to pay for things like fines, restitution, child and family support, taxes, and sometimes room and board. Oregon is a case in point. "[T]he state's inmate work program is run as a for-profit business under an assumed business name, Inside Oregon Enterprises. It . . . leases inmates to companies in need of labor. Although the inmates must be paid market wages, employers" do not pay benefits (Hallinan, 2003: 144). One of the most well-known employers of convict labor is Oregon-based clothing manufacturer Prison Blues (www.prisonblues.com). Started in 1989, the company produces blue jeans, yard coats, work shirts, and related apparel. The "tough guy" image, besides the fact that prisoners make the clothing, helps in its widespread popularity among some consumers. There is apparently a three-year-long waiting list among inmates at Eastern Oregon Correctional Institute to perform this work where the articles are manufactured.

EDUCATION

Most prisoners typically and desperately need to upgrade their formal education. In some correctional facilities the majority of inmates are high school dropouts. In prison, however, opportunities for receiving some form of formal education are in short supply, and dwindling (Taylor and Tewksbury, 2002).

The Setting

Typically, prisons may have an education section or department that occupies a floor or wing of a building. This may include a small library and a few classrooms. It might be staffed by teachers, COs, and convict clerks, with a range of certifications and training. The utility of the program depends as much on the skills of the officers or teachers, as the determination of the individual prisoners (e.g., Fisher-Giorlando, 2003; Tregea, 2003). The quality of educational programs generally varies based on the security level. Most maximum-security or Supermax prisons' educational programs are limited to Adult Basic Education (ABE eighth grade), and the General Education Development (GED) certificate, basically a high school diploma.

Difficult to Pursue

Most convicts are lucky to receive basic instruction that would lead to the achievement of a GED. The education programs are mostly inadequate. Very few resources (staff, space, etc.) are devoted to "inmate education." Prison administrators rarely support higher education. Most wardens, even those who publicly portray themselves as dedicated to rehabilitation, see outside instructors as potential threats to the security and smooth running of the institutions. Convicts taking college classes also may be subject to frequent cell searches and disciplinary transfers to administrative detention (solitary confinement) or other institutions. This disrupts their ability to regularly take classes.

Wardens may consider educated convicts to be a threat to their authority because they may be more knowledgeable, skilled, and appear more credible than other prisoners particularly in their communications with outsiders (e.g., the media and oversight agencies). In short, educated inmates may report on poor prison conditions, corruption, and incompetent administrators. Then again, on the other hand, educated convicts may be easier to deal with because they may distrust rumor, and respond better to reason, facts, and empirical support.

Up until the summer of 1995, Federal Pell Grants were available for prisoners in both state and federal prisons, as a means of paying college tuition for courses taught inside its walls or by correspondence. This benefit was not without its problems. Occasionally, some inmates applied for the grants, but never received the support, because they were transferred to another correctional facility. Alternatively, prisoners may have applied for a Pell Grant and the education office at the prison, and not themselves, actually received the funds, which could be spent by the institution on anything that remotely could be interpreted as educational (e.g., basketballs, pencils, and flower gardens).

Those who serve time no longer have to worry about the hassle of Pell grants, because the grant program has been canceled. The *Violent Crime Control Act* (aka *the Crime Bill*) passed in 1994, during the Clinton Administration, cut off the primary funding for postsecondary correctional education to prisoners. As if to add insult to injury, in 1998 the *Drug Free Student Loan Act* was passed, which denied student loans or work-study programs to individuals who had been convicted of drug offenses whether this was at the misdemeanor or at the felony level.

SOLUTIONS

In every jail or prison there are a dedicated group of inmates, many of them college educated, some of them former teachers, who tutor other men for their ABE or GED. Many DOCs and the FBOP emphasize the need for prisoners to complete these basic educational requirements. Meanwhile there are multiple opportunities for self-education and sometimes formal education.

Self-Education

Numerous possibilities exist for inmates to educate themselves, not only by reading appropriate books but by participating in informal classes with other prisoners.

Books to Read
Convicts often have more free time to read than they have ever had in their lives.[1] They generally have two options. They can borrow the worn, tattered, and outdated books in the prison library. Oftentimes, the good books are missing. Even amid volumes of so-called trashy fiction, prisoners will always find a few worthwhile books. On the other hand, since inmates rarely have access to well-stocked library collections, prisoners need to ask outsiders to purchase books from book stores or publishers, then have those businesses mail them in to convicts. In communications with outsiders convicts may ask for the classics and college textbooks. This reading material may help convicts prepare themselves if they are planning to go to school upon eventual release (Richards, 2004).

Convict-Taught Classes
Semiformal classes are sometimes organized by prisoners on a wide range of topics. Many of these are taught by men convicted of white-collar offenses. Included are entrepreneurial subjects like writing business plans, applying for small business loans, and operating a company. Many convicts are foreign born. Thus, it is relatively easy to find a tutor to help inmates learn a foreign language. Also worth noting are the

instructions by jailhouse lawyers in writing administrative remedies, writs, motions to court, and appeals. Such classes taught by convict volunteers are unofficial, with no assistance from prison authorities.

Formal Education

Considerable academic research clearly demonstrates higher education is the single most effective means to lower criminal recidivism rates (Tregea, 2003). Simply stated, prisoners who complete a year or more of college courses while incarcerated are much less likely to violate parole or be returned to prison on a new conviction. Nevertheless, formal classes, beyond the GED, with rare exceptions, are not available in jails and prisons. Most correctional systems do not have postsecondary education offerings.

The only institutional program worth taking may be a computer repair class, operated on contract by an outside corporation. Convicts may enjoy learning about computer architecture and program languages, but spend most of their time teaching remedial math classes to fellow inmates. Some of them may actually learn enough basic algebra to pass the computer course exams. Unfortunately, this unique prison program is often discontinued when the funding expires.

Occasionally, cash-strapped or entrepreneurial local institutions of higher learning might offer introductory college-level courses. These programs are often dependent on the resources and the predicted and actual financial incentives that the educational institution receives and the whims of the warden. In any event, they only serve a few dozen prisoners at a time who can somehow scrounge up the funds to pay the tuition. The college or university often terminates the program when they discover that the convicts cannot afford the courses and/or when they lose patience with the bureaucrats who manage the penitentiary. Alternatively, the DOC is slow with the payments and the school feels that it is not economically viable to continue (Ross and Richards, 2002).

College Credit by Correspondence

As most prisons do not offer college courses or actively support prisoners who pursue postsecondary education, an alternative is for prisoners to take self-paced college classes by correspondence. Most of these university programs do not have admission requirements and do not require a GED or high school diploma to begin classes. Almost every correctional facility has a small group of prisoners who take these classes by mail. They usually hang out in the main prison library or law library where it is quiet, and they might have access to typewriters and copying machines.

How quick it takes prisoners to complete a course of studies depends on the time limits established by the correspondence school; the inmates' funds to pay for courses, books, and stamps; scholastic ability; determination; and the conditions of confinement, including distractions. Convicts will have to figure out how to pay for the college credit courses and what classes to take. Inmates may use the meager amount of money they earn inside the prison, or ask for outside help (e.g., family or friends) to pay for courses.

Inmates also need to have the prison case manager, counselor, or free world friend make arrangements to pay the university. Another idea is to have outside family or friends pay for the first course, and then reimburse them later, and/or when the prisoner is released.

Typically, inmates are subject to many security restrictions that complicate their efforts, including no more than a handful of books in cells, limited use of typewriters or computers, or photocopy machines, and mail procedures. Some mail, coming and going, is opened, read, and copied by COs. In years past books mailed to convicts from friends and families typically had the covers ripped off by prison employees to prevent the entry of contraband into the institution.[2] Now the only way convicts can receive books is from a reputable publisher or bookseller.

College credit courses are not for everybody. Prisoners, just like first-year students on college campuses, have a high rate of failure. On the other hand, inmates have lots of time to read, room and board is provided, and depending on the conditions of confinement there may be few distractions. Cons who fail to complete a course of studies while incarcerated may finish college degrees at universities when and if they are released from jail or prison. Meanwhile, two alternative educational programs have been recently created: Inside-Out and Inviting Convicts to College.

Inside-Out Prison Exchange Program

College students pursuing bachelor degrees in criminology and criminal justice take university-level classes in prison alongside inmates, formally known as *The Inside-Out Prison Exchange Program: Exploring Issues of Crime and Justice Behind the Walls*. Piloted in 1997, by Lori Pompa, a licensed social worker and current instructor in the Department of Criminal Justice at Temple University, with the support of the Philadelphia Prison System and Temple University, the program boasts over 300 college students and 400 inmates having participated in the experience. In 2002, Pompa received a year-long Soros Justice Senior Fellowship, to expand Inside-Out nationwide. In 2004 she stated, "After relatively limited outreach, 75 instructors have expressed interest in being trained in this approach. The first Training Institute, scheduled for mid-July 2004, will be attended by 20–25 instructors from a dozen different states" (www.temple.edu/inside-out/). Since then "there have been 130 instructors from 82 colleges/universities in 32 states" that have taken the course.[3]

The program incorporates the pedagogy of community-based service learning (i.e., a kind of pedagogy that combines classroom teaching with performing some sort of valuable service). Pompa says, "This unique educational experience provides dimensions of learning that are difficult to achieve in a traditional classroom. At its most basic level, Inside-Out allows the 'outside' students to take the theory they have learned and apply it in a real-world setting, while those living behind the walls are able to place their life experiences in a larger academic framework." The Inside-Out Prison Exchange Program "was established to create a dynamic partnership between institutions of higher learning and correctional systems, in order to deepen the conversation about and transform our approaches to issues of crime and justice." "This semester-long course provides a life-altering experience that allows students to contextualize and rethink what they have learned in the classroom, gaining insights that will help them to better pursue the work of creating a more effective, humane and restorative criminal justice system. At the same time, Inside-Out challenges men and women on the inside to place their life experiences in a larger social context, rekindles their intellectual self-confidence and interest in further education, and encourages them to recognize their capacity as agents of change—in their own lives as well as in the broader community."

The students meet "once a week . . . through which 15–18 undergraduate students and the same number of incarcerated men or women attend class together inside prison." All participants read a variety of criminal justice texts and write several papers; during class sessions, students discuss issues in small and large groups; and, in the final month of the class, students work together on a class project. Crucial to the Inside-Out pedagogy is the powerful exchange that occurs between "inside" and "outside" students. It is the reciprocity and authenticity of this exchange that makes Inside-Out unique. In 2006 Inside-Out "became an established program in the College of Liberal Arts at Temple University" (www.temple.edu/inside-out/).

Inviting Convicts to College Program

In 2004, Susan Reed, Chris Rose, and Stephen C. Richards (who received a Soros Justice Senior Fellowship in 2001), criminal justice professors at the University of Wisconsin–Oshkosh (UWO), coordinated the first "Inviting Convicts to College" program in two state prisons (Rose, Reed, and Richards, 2005; Richards, Rose, and Reed, 2006; Richards and Ross, 2007). On a weekly basis pairs of undergraduate or graduate student teachers visit a number of medium- and maximum-security prisons in the state and teach a class about crime, criminals, and prisons. The university students learn to teach, by writing their course syllabi, giving lectures, administering examinations, grading their own class of prisoner-students, and receiving internship credits in return. The prisoners get a free education that is relevant to not only their backgrounds, but possible future careers.

The curriculum is composed of three free noncredit college courses that use the textbook *Convict Criminology* (Ross and Richards, 2003) in the first two courses. Half of the text includes chapters authored by former prisoners who were or are now university professors. The book inspires the prisoner-students to plan on attending colleges and universities upon completion of their prison sentences. Prisoner-students discuss the readings and write papers. The third course "College Preparation and Enrollment" is devoted entirely to teaching prisoners how to transition from prison to college, including completing college admissions and financial aid forms.

Upon finishing the three courses, the prisoner-students receive a certificate of completion from the university. Students show letters notifying them of acceptance to college to their fellow convicts, and this, in turn, has inspired more prisoners to take the course. Their "release plan" may include attending college or university where their financial aid checks are waiting.

The "Inviting Convicts to College" program includes a number of innovative ideas. The classes are free because they are taught by undergraduate or graduate students. University departments that include student internship programs may find this model an attractive idea for placing students as classroom instructors in prison. Deploying students in this manner means universities do not incur the expense of reassigning faculty to teach the classes. The use of student interns as instructors was the key to keeping the university and departmental costs to a minimum. The faculty members, in turn, supervise a number of internships, including multiple placements of student interns in different prisons. The model is relatively easy to implement, thus making it easily employed at no expense in many correctional facilities across the country. As of July 2007, the program boasted having deployed 13 student teachers with 120 convict students. In the fall 2007 and spring 2008 they will add 8 more teachers and 60 students.[4]

Summary

A prison record and a GED provide men and women released from prison with few long term career prospects other than minimum-wage jobs. That is why college courses may improve their opportunities for getting a better jobs. After getting out of prison, one possible path for former inmates is to go to college (Ross and Richards, 2003). As a former prisoner, ex-cons are already institutionalized, accustomed to dormitory living, and bureaucratic rules. Considering ex-cons are probably without a job, have no income, and have not paid taxes in years, depending on the crimes for which they were convicted, they might qualify for nongovernmental student loans and possible grants.

Faith-Based Programming

As mentioned earlier, during the past four years in American prisons, there have been attempts to integrate more religious programming (primarily Christian) and to get faith-based communities involved in prisoner reentry programs. This may include the promise of housing, meals, and work once the prisoner is released. Although there is a long history of religious community's involvement with prisons, this current iteration can be traced back to the time when current president George W. Bush was governor of Texas. He allowed the Prison Fellowship Ministries (led by Charles W. Colson, a former convict, who had done time because of his role in the 1971 Watergate break-in scandal) entrance into the Texas Department of Corrections to run a program called InnerChange Freedom Initiative, which was "a Bible-centered prison-within-a-prison where inmates undergo vigorous evangelizing, prayer sessions, and intensive counseling" (Kleiman, 2003). To date, there have been few evaluations of the success of these programs. One of them, produced by the University of Pennsylvania's Center for Research on Religion and Urban Civil Society, that touted the program as a success was severely criticized for selection bias (Kleiman, 2003). Meanwhile, several of the programs have been under the watchful eye of civil libertarians because of allegations of using state funds for religious purposes (Henriques and Lehren, 2006).

Therapy in Prison

Many prisons have a variety of alcohol and drug treatment programs. Too often, the programs are run by staff or inmates who are unqualified. "Departments of corrections frequently encourage inmates to establish self-help programs. These are run primarily by the inmates themselves and often express ethnic and cultural goals. Self-help groups meet in the evenings and on weekends. They usually are required to have a staff sponsor and to establish governing bylaws and procedures" (Bartollas, 2002: 314). Needless to say, there are many problems with drug treatment behind bars (Austin, 1998).

Some of the more successful are Alcoholics Anonymous (AA) and Narcotics Anonymous. These programs, sometimes with the assistance of outside volunteers, teach and support prisoners in a "twelve-step program." This involves both psychological and lifestyle changes. There is a certain continuity with these programs because when inmates are released on parole, their officers may require ex-cons to attend these meetings and/or one of the conditions of parole is to attend AA (Austin, 1998). In fact, many individuals in AA are ex-cons. Anger Management Programs, on the other hand, have been found to be of questionable utility (Terry, 2003: 160–183). Once again and unfortunately, in the recent get-tough era, however, state governments have cut back funding in providing competent therapy.

Boot Camps

Other solutions for rehabilitation have been the creation of boot camps in state-run facilities (Armstrong, Gover, and Mackenzie, 2002). As mentioned earlier in this text, also known as shock or intensive incarceration, they started in Georgia in 1983. Essentially these programs, operating in approximately 39 states, which are separate from the main facility, last a maximum of 120 days and involve a military or paramilitary regimen. "Most are residential facilities for juvenile delinquents or adult criminals with military style structure, rules, and discipline. Boot camp programs are expected to reduce prison crowding and related costs. They are also intended to reduce recidivism and antisocial behavior. Finally it is commonly believed that they can deter individuals from future offending while also helping to rehabilitate them through the imposition of discipline" (Odo, Onyeozili, and Onwudiwe, 2005: 79). Unfortunately, rigorous evaluations have discovered that inductees do no better in the boot camp environment than others sent to traditional correctional institutions (Armstrong, Gover, and Mackenzie, 2002: 126). Moreover, it does not appear that benefits are accrued in the reduction in prison space (overcrowding) (Mackenzie and Souryal, 1991).

Programs on the Horizon

In April 2007 Congress was about to consider the passage of the *Second Chance Act of 2005* (H.R. 1593), a bill that is "designed to ensure the safe and successful return of prisoners to the community." Recently passed by the House Judiciary Committee, this bill has existed in earlier drafts since the spring 2005 when it was originally tabled in Congress. In general, the *Second Chance Act* has received considerable bipartisan support including endorsements from over 200 organizations. Needless to say, this bill has faltered before. On December 6, 2006, Senator Coburn (R-OK) put a hold on the bill. He argued that "there is no federal role in prisoner re-entry" and that his state was doing perfectly fine in minimizing recidivism and reintegrating ex-offenders back into society.

The bill, earmarked at $65 million, helps with state and county reentry initiatives, funds community and faith-based groups to deliver services to ex-convicts, and encourages drug treatment programs. Finally, it is aimed at ensuring adequate housing, work, substance abuse counseling, mental health treatment and support for families and children.

The need for this bill is fairly self-evident. Approximately 7.65 million people are released from jails and prisons each year and about two-thirds of all inmates who are released from state prisons are rearrested and are sent back to state prisons. Communities do and must take an active role in the reintegration of prisoners. There needs to be more coordination at the federal level. And money needs to be appropriated to determine how successful these programs are.

CONCLUSION

Prisoner rehabilitation is clearly lacking. This should not come as a surprise (e.g., Martinson, 1974). The emphasis in jails and prisons is disproportionately on punishment and the external benefit is supposed to be community safety. Still as this chapter has outlined, there are opportunities for both administration- and convict-led efforts for prisoners to improve themselves.

One must guard against the perception, however, that treatment effects are too idiosyncratic to implement programs with broadly positive effects. Although there are "responsivity" issues (individuals react differently depending on how treatment is delivered), there is growing evidence (as noted earlier) that most people convicted of a crime are generally responsive to cognitive-behavioral interventions. (Andrews et al., 1990).

Meanwhile, periodically, well-meaning individuals and organizations gain access to prisons and, with the blessing of the warden, senior correctional personnel, or the DOC, manage to get their "rehabilitative" programs implemented. Unfortunately, this "correctional quackery" often suffers from poor science. Their beneficial claims are made based on anecdotal rather than empirical evidence. It is also difficult for them to compare the advantages of their experiment to other programs that can be introduced. For example, how do these skills and experiences transfer to something that is tangibly useful on the outside (Latessa, Cullen, and Gendreau, 2002)?

Understandably, "some rehabilitation programs work better than others, but no program works all the time—or even most of the time. The best success rate for the best programs is only about 20 percent, and even this figure can be misleading. Different programs measure 'success' in different ways. For some, success means a complete halt to criminal activity. The inmate, after his release, never again has a brush with the law. For others, an inmate may be considered rehabilitated if the 'rate' of his criminal activity declines: He may be rearrested (or reconvicted or reimprisoned) and still be considered 'rehabilitated' so long as he is not rearrested as often as he might have been had he not participated in the rehabilitation program. The consensus is that programs that work best tend to be those that teach so-called life skills like balancing a checkbook and those that stress family involvement" (Hallinan, 2003: 133).

KEY TERMS

boot camp
correctional quackery
faith-based programming
General Education Development (GED)
"Inside-Out Prison Exchange" Program
"Inviting Convicts to College" Program
jailhouse lawyer

net widening
No Frills Prison Act
Pell Grant
rehabilitation
responsivity
Second Chance Act

REVIEW QUESTIONS

PART 1: MULTIPLE-CHOICE QUESTIONS

1. Who established the Walnut Street Jail?

   a. the government
   b. Quakers
   c. Puritans
   d. Lutherans
   e. none of the above

2. In a typical prison, what percent of inmates work?

   a. 10–20
   b. 25–30
   c. 35–40
   d. 45–50
   e. 55–60

3. Semiformal classes are sometimes organized by prisoners on a wide range of topics. Of what types of crimes have these convict teachers typically been convicted?

   a. murder
   b. white-collar crimes
   c. rape
   d. tax crime
   e. some of the above

4. Many prisons have a variety of alcohol and drug treatment programs. What is/are the most successful one/s?

   a. Gamblers Anonymous
   b. Alcoholics Anonymous
   c. Anger Management
   d. some of the above
   e. none of the above

5. Who or what entity is the major consumer of products manufactured by prison industries?

    a. blue-chip companies
    b. clothing manufacturers
    c. furniture chains
    d. state and federal government
    e. quarries

6. In prison, of what does vocational training generally consist?

    a. kitchen duty
    b. maintenance work
    c. groundskeeping
    d. all of the above
    e. none of the above

7. What is the name of the clothing manufacturing company that uses convicts to produce its line of blue jeans?

    a. Gap
    b. Lee
    c. Levis
    d. Prison Blues
    e. Victoria's Secret

8. What is the name for an inmate who helps other convicts in lawsuits?

    a. inmate litigator
    b. jailhouse lawyer
    c. prison advocate
    d. trustee
    e. none of the above

9. What is a Pell Grant?

    a. document used in transferring inmates from one institution to another
    b. immunity from prosecution
    c. money that is given to a student pursuing college education
    d. money used by prisons for GEDs
    e. none of the above

PART 2: SHORT-ANSWER QUESTIONS

1. What is a jailhouse lawyer?
2. Who was Robert Martinson and why is he important in the field of corrections?
3. List three things convicts can do to take control of their own rehabilitation.
4. Who was Zebulon Brockaway?

PART 3: ESSAY QUESTIONS

1. How can rehabilitation be best used to minimize recidivism?

2. How would you evaluate the success or failure of a program designed to rehabilitate inmates?

3. How would a DOC determine if an inmate is rehabilitatable?

NOTES

1. This presupposes that they are relatively literate. As many studies have demonstrated, reading and writing ability among prisoners are very low.
2. The staff is concerned about drugs (e.g., sheets of LSD, heroin, or cocaine), weapons (e.g., razors or hacksaw blades), or money being hidden in the cloth or paper cover.
3. Personal correspondence with Lori Pompa, August 3, 2007.
4. Personal correspondence with Stephen C. Richards, July 16, 2007.

Chapter 9

Overburdened Community
Corrections System

INTRODUCTION

Community corrections consists of a number of different types of programs and sanctions for individuals who have either been charged with or convicted of a crime, or served jail or prison time, but still under the supervision of the criminal justice system (McShane and Krause, 1993; Ellesworth, 1996; McCarthy and McCarthy, 1997). As reviewed in Chapter 3, there are various community corrections options including prerelease, supervised release, probation, intermediate sanctions, parole, and mandatory release. The problems experienced by community corrections are not only for the agencies and officers, but also for the individuals who are awaiting their trials, people who have been convicted of a crime, but sentenced to probation, inmates who are released from jail or prison on parole, and their families and loved ones. Over the past decade, this noninstitutional approach has encountered and/or experienced numerous problems. These difficulties have occurred after repeated criticisms during the 1980s and 1990s that community corrections programs have been too lenient and that tougher sanctions and forms of control needed to be implemented (e.g., Morris and Tonry, 1990).[1] Community corrections now stresses programs that make probationers and parolees more accountable and the public better protected (e.g., through intensive probation, electronic monitoring [EM], and house arrest) (Feeley and Simon, 1992; Lucken, 1998). These gains, however, have come at a cost. Probation and parole agents spend a considerable

This chapter has benefited from the comments of Ginger Duke-Miller, Ernest Eley, Mike Johnson, Alicia Peak, and Dana Valdivia.

amount of their time writing reports, receiving training, going to court, attending probation and parole revocation hearings, talking with program providers, all of which take time away from actually supervising their caseload.

THE PROBLEMS

Introduction

Several difficulties confront the modern practice of community corrections (e.g., Finn and Kuck, 2005). These include role conflict; the location of community corrections offices; rigid, bureaucratic, or inflexible supervisors; the failure to make a meaningful reduction in recidivism; high levels of work-related stress; violence by probationers and parolees against their officers/agents; overcrowded/overburdened probation and parole officers/agents; and lack of adequate funding.

Role Conflict

One of the problems for some probation and parole officers is that they suffer from role conflict. On the one hand, they perform some of the duties of social workers; on the other hand, they are law enforcement officers. "The majority of officers used to see themselves in the counselling role. Personal involvement in the supervision of offenders was emphasized" (Bartollas, 2002: 132). During the 1970s, the reintegration model emphasized probation officers as resource brokers instead of counselors. Increasingly, their role as law enforcement officers is being stressed. This may have something to do with the fact that in the past many community corrections workers earned degrees in the fields of social work, psychology, and sociology. Now they are disproportionately drawn from individuals with community college diplomas or university degrees in criminology and criminal justice. These factors combined means that, compared to past practices, probation and parole officers are more likely to violate probationers or parolees who do not comply with their court-sanctioned requirements. In sum, over time, the probation/ parole officer role has changed to being more focused on public safety functions, emphasizing surveillance, control, and ensuring that their charges comply with the numerous court-mandated orders.

Location of Community Corrections Offices and Institutions

Although some probation and parole offices are located in or next to courthouses, most of the agencies, as well the facilities that are established to help ex-cons (e.g., residential treatment centers and halfway homes), are located close to or within parts of town where the probationers and parolees live. These neighborhoods are typically poor or economically depressed. On the one hand, it makes sense to locate community corrections-related offices and institutions in these locations. Rent and land are relatively cheap in these parts of the city, allowing typically cash-strapped probation and parole departments to take advantage of these cost savings. Additionally, it's easier for probationers and parolees to access these programs; it does not require them to hop on a bus or subway, and spend half a day traveling across town or downtown just to speak to their officer or agent. Also it must be understood that probation and parole offices and related services experience a lot of community backlash, particularly in middle-class residential areas or upscale commercial parts of a city, as a result of their office location and thus many land-lords refuse to rent to probation and parole agencies. Residents and business own-ers argue or worry that probationers and parolees commit new crimes close to their offices.

On the other hand, arguments can also be made that locating community corrections offices and related services in poorer parts of town only contributes to the cycle of poverty and crime that these communities experience. In short, the offices are often located in poorer areas because the communities in more upscale areas generally complain that they don't want ex-cons wandering in their neighborhood. Needless to say, where the probation and parole office is located is a major and real challenge for probationers and parolees in rural parts of states and places without access to adequate public transportation. Consequently, we see a number of technical violations for failure to report.

Rigid, Bureaucratic, and/or Inflexible Supervisors

An additional difficulty that has plagued community corrections is that officers routinely complain about unnecessarily rigid, bureaucratic, and/or inflexible supervi-sors. Many administrators forget what it was like when they were line parole or probation officers. "The overall pattern of probation in the late 1980s and 1990s showed much defensiveness on the part of administrators and little tolerance for innovation. All too often, probation officers are told that the first commandment of working in the office is not to embarrass the agency" (Bartollas, 2002: 141). A corollary problem is that advancement possibilities are limited. Administrators seem to remain in their positions for long periods of time, and when a few positions open up, there is considerable competition.

Failure to Make a Meaningful Reduction in Recidivism

One of the effects of an overburdened community corrections system is the high rate of recidivism. But recidivism, as was previously discussed, is a complex phenom-enon that difficult to define and measure (Austin, 2003). Moreover, because of the human element, there is only so much a probation or parole officer can do to help a probationer or parolee to change their attitudes and behavior. This is perhaps why most community corrections agencies try to shy away from using the term recidi-vism and evaluate the progress of their clients in terms of whether they have *successfully met the conditions of the supervision.* In the end, these factors contribute to a considerable amount of stress on the part of the officers, and this leads to job burnout and high turnover rates.

Stress

Almost all of the problems with community corrections had led to increased levels of psychological and physical stress on probation and parole officers and related correctional staff (Finn and Kuck, 2005). Undoubtedly, the amount of stress varies based on the job detail and the kinds of individuals the community supervision workers are responsible for. It also depends on the maturity level, the work attitudes, and experience of the probation and parole officers. This problem has been recognized not only by workers and management, but also by the federal government. During the mid-2000s, the National Institute of Justice (NIJ), for example, funded a series of studies examining stress in this job category. Most of the sources of stress are embedded in this discussion.

Violence by Probationers and Parolees

Few probationers and parolees welcome visits by their officers. This is especially true if there is a possibility that their status (i.e., probation or parole) will be revoked and the freedom to live in the community (i.e., outside a correctional facility) is in peril. According to Finn and Kuck (2005), somewhere "between 39 and 55 percent of officers have been victims of work-related violence or threats" (p. 1). Supervision means that many officers make home and work visits in poorer and more dangerous parts of a city and/or state. This places them in contact with all sorts of unsavory elements of society and the risk of victimization, particularly assaults are greater in these situations.

Overcrowding/High Caseloads

The number of people in community corrections depends on a variety of factors including the population of the state, "differences in sentencing philosophies, and the availability of probation resources within the state" (McCarthy and McCarthy: 108). It stands to reason, however, that if a significant number of people are being sent to correctional facilities and these places are overcrowded, then community corrections will be utilized for those individuals when judges and parole boards deem them suitable for this sanction. Thus, the majority of individuals sent to jail and prison will eventually be released back into the community (aka *reentry*), and many will serve the balance of their sentence on parole. The simple result is that there have been too many people for probation and parole agencies to handle, and funding has not increased proportionally to the number of individuals on probation or parole needing supervision.[2] In short, this translates into higher caseloads than normal. Overcrowding means that there is more paperwork and deadlines, both planned and unexpected (Finn and Kuck, 2005).

EXHIBIT 9.1

Classics in Corrections

Richard McCleary's *Dangerous Men*

Ex-convict and current professor of Sociology and Criminology at the University of California–Irvine provides an in-depth account into the decisions and actions of parole officers. This early ethnographic study outlines the positive and negative aspects of working as a parole officer. McCleary (1978/1992) develops a useful typology of ex-cons on parole. According to the author, a dangerous man is one who cannot be influenced by the parole officer and is most likely to have his parole revoked. Since the book has been written, there have been several changes in the DOCs. These include the kinds of laws that they are subjected to. The actors may change in their field, but the characters titles remain the same. They want the flexibility in their jobs and rely on each other to help with their caseloads.

Lack of Funding

As in case of institutional corrections, budget cuts and increased numbers of people on probation and parole have meant that over the past two decades community corrections agencies have had to do more with less. This means that staff are frequently stretched too thin, and that facilities and offices like many inner-city public schools in the United States are dilapidated, shoddy, or in need of renovation, and equipment is either broken or technologically outdated. Although some money is recouped by charging probationers or parolees for services like urine tests, electronic monitoring, and house or work visits, it is clearly not enough. Most states, like Maryland, charge a supervision fee of approximately $40.00 per month for everyone under supervision. In many state systems, community corrections workers put in a couple of years and, if they are lucky, transfer out to the federal parole system where salaries and benefits are higher and working conditions are significantly better. Increasingly, money is being cut for community corrections. This means that when the lion's share (typically 85 percent) of the agency's budgets goes for salaries and fringe benefits, little money is left for meaningful programs for the people who need it the most, in particular convicts who have been released.

SOLUTIONS

Introduction

In order to deal with the overburdened community corrections system, important changes have been implemented. The following discussion reviews the most salient of these initiatives. These innovations include community corrections officers carrying weapons, utilizing private-sector therapeutic communities, user fees for probationers/parolees, redistributing the workload, new classification levels, enlisting faith-based communities, experimenting with technocorrections, and specialized caseloads.

Carrying Weapons

It goes without saying that most people who are under probation or parole are hostile to community corrections workers. Officers are sometimes in jeopardy of being assaulted or killed (Parsonage and Bushey, 1989; Parsonage, 1990). Most jurisdictions are now allowing probation and parole officers to carry weapons (Camp and Camp, 1999). Since the late 1980s, some states and the federal probation system, community corrections workers have allowed to carry guns. Likewise, some community corrections workers (e.g., Maryland) are now wearing body armor when they affect arrests or go into what they believe are dangerous situations, and in some jurisdictions arrests of probationers and parolees are now only done by municipal and state police officers instead of probation or parole officers.

Residential Programs/Therapeutic Communities

Part of the solutions to overburdened community corrections also includes the use of residential programs or therapeutic communities. Similar to halfway houses, these typically nonprofit organizations generally provide vocational training and counselling to excons. Some are run by government corrections departments while others are administered by private self-help organizations. One of the most respected private initiatives is the San Francisco-based Delancy Street Foundation (www.grass-roots.org/usa/delancey.shtml). The residential organization is ostensibly run by its 450 residents. On average, Delancy Street participants have served four terms in prisons, have 18 criminal convictions, and have been substance abusers for ten years (Mieszkowski, 1998). "Today the foundation has 1,500 full-time residents in five self-run facilities around the United States—including a spectacular 350,000-square-foot complex on San Francisco's waterfront, and a rural ranch in San Juan Pueblo, New Mexico."

When the residents leave, they are expected to have two marketable skills that they learned through this program. Its graduates have become "lawyers, doctors, small-business owners, restaurateurs, mechanics, contractors, and salespeople." In sum, many of these private programs have been met with praise, especially because they have a visible impact on recidivism.

User Fees for Probationers and Parolees

Increasingly, in order to deal with the additional financial burden that has been placed on community corrections offices, probationers and parolees, in some jurisdictions, are now being charged user fees (e.g., for urine tests)—a nominal amount these individuals, under supervision, must pay for partaking in this sanction. In Maryland, for example, the Division of Probation and Parole charges a flat rate of $120.00, payable over time. Needless to say, this is an imperfect solution. Ex-cons struggling to find gainful employment now are saddled with extra financial obligations that cut in their meager earnings. No wonder that in some jurisdictions ex-cons refer to probation and parole officers as collection officers.

Redistributing the Work

Caseload Standard

In the past, an ideal caseload for probation and parole officers was between 35 and 50 adults (American Probation and Parole Association [APPA]). Unfortunately, "no empirical evidence shows that this range is ideal or that it is regarded as such any longer. In practice, caseloads vary widely. *The Corrections Yearbook: 1999* reported that the average caseload of adult probationers was 124. Caseloads ranged from 54 in Wyoming to 352 in Rhode Island. Intensive supervision probation caseloads average 25 offenders, ranging from 9 in Arizona to 51 in Rhode Island" (Cromwell, Del Carmen, and Alaird, 2002: 128).

Over the past three decades, different "ideal numbers" have been proposed. In 1973, for example, the President's Commission on Law Enforcement and Administration of Justice (National Advisory Commission on Criminal Justice Standards and Goals, 1973) recommended that probation/parole caseloads should be 35 clients per officer. They argued that "[h]igh caseloads, combined with limited training and time constraints forced by administrative and other demands, culminate in stop-gap supervisory measures. 'Postcard probation,' in which clients mail in a letter or card once a month to report on their whereabouts and circumstances, is an example of one stopgap measure that harried agencies with large caseloads use to keep track of their wards" (Schmalleger, 1999: 350). Additionally, most probation and parole agents work for small agencies administered by a handful of managers (Schmalleger, 1999: 351).

Across America, there is a considerable range with respect to the number of cases assigned per officer. In one recent survey, officers in Arkansas supervised 154 individuals, whereas those in Wisconsin were responsible for 51 (Cromwell, Del Carmen, and Alaird: 129). "[T]he average [number of] face-to-face contacts between officer and probationer was 18 in 1998. Offenders under intensive supervision averaged 114 contacts per year" (p. 128).

Workload Standard

Caution, however, must be exercised, as "not every offender needs the same type or amount of supervision to achieve the goals of probation or parole. There are a number of proven and accepted methods for determining the type and amount of supervision, but the key is that in order to be most effective and efficient, there must be varying amounts of supervision provided to offenders" (APPA).

The APPA "recommends a 'workload standard' instead of a caseload standard. It does not make sense, the APPA argues, to count every case as equal. A case requiring maximum supervision effort may require, for example, four hours of the probation or parole officer's time per month. A medium supervision case may require two hours per month to effectively supervise. A minimum supervision case may only require one hour or less per month of the probation or parole officer's time" (Cromwell, Del Carmen, and Alaird: 128).

They add, "Depending on the makeup of the caseload, the officer could effectively and efficiently supervise 30–40 maximum supervision cases, 60 medium cases, and as many as 120 minimum cases. In practice, caseloads contain offenders at every level of supervision need. The ideal caseload then is calculated by determining how many hours are available to the officer and adjusting the caseload to account for the various supervision requirements of the persons being supervised" (Cromwell, Del Carmen, and Alaird: 128).

Workload versus Caseload Standard

The workload standard takes into consideration the fact that probation and parole officers have other duties beyond supervising clients. These may include writing presentence investigation (PSI) reports and traveling across a wide geographic region (Cromwell, Del Carmen, and Alaird: 128). Occasionally, probation and parole officers working in large states like Texas supervise a caseload that are spread out over 300 miles. Alternatively, there will be community corrections officers who have caseloads in large inner cities that are confined to 12 city blocks (p. 128). In sum, it is very difficult to set an ideal caseload number, but the workload standard helps managers and researchers make better comparisons among probation and parole officers and help administrators better apportion the workload to make things fairer among employees (p. 128). It must also be understood that some probation and parole officers have mixed caseloads including probationers, excons on parole or mandatory release. In Maryland, for instance, the Division of Parole and Probation currently only has intensive and standard (aka *minimal*) levels of probation. Sometimes, however, the "standards" consume more time than the intensives.

Another issue is that with some cases, contact will not happen for weeks and this has led to a lackadaisical approach to handling probationers and parolees. This practice has been pejoratively labeled *postcard probation*, in which officers and parolees/probationers will chiefly communicate through the mail, and rarely by phone or in person.

PSIs Written by Other Community Corrections Professionals

One of the biggest problems with probation is that in many offices the individual who is supervising probationers is the same person writing up the PSI. Rarely is this recognized as a conflict of interest. Why? Because the impact of these recommendations will affect the office's workload. So, for example, if the division needs more individuals to supervise, PSI writers could simply recommend probation. If the probation offices are overwhelmed, then they may favor incarceration (Czajkoski, 1973; Campbell, McCoy, and Osigweh, 1990). This is partially the reason why the task of writing PSIs is being taken out of the hands of probation officers and given to other correctional professionals. In Maryland, for example, parole agents no longer write PSIs, investigators do. And the investigators do not supervise offenders.

New Classification Levels

Workloads have also been coupled with the development of new classification levels. These are typically broken down into intensive, medium, or minimum supervision. Most of these categories are modeled after the Wisconsin Classification System, or the NIC Model Probation Client Classification and Case Management System (Bartollas, 2002: 128). This approach may help decrease the burden on probation and parole officers.

The Enlistment of Faith-Based Communities

Undoubtedly, there is a prisoner reentry problem (Petersilia, 2003). State and federal correctional services are worried about the increasing number of individuals who are being released from jails and prison and fear that there are not enough resources in place to manage this population. Even President George W. Bush acknowledged this in his January 20, 2004, State of the Union Address. Bush outlined how he intended to utilize faith-based groups to help the federal government successfully manage the reentry of prisoners into the community. According to the President, "This four-year, $300 million initiative will provide transitional housing, basic job training, and mentoring." Although it is recognized that religious groups (particularly Christians) have historically been involved in rehabilitating prisoners, to date no unbiased evaluations has been done on the current faith-based initiative. At the time of this writing there are numerous popular media accounts of these initiatives, but evaluations looking at a comprehensive array of these unique programs using social scientific methods have not yet been done.

Technocorrections

During the 1980s, specialized technology improved in order to allow for the possibility of keeping more inmates out of jails and prisons and instead supervised in the community (Fabelo, 2000). Methods include EM systems and pharmacological treatments. In general, EM is a tracking device (like a wrist or ankle bracket) worn by the probationer or parolee, and it is sometimes combined with home confinement. It consists of a control computer, a receiver, and a transmitter. Communication can be established through a landline, cell phone, or satellite. If probationers/parolees leave a proscribed area, or enter into a prohibited one, a signal is emitted to their probation or parole officer. The community corrections office then asks the probationer/parolees to get in touch.

Electronic monitoring use has grown considerably, from approximately 95 individuals in 1986 in Florida to about 70,000 individuals monitored by local, state, and federal entities. But EM is not without its difficulties. During the 1990s, reports surfaced that cited problems with the devices and the practice of using EM (Corbet and Marx, 1991; Hoshen, Sennott, and Winkler, 1995). These included substantial up-front costs, the cost of running the system effectively, and community reaction to criminals who are on EM. Moreover, parolees are released into neighborhoods that do not feel comfortable with the individuals, and do not feel that EM does an adequate job tracking these people, and "bugs" within the EM technology.

Nevertheless, one variant of EM is the Secure Continuous Remote Alcohol Monitor (SCRAM), an ankle bracelet that analyzes a person's sweat for the presence of alcohol in the bloodstream. It is increasingly being used as a condition of probation or parole in several jurisdictions in the United States. SCRAM was introduced in 2003; by summer of 2007, its manufacturers claimed that it has been used by 40,000 individuals. Part of the rise of popularity of this sanction and control is because it has been sported by well-known American celebrities like actors Lindsay Lohan, Tracey Morgan, and Michelle Rodriguez (Zumbrun, 2007).

Another kind of technocorrections involves the use of drugs. Since the mid-1990s, states such as California, Georgia, Florida, Texas, and Wisconsin require individuals (i.e., men) convicted of sexual offenses with minors, when released from prison into the community, to register with the local police, and be chemically castrated. Males receive shots of Depo-Provera, a drug that lowers the body's production of testosterone and hampers the sex drive (Fabelo, 2000). EM and drugs are not supposed to offer a solution to overburdening, but they decrease the need to personally monitor those individuals on the probation or parole officer's caseload.

Specialized Caseloads

The probation and parole profession has recognized that ex-cons (with similar characteristics) can benefit by dealing with specialist probation and parole officers. This includes probationers and ex-cons who have alcohol and substance abuse problems, dangerous offenders, sex crime offenders, and those who have mental health issues (Cromwell, Del Carmen, and Alaird, 2002: 130). Thus, there has been increasing specialization amongst probation and parole officers and the system benefits through more efficient case management.

Rhine, Smith, and Jackson (1991) reported "that, by 1990, specialized parole caseloads were being used in 25 states." "Fourteen states were using specialized caseloads for sex offenders, 12 for drug offenders; 10 for offenders with mental disabilities, five for 'career criminals,' and 2 for violent criminals. Specialized caseloads for DWI . . . offenders were established in Texas in 1983 and now exist in virtually every medium-to-large probation department in the nation. Although few empirical studies have been conducted of the efficacy of specialized caseloads, anecdotal evidence supports the concept" (as quoted in Cromwell, Del Carmen, and Alaird, 2002: 130).

CONCLUSION

Through the implementation of sound policies and practices, coupled with the professionalization of probation and parole, along with rigorous empirical research, we may be able to minimize the problems of the overburdened community corrections system. But this is extremely difficult in an environment where government cutbacks exist, and an increasing number of people are being incarcerated and/or placed on community corrections programs each day. Finally, the community corrections system needs more resources—particularly funds to be earmarked to this vital service, trained professionals who are capable of doing a proper job, and more emphasis on rehabilitation rather than on simple reporting requirements.

KEY TERMS

American Probation and Parole
   Association (APPA)
caseload standard
Depo-Provera
electronic monitoring

postcard probation
role conflict
technocorrections
therapeutic community
workload standard

REVIEW QUESTIONS

PART 1: MULTIPLE-CHOICE QUESTIONS

1. What role conflict do probation and parole officers sometimes suffer from?
    a. they are often both fathers and sons
    b. they are one part jail guard and one part corporate manager
    c. frictional and fractional
    d. sometimes they act like police officers and at other times social workers
    e. none of the above

2. Which of the following is a problem with electronic monitoring?
    a. start-up costs
    b. system malfunctions
    c. few probation and parole agencies are willing to use it
    d. all of the above
    e. none of the above

3. Who argued that for community corrections to improve there must be three approaches?
    a. Regan
    b. Green
    c. Richards
    d. Greenberg
    e. none of the above

4. What is the most important factor determining an inmate's eligibility for parole?
    a. the age of an individual
    b. the person's health
    c. the type of crime committed
    d. requirements set by law and the sentence imposed
    e. all of the above

5. Community corrections programs that require only part-time incarceration include

   a. intern programs
   b. educational release programs
   c. house arrest
   d. all of the above
   e. b and c only

6. To which practice does community-based corrections refer?

   a. the diversion of accused offenders from the criminal justice system before prosecution
   b. sentences that impose restrictions on convicted offenders while maintaining them in the community
   c. programs designed to smooth the transition of offenders from prison to the community
   d. all of the above
   e. none of the above

7. Why are sentencing guidelines used?

   a. because federal crimes are more severe
   b. because judges are not that creative
   c. to reduce arbitrary decision making
   d. most PSIs are not the helpful
   e. to save resources

8. Which of the following is a problem with the probation system?

   a. understaffing
   b. little funding
   c. large caseloads
   d. too many people in the system
   e. all of the above

9. Which of the following state/s was/were among the first users of the electronic monitoring systems?

   a. Florida
   b. Illinois
   c. Miami
   d. a and b
   e. b and c

10. The electronic monitoring system comprises which parts?

    a. a control computer
    b. a receiver
    c. a transmitter
    d. all of the above
    e. none of the above

11. What is the name of the therapeutic community that was originally established in San Francisco to support ex-felons and ex-addicts and where the residents run the programs?
    a. Residential Transition House
    b. Sylvan Beech Foundation
    c. The Delancy Street Foundation
    d. Volunteers for America
    e. Soros Foundation

PART 2: SHORT-ANSWER QUESTIONS

1. List six strategies that have been used to deal with an overburdened community corrections system.
2. What does the acronym PSI stand for, and why is it written?
3. Why was President George W. Bush's January 20, 2004, State of the Union Address significant for community corrections?
4. What is Depo-Provera?
5. What is postcard probation?

PART 3: ESSAY QUESTIONS

1. How would you improve community corrections?
2. Which standard is better to organize a probation officer's job duties? And why?
3. Should probation and parole officers be allowed to carry guns?
4. Should governments locate services for ex-convicts in economically depressed areas, thereby creating crime-ridden ghettos, or is this simply a prudent measure by bringing the services close to the individuals who need them the most?

NOTES

1. One of these innovations was the use of intensive probation.
2. This chapter does not review the problems faced by residential treatment centers. For an analysis of some of these, see, for example, Bartollas (2002: 112–113).

Chapter 10

Crowding/Overcrowding

INTRODUCTION

It should come as no surprise that America's jails and prisons are severely crowded and overcrowded. In some facilities, four prisoners are sleeping in cells originally designed for one person. Other correctional institutions have converted their halls, recreational areas, and classrooms into dormitories with double and triple bunking. "By 1980, two-thirds of all inmates in this country lived in cells or dormitories that provide less than sixty square feet of living space per person—the minimum standard deemed acceptable by the American Public Health Association, the Justice Department, and other authorities. Many lived in cells measuring half that" (Hallinan, 2003: 97). Fortunately, many of these are only temporary and after a while a jurisdiction must look for longer lasting alternatives to the shortage of cell space.

Many experts might say that underfunding is the biggest problem facing corrections. And if the correctional departments at the municipal, regional, state, and federal levels had more money, then new facilities would be built, more and better qualified correctional officers (COs) would be hired, and overcrowding would no longer be an issue. This presupposes that this money will be spent properly and that qualified persons can be hired and trained throughout the ranks. Regardless of this chicken-and-egg problem, there are several causes for the overcrowded conditions in our jails and prisons (Bartollas, 2002: Chapter 18).

Overcrowding is recognized as a problem by a wide cross-section of individuals with expertise in the corrections field. This reaction is not simply that of well-intentioned do-gooders; among those who advocate reducing overcrowding are state and federal judges. For example, Frank M. Johnson Jr., the late Alabama judge, wrote in a 1976 opinion that "[o]vercrowding, . . . is primarily responsible for and exacerbates all the other issues of Alabama's penal system." These conditions, Judge Johnson wrote, "create an environment that not only makes it impossible for inmates to rehabilitate themselves, but also makes rehabilitation inevitable" (Hallinan, 2003: 97).

However, the sentiments of Johnson and other jurists have been overruled by the Supreme Court. The court argued in *Bell v. Wolfish*, 99 S. Ct. 1861, 1875 (1979), a landmark overcrowding case, argues that the constitution does not provide for the - "one man, one cell" ethos. If states wished to put two men in a cell designed for one, they were free to do so. The Supreme Court added, in *Rhodes v. Chapman*, 101 S. Ct. 2391, 2400 (1981), that the constitution does not guarantee inmates "comfortable prisons."

It should be understood that this problem varies from state to state and between the states and the federal system. Nevertheless, crowding/overcrowding is not an either-or situation. There is considerable nuance in determining whether a facility is crowded or overcrowded. In order to assess whether crowding or overcrowding exists, the corrections field has developed three complementary standards: a facility's *rated capacity*, *operational capacity*, and *design capacity*.

The first figure is the number of prisoners or beds a facility can handle as judged by a qualified expert who is responsible for making this determination. The second approach refers to the number of inmates a correctional institution can accommodate given the amount of staff, programs, and services available. The final benchmark is the number of convicts that the original planners, designers, or architects envisioned that the facility would be able to house (Schmalleger, 2006: 366; McKinnon, 2004: 656). In general "[r]ated capacity estimates usually yield the largest inmate capacities, while design capacity . . . typically shows the highest amount of overcrowding" (Schmalleger, 2006: 366).

What many analysts fail to consider is that the number of jails is decreasing. In their place, newer and bigger jails are being built to address overcrowding. However, capacity has not kept up with the actual numbers of inmates (Allen and Simonsen, 2001: 168). What these figures typically ignore is the total number of convicts per correctional facility. This can be represented by a simple fraction: number of institutions/cells. If, in the construction of big facilities, the number of cells decreases, then administrators have an overcrowding problem. If, on the other hand, the number of cells increases, then the situation is better for the prisoners and staff.

Overcrowding leads to many, if not most, of the other problems facing the correctional system including

1. hostility, anger, and violence by convicts toward other inmates and COs;

2. compromised security for both convicts and staff—in particular, it fuels gang activity (Hallinan, 2003: 98–100);

3. ability to follow through with classification plans;

4. rehabilitation taking a backseat to the demands of running a safe and secure institution;

5. strain on the infrastructure of the institution and services that are provided to inmates (Things break down more often because they are overused or abused by frustrated cons. Inmates typically take their aggression out on other inmates, correctional staff, the building, and on the equipment.); and

6. pressures to build more facilities (see Exhibit 10.1).

CAUSES

There are several interrelated reasons that have led to the problem of overcrowding. These include moratoriums on the death penalty, zero tolerance policing, the aging prison population, the closing of correctional facilities, demographic shifts, the increased costs of running jails and prisons, public and political apathy, and new sentencing laws.

Moratoriums on the Death Penalty

In some states (i.e., Alaska, District of Columbia, Hawaii, Iowa, Maine, Massachusetts, Michigan, Minnesota, North Dakota, Rhode Island, Vermont, West Virginia, and Wisconsin) and the federal system where they have put a moratorium on the death penalty, it has led to some slight increase in the prison population. Prisoners given the death penalty typically have to wait a little over seven years before their sentence is carried out. In the meantime, those sentenced to death and their lawyers usually appeal their sentence on a number of grounds. However, this number is marginal. Alternatively, in some states where there is a long wait on death row there is an overcrowding problem.

Zero Tolerance Policing

Likewise, the use of zero tolerance policing (where law enforcement officers are not allowed to use discretion) has been argued to increase the number of people behind bars. Much has been discussed about zero tolerance policing (e.g., Dennis, 1997). It is the notion that in some jurisdictions, parts of a city, or with some types of crime, police officers will stop, question, issue a citation, or a summons, or arrest an individual if they believe the individual has committed a crime. Zero tolerance policing is connected with the policing of hot spots, and identification of High Intensity Drug Trafficking Areas.

The Aging/Greying Prison Population

As previously reviewed, the population of prisoners 55 years and older is increasing. This is not simply because the elderly are committing more crime. The tendency of inmates to live longer means that more will be housed in correctional facilities. In some prison systems institutions have been specially created for the elderly. As people age, they typically need more health care and specialized facilities. The Federal Bureau of Prisons (FBOP) has two medical units for male inmates: one located in Fort Worth, TX, and another in Springfield, MO. Overall, the problem is more acute with states that have life without parole (Flynn, 1992).

The Closing of Correctional Facilities

Albeit a rare occurrence, states do periodically close jails and prisons. This type of action—often opposed by most COs and their unions—usually only takes place after serious attempts by the state to renovate one or more correctional facilities. This explains why so many jails and prisons built so long ago are still operating. Exceptions do occur. For example, in March 2007, the State of Maryland finally closed the House of Corrections located in Jessup. Over the past decade, the 128-year-old prison pejoratively referred to as *The Cut* had experienced several officer stabbings. The 800 inmates were dispersed to different facilities throughout the state.

Demographic Shifts

In general, the number of people convicted of committing crimes has increased over the past few decades. This is largely due to shifting birth rates, which started some 18–35 years ago. "This is seen as the population at risk, because crime is usually a young man's activity. That group is a direct result of the baby boom following World War II, which clogged the school systems of America in the 1950s and 1960s and has now affected yet another area—urban crime. That group is also the one with the highest unemployment rate, and in time of general underemployment, will continue to commit crime out of proportion to its size" (Allen and Simonsen: 243).

Increased Costs of Running a Facility

Over time, because of the professionalization of COs, union pressures, legal suits, and other factors, it has become more expensive to run a jail or prison. It requires enormous resources to efficiently and legally operate correctional institutions. Conterminously, governments are freezing the budgets of jails and prisons or are imposing budgetary cutbacks. Underfunding means that prisons must generate more money from other sources or do without. Correctional planners often assume that costs will be saved if prisoners and functions were consolidated in the same physical building. Additionally, through their use, however, facilities deteriorate, causing health and safety issues for convicts, COs, and correctional administrators alike. If conditions become too unsafe, because of the threat or reality of successful lawsuits or public outcry, inmates are transferred to other existing jails and prisons. Unless regular maintenance, upgrading, and planning are done, correctional institutions are disproportionately at the whims of each and every subsequent state director of corrections and state legislature.

Political and Public Apathy

Politicians, political candidates, and the general public have become apathetic about allocating more funds to corrections if it means improving prison conditions or rehabilitative programs. It's easier for convicts to remain "out of sight, out of mind." And no politician who appears to be soft on crime is likely to be reelected or reappointed. On the other hand, politicians are actively writing and passing laws to increase penalties for criminal behavior. However, they are rarely cognizant of (or unwilling to publicly admit) the unintended consequences of their activities; or they do not care what happens a decade later because they may not be in office. Likewise, as reviewed in Chapter 2, the public is generally poorly informed and plagued with all sorts of myths about both who is incarcerated and what goes on behind bars. Thus they remain apathetic (Ross, 2000c: Chapter 7).

Sentencing Laws and Practices

The growth in prison populations is attributable to a number of previously reviewed factors, including severe sentencing laws and practices and the fact that both the federal government and many states abolished parole, thus forcing inmates to stay longer in their correctional facilities. The *Sentencing Reform Act of 1984*, in particular, put an end to parole at the federal level, and reduced good time, mandatory minimums, and determinant sentencing. Similar initiatives were then implemented in several states. In addition to the aforementioned mandatory sentencing laws, Congress passed *Aimee's Law* in 1999. Named after Aimee Willard, a university student living in Philadelphia, who was raped and killed by a Nevada state parolee, this law holds states financially liable if they release an inmate and that person commits another felony in a different state. The "release states" are now obligated to pay any arrest, prosecution, and imprisonment costs incurred by another state, in addition to $100,000 to the victim's family. Thus states are now under the obligation to either successfully rehabilitate the individual or prevent them from release (www.usdoj.gov/ovw/laws/vawo2000/aimee.htm). All told, this prevents states from releasing more inmates.

EXHIBIT 10.1

Causes and effects of overcrowding

Causes	*Effects*
Demographic shifts	Increased wear and tear on prison facility
Underfunding	Security of facility compromised
Changes in sentencing	Violence
Closing correctional facilities	Rehabilitation curtailed
Increased costs	

SOLUTIONS

By far the most frequent solution proposed by state and federal correctional planners to the problem of crowding and overcrowding has been the construction of new correctional institutions, which cost millions of dollars each.

Understandably, estimates on the cost of new jail and prison construction vary. Some reports place the average cost to build one bed space for a prisoner at $54,000. This figure, however, does not include the amount of money the state or FBOP needs to finance the construction of the correctional facility, nor to feed, clothe, and "rehabilitate" inmates. The increase in the number of jails and prisons built has increasingly put many states into debt. "California, for example, between 1980 and 1990 spent more than $5 billion building new prisons. . . . Across the nation, prison construction has outpaced the construction of new schools. Moreover, while construction addresses overcrowding, it has no impact on reducing prison populations and may actually contribute to growing incarceration rates. . . . Critics argue that the construction strategy is based upon an 'If you build it, they will come' philosophy; that is; the more prisons that are built, the more inmates will be found to fill them" (McKinnon, 2004: 657).

Meanwhile, it appears as if there is always a budget crunch within state departments of corrections (DOCs). As a response, officials often cut overtime for officers, try to reduce benefits, and compromise officers' safety. Correctional facilities need to be more creative in developing methods of staffing the institutions, maintaining the institutions, and funding programs for inmates.

Nevertheless, how have local correctional systems dealt with the problem of overcrowding? The eight solutions most often used include

1. purchasing abandoned buildings (e.g., motels);
2. using manufactured housing units (e.g., trailers);
3. erecting tents;
4. using jail barges;
5. renting spaces from other jurisdictions;
6. placing prisoners under house arrest;
7. using electronic monitoring; and
8. double and triple bunking.

Sometimes it takes an innovative leader to deal with the problem of overcrowding. In the 1990s, shortly after the new jail was opened in Kings County in Seattle, WA, and it almost immediately became filled to capacity, the manager invited senior representatives from different local criminal justice agencies to meet once a month at a local restaurant to help him manage this problem. These informal and informational conversations led to a concerted effort amongst judges, police officials, and prosecutors to either lessen the number of people going to jails or hold the jail population constant (Coleman, 1998).

Other Ways to Get Out of Prison

Introduction

With the exception of escaping and/or death, there are three other basic legal ways individuals can get out of prison: commutation, amnesty, and pardon. All of these fall under the broad category of clemency. The final issue discussed is prison abolition.

Commutation

Commutation is when the executive (i.e., president, governor, or board of pardons) reduces the sentence of a person convicted of a crime. This practice can occur before the individual enters a correctional facility or during the time the person is incarcerated. Often the reduction is made "based on time already spent in jail and prison and results in almost immediate release of the petitioner" (Allen and Simonsen: 614). These kinds of executive actions are often controversial. In the spring of 2007, for instance, President George W. Bush commuted the prison sentence of Chief of Staff, for Vice President Dick Cheney, and White House insider I. Lewis (Scooter) Libby for obstruction of justice, perjury, and making false statements to federal investigators.

Pardon

In general, a pardon "nullifies an original sentence and can occur while an offender is incarcerated, or while on parole or probation. A pardon can also be issued after a full sentence has been completed, or even granted posthumously" (Thomas, 2005: 135). There are two basic types of pardons: full/absolute or conditional. The first "applies to both the punishment and guilt of the offender" and eliminates "the existence of guilt in the eyes of the law. It also removes his or her disabilities and restores civil rights. The conditional pardon generally falls short of remedies of full pardon, is an expression of guilt, and does not obliterate the conviction" (Allen and Simonsen: 700).

Pardons are also acts of the executive who have the power to grant these orders. At the federal level it is the president and at the state level it is the governor. In both cases they review cases after they have been vetted by a pardon board. In general, there are three reasons for pardons. "(1) to remember a miscarriage of justice, (2) to remove the stigma of a conviction, and (3) to mitigate a penalty. Although full pardons for miscarriages of justice are rare, . . . some individual who has been released from prison after it has been discovered that he or she was incarcerated by mistake" (Cole, 1994: 668–669).

Amnesty

Amnesty is a form of pardon typically "granted to a group or class of offenders." In the United States amnesty is frequently given after wars, "to soldiers who deserted or avoided service." This is done to curry favor with potential voters in upcoming elections (Allen and Simonsen: 614). For example, in 1979 under President Jimmy Carter, Vietnam veterans who had evaded the draft (*most of whom escaped to Canada*) were offered amnesty. Similarly in 1997, President Bill Clinton "gave amnesty to qualified Central American aliens residing in the United States" (Thomas, 2005: 135).

Prison Abolition

No sooner than the first prison was constructed, there were calls for its reform. One of the most radical positions has been the prison abolition movement that "want[s] to either eradicate whole elements of the current punishment system or bring an end to it entirely. They also advocate for a variety of alternatives" (Greene, 2005: 2). In the forefront of this movement are "activists, ex-prisoners, academics, religious actors, politicians, inmates and their families" (Greene, 2005: 2). The modern origins of prison abolition started during the 1960s in Scandinavia and soon spread to other western countries. In the United States, the prison abolition movement started in 1976 with the help of Quaker and prison minister Fay Honey Knopp, who started an organization called the Prison Research Education Project, that later authored a well-known book *Instead of Prisons: A Handbook for Abolitionists*. In 1981 the Canadian Quaker Committee for Jails and Justice started advocating prison abolition, and in 1983 the very first International Conference on Prison Abolition (ICOPA) was held in Toronto (Ross, 1983). Since then, the organization has changed respectively what both the C and the P in the name mean from Conference to Circle and from Prison to Penal.

NIMBY

Often, when it comes time to locate or build a jail or prison, correctional administrators and planners have difficulty finding an ideal spot. Local residents are not happy with the facility being built so close to where they work or live, or to where their children go to school. This phenomenon is usually referred to by its acronym NIMBY (i.e., Not In My Back Yard), which alludes to citizen's concerns about the negative effects, especially safety and/or the impact on their property values. Often, the neighborhoods in which correctional facilities are housed are the poorer ones. In 1998, in Washington, D.C., for example, the Corrections Corporation of America (CCA) had purchased 42 acres in the historically impoverished southwest part of the city, in order to build a much-needed prison for the District. In part because the corporation was criticized because of the way it had run its prison in Youngstown, OH, residents of Ward 8, arguably the most poverty stricken in District, where the parcel of land is located, were upset with the decision to build the facility there and mounted a spirited campaign against it being built (Thompson, 1998: B1, B9). Locations such as this one make sense for developers of jails and prisons. It is often a matter of economics. The land is cheaper there. Needless to say, CCA's plans for the jail were never approved by the D.C. government.

Then again, many economically depressed communities either lack a political voice to prevent the construction of a nearby jail or prison, or are all too happy to have correctional facilities be built in or relocate to their town, city, or region. For example, an archipelago including the city jail and state prison buildings with various security classifications has been established in an impoverished section of downtown Baltimore. Various businesses (e.g., store front bail bonds operations) have sprung up almost next door that are dependent on the existence of the correctional facilities. The nearby residents of this section of town are typically transient and thus rarely participate in the local politics.

On the other hand, some local or regional bodies will lobby their elected and appointed officials to attract a new jail or prison. This was true in Florence, CO, where during the early 1990s the residents bought land and donated it to the federal government for the purpose of building a Supermax prison. Similar situations exist. As portrayed in Michael Moore's *Roger and Me*, shot in Flint, MI, the residents lobbied the state government to have a new prison situated there to pick up the slack from a faltering economy largely caused by the closing of the local General Motors plant (1989). Similarly, in Weed, CA, "supporters of a proposal to build a prison in their town have held prison rallies and barbeques to raise money to hire a public relations expert to argue their case to state officials" (Welch, 1998: 110–111).

CONCLUSION

In many states that have determinant sentencing the DOCs engage in a process known as collective incapacitation. In this system almost all those charged with a criminal offense that involves jail or prison time complete their entire sentence behind bars. In systems where there is selective incapacitation, on the other hand, only those individuals that a judge determines will benefit from incarceration, or they believe is becoming a career criminal will be placed behind bars (Schmalleger, 2006: 367). Regardless, both these practices contribute to the increased number of people incarcerated.

Several factors are taken into consideration when a new jail or prison is built, including the conditions of existing institutions, the cost of maintaining the old ones, demographic shifts, cash flow, and other economic uncertainties. Although many people advocate rehabilitation programs like drug treatment, education, and vocational skills, it is difficult to realistically provide them if there is overcrowding (especially when it results in waiting lists for popular and needed programs).

Policies and practices in connection with life sentences should be reexamined (Liptak, 2005). It must be understood that for one reason or another, some people who are given a criminal sanction do change, while others no matter how long the sentence or severe the punishment is may never mend their ways. Notwithstanding, over the past two decades, our state and federal prison populations have grown at exponential rates. This makes it difficult to implement rehabilitative programs. It also makes the job of a CO and other correctional workers more dangerous. Parole boards and sentencing commissions must reexamine the purpose, intent, and effects of life sentences and governors should start reviewing cases for executive clemency. Overcrowding will be a dominant problem in the U.S. correctional system for the foreseeable future.

KEY TERMS

Aimee's Law   NIMBY (Not In My Back Yard)
capacity   operational capacity
clemency   pardon
collective incapacitation   rated capacity
design capacity   selective incapacitation
jail barge   zero tolerance policing

REVIEW QUESTIONS

PART 1: MULTIPLE-CHOICE QUESTIONS

1. Even if money is appropriated to correctional departments at the municipal, regional, state, and federal levels, what caveats are in order?

    a. that the money will be available in the appropriate denominations
    b. this money will be spent properly
    c. qualified persons can be hired throughout the ranks
    d. both b and c
    e. none of the above

2. What is Aimee's Law?

    a. a law protecting the rights of children
    b. a law regarding kidnapping
    c. a law that holds states liable if a prisoner is released and they commit a crime in another state
    d. all of the above
    e. none of the above

3. Which municipality purchased land and gave it to the federal government in order for the FBOP to build a Supermax prison?

    a. Baltimore, MD
    b. Florence, CO
    c. Colorado Springs, CO
    d. Marion, IL
    e. Washington, D.C.

4. Which federal legislation contributed in a large part to overcrowding in correctional facilities?

    a. *Sentencing Reform Act of 1984*
    b. *Sentencing Tribulation Act*
    c. Reinstitution of the death penalty
    d. Three strikes you're out
    e. none of the above

5. How can lifers who are no longer perceived to be threats to the community be released from prison?

   a. clemency
   b. pardon
   c. sentencing reform
   d. all of the above
   e. none of the above

PART 2: SHORT-ANSWER QUESTIONS

1. List five causes of overcrowding.

2. List four effects of overcrowding.

3. List five solutions that have been implemented to address overcrowding.

4. What does the acronym NIMBY stand for?

5. What is collective incapacitation?

6. What was the ruling in *Rhodes v. Chapman*?

PART 3: ESSAY QUESTIONS

1. Are correctional reformers wasting their time when they complain about overcrowding only to have the supreme court find legal justifications that seem to sanction this problem?

2. Some ideologues argue that understanding how overcrowding is determined is simply a case of smoke and mirrors. Do you agree with this statement? Your answer should demonstrate understanding how overcrowding is calculated.

3. What are three ways we can reduce overcrowding in prisons?

PART III

Problems for Correctional Officers and Administrators

Chapter 11

Hiring Standards, Requirements, Practices, and Training

INTRODUCTION

Working as a correctional officer (CO) is not easy. Several challenges are in store for a person choosing this profession. In order to better understand these difficulties, this chapter reviews the number of COs working in the United States, their basic demographic characteristics, their motivations for working in this field, the process of getting hired, educational requirements, age restrictions, the pay, and some of the problems with hiring. The latter part of the chapter examines the training that COs receive.

NUMBER OF CORRECTIONAL OFFICERS IN THE UNITED STATES

Over the past four decades, the number of COs hired by federal, state, and local correctional systems has increased but not at a level commensurate with the amount of people incarcerated. What does this mean? In short, correctional systems increasingly have to do more with less.

According to the U.S. Department of Labor, "[b]ailiffs, correctional officers, and jailers held about 484,000 jobs in 2004. About 3 of every 5 jobs were in State correctional institutions such as prisons, prison camps, and youth correctional facilities. About 16,000 jobs for correctional officers were in Federal correctional institutions, and about 15,000 jobs were in privately owned and managed prisons" (www.bls.gov/oco/ocos156.htm).

DEMOGRAPHICS

Although the number of male, female, and visible minorities COs vary from state to state, statistics on their representation is spotty. In 2001, it was reported that "[s]eventy-six percent were male, 65 percent were white, 23.8 percent were black, and 8.2 percent were Hispanic" (Champion, 2005: 525–526). One of the fastest growing segments is women and nonwhites.

A number of reasons can be attributed to the increased number of women and minorities in the field of corrections including the passage of the *Civil Rights Act of 1964*, which prohibited discrimination in hiring based on race and ethnicity; the 1972 amendment (Title VII) to this act, which made it illegal in hiring and firing processes to discriminate based on race, color, religion, sex, or national origin; and numerous civil suits by minorities and women, which have backed up this legislation. Clearly, women COs experience the job differently than men (Zupan, 1986; Belknap, 1995; Pogrebin and Poole, 1997; Lawrence and Mahan, 1998; Farkas, 1999). These issues concern discrimination, stress, and the way they relate both to male prisoners and to fellow COs.

GETTING HIRED

Most jails and prisons consider candidates who are U.S. citizens, between the ages of 18 and 21 years, who have completed high school or obtained its equivalent education (e.g., GED), have not had any felony convictions, and have two years' work experience (www.bls.gov/oco/ocos156.htm).

The Federal Bureau of Prisons (FBOP), in particular, want their recruits to have either an undergraduate degree or three years' experience in a field delivering "counseling, assistance, or supervision to individuals." They also must be in good health and meet the requirements of "physical fitness, eyesight, and hearing" (www.bls.gov/oco/ocos156.htm).

Typically, those wishing to work as a CO:

1. fill out an application with the relevant state or federal agency;

2. sit for a written test, a paper-and-pencil psychological examination (like a Minnesota Multiphasic Personality Inventory [MMPI] test or California Personality Inventory [CPI]), perform a physical test, and be subjected to a urine (i.e., drug) test;

3. submit to a criminal background investigation;

4. have a medical exam;

5. perform a physical ability/agility test;

6. have a face-to-face psychiatric test; and

7. have a personal interview (Freeman, 2000: Chapter 12).

This last step is often the most important, as seasoned human resource personnel suggest that the suitability of the candidates is best disentangled during the face-to-face interviews. Upon acceptance, officer recruits will undergo some sort of in-class training either at the institution where they will work or at a state training academy/facility.

AGE RESTRICTIONS: PROBLEMS AND SOLUTIONS

Most correctional systems require their candidates to be between the ages of 18 and 21. Many COs get into the field at a relatively early age. Some correctional professionals worry that younger recruits are more immature, and might be susceptible to being manipulated or corrupted by convicts under their watch. At least by 21 the person has matured more, graduated from high school, had a number of life experiences, and possibly experienced the challenges and rewards of marriage and parenting and/or frustrations of being unemployed, separated, or divorced.

EDUCATIONAL REQUIREMENTS: PROBLEMS AND SOLUTIONS

There is considerable variability with respect to the educational requirements that states have for hiring recruits. In 1997, "13 states (25.2 percent), less than a high school diploma was considered adequate" (Sechrest and Josi, 1999). In 22 (42 percent) states, a GED or high school diploma was considered adequate to qualify for CO employment. Only 16 states (31.4 percent) required a high school diploma or its equivalent for CO work. In 1997, 38 states indicated that their current correctional staffs had less than 30 units of college. The greatest emphasis on college education was among the Midwest prisons (Sechrest and Josi, 1999: 54).

Pursuing and obtaining a college diploma or university degree is usually thought to be more professional. Research is not clear just how much a diploma or degree helps criminal justice practitioners. However, having education beyond a high school diploma is seen by correctional administrators as a stepping stone to entering middle and senior management positions. At the very least it helps narrow down the pool of potential applicants (Champion: 489, 493).

Some correctional professionals argue that having a four-year degree means that officers will have a better understanding of the job. This presupposes that the courses that COs take are specifically geared to the profession, dealing for example with operating facilities, supervising different inmates, writing reports, public speaking, and working with diverse cultures. The classes offered to correctional workers should be evaluated on a continual basis in order to keep up with the constant changes in the field. There should also be some sort of review board that consists of Department of Public Safety representatives, COs, and administrators to decide what information is taught, how it should be delivered, and how students should be evaluated.

Many correctional professionals say that a two-year diploma from a community college is sufficient. But what if applicants' degrees are in supposedly unrelated fields like computer science? Should they be denied entrance as prospective candidates or will they be able to find a proper position with a department of corrections (DOC)? All of this is debatable as people from all kinds of subject fields become successful COs. Moreover, institutions of higher learning, and the courses they offer, are not all created equal; thus those that emphasize critical thinking skills would be preferable. Other difficulties arise due to the shifts that COs are expected to work. It does not make it easy for them to go to classes held at times they have to work or should be sleeping, particularly when a supervisor asks them to stay late and/or do a double (i.e., two shifts back to back). There also needs to be programs in place where DOCs and the FBOP give tuition remission to COs so they can pursue higher education.

Moreover, it is recognized that training geared specifically for COs is insufficient. Frequent complaints include that it is either too short or does not emphasize the right kinds of knowledge or skills and may be unrealistic. COs and administrators are well aware of recruits who after making it through the academy and after one day or week on the job quit. They argue that if the recruitment and training was more realistic about the field of corrections, then this problem would be mitigated. A final problem is that many people do not want to be COs because of the numerous myths and misconceptions people have heard about the field.

PAY: PROBLEMS AND SOLUTIONS

Pay of correctional workers varies considerably based on the type of institution an officer works at, their seniority, and whether the employee works for the federal, state, or municipal correctional services or for private companies like Wackenhut or Corrections Corporation of America (CCA). On the other hand, if, for example, officers are employed by a local jail in the Deep South, their hourly rate may very well be just a little higher than the minimum wage. If, however, the person works for the federal system, they may make an amount that is comparable to what someone may earn as a federal law enforcement officer (e.g., FBI and Department of Homeland Security).

Nevertheless, the most recent salary surveys available indicate that COs make anywhere between $19,000 and $40,000 a year, with an average salary of $27,000. They also typically cap out at an average maximum salary of $43,000 (Camp, Camp, and May, 2003; American Correctional Association, 2004). Moreover, "[t]he national average entry-level pay of about $21,000 is not bad when one considers that the current minimum qualifications for applicants is usually only a high school diploma or equivalent (GED) and no criminal record" (Allen and Simonsen: 12, 363). This does not include the money they can make working overtime.

Finally, "standard benefits included a retirement plan, annual and sick leave, insurance programs, and deferred compensation. Officers also received uniform allowances, longevity pay, tuition assistance, optional insurance packages, and other incentives. (Champion: 493)"

AVAILABILITY OF JOBS: PROBLEMS AND SOLUTIONS

Some correctional facilities have difficulty staffing positions. The supply and demand for COs varies from one DOC to another. In some places jobs go unfulfilled, with COs regularly being asked to work overtime. The need to fill CO spots is also dependent on a number of factors including, but not limited to, the health of the local economy and labor market, the proclivity for individuals to move in search of new employment (i.e., some people, particularly young adults with minimal family commitments, are more willing to take a job somewhere else), the attrition rates (i.e., turnover in personnel) in DOCs, the mobility of the population, the speed with which DOCs can adequately train new recruits, and changes in the prison population.

Meanwhile, correctional supervisors throughout the United States constantly ask COs to work additional shifts. Less an issue today, than it was a decade ago, concerns mandatory overtime. COs forced to work doubles get overtired, are subject to accidents, sloppy paperwork, and thus cannot do their job properly. Meanwhile, overtime eats into already stressed budgets.

Furthermore, legislators are reluctant to increase budgets for DOCs believing simultaneously that criminals deserve their just deserts, and the fear that any increase in correctional budgets will be used to improve "nonessential" prison conditions (which they are opposed to) and, with respect to COs, feel that their benefits are too much anyways (Allen and Simonsen: 363).

One of the more recent innovative ways to hire COs has been through federal and state job corps programs. According to the U.S. Department of Labor, job corps is a "no-cost education and vocational training program administered by the U.S. Department of Labor that helps young people ages 16 through 24 get a better job, make more money, and take control of their lives. At Job Corps, students enroll to learn a trade, earn a high school diploma or GED and get help finding a good job. When you join the program, you will be paid a monthly allowance; the longer you stay with the program, the more your allowance will be. Job Corps provides career counseling and transition support to its students for up to 12 months after they graduate from the program" (http://jobcorps.dol.gov/about.htm).

For the time being, this program, however, is limited to one particular geographic location. Operating since 2002, with its first class in 2003, the Gary Job Corps Training Academy Program (in San Marcos, TX) trains candidates to work in prisons operated by the Texas Department of Criminal Justice.[1] Alternatively, students are eligible to work in one of the many private prisons in the lone star state. Since its opening, the program has trained 95 students with 20–25 graduating each year.[2] These are similar to the police cadet programs that were started during the mid-1990s, which were introduced in the wake of the community policing movement (Nink et al., 2005).

According to the Bureau of Labor statistics, the federal agency that tracks employment-related data, "Employment of correctional officers is expected to grow *more slowly than average* for all occupations through 2014." They caution that the increasing "demand for correctional officers will stem from mandatory sentencing guidelines calling for longer sentences and reduced parole for inmates, and from expansion and new construction of correctional facilities. However, mandatory sentencing guidelines are being reconsidered in many states because of a combination of budgetary constraints, court decisions, and doubts about their effectiveness. Instead, there may be more emphasis on reducing sentences or putting offenders on probation or in rehabilitation programs in many states. As a result, the prison population, and employment of correctional officers, will probably grow at a slower rate than in the past. Some employment opportunities will also arise in the private sector, as public authorities contract with private companies to provide and staff corrections facilities" (www.bls.gov/oco/ocos156.htm).

TRAINING: PROBLEMS AND SOLUTIONS

Introduction

There are considerable differences with respect to how and where CO candidates get trained. At a minimum DOCs design their training based on "guidelines established by the American Correctional Association and the American Jails Association. Some States have regional training academies that are available to local agencies" (www.bls.gov/oco/ocos156.htm).

Initial training may occur at formal state-run academy and then the balance of knowledge, skills, and training is delivered at an actual correctional facility. At the academy and/or at the correctional facility at which they are assigned, CO candidates get instruction in self-defense, firearms, "institutional policies, legal regulations, and operations, as well as custody and security procedures" (www.bls.gov/oco/ocos156.htm).

While on the job, recruits will typically serve out a probationary period, and be subject to random drug testing. "Officer trainees typically receive several weeks or months of training in an actual job setting under the supervision of an experienced officer" (www.bls.gov/oco/ocos156.htm). In the BOP, recruits "must undergo 200 hours of formal training within the first year of employment. They also must complete 120 hours of specialized training at the U.S. Federal Bureau of Prisons residential training center at Glynco, GA, within 60 days of their appointment" (www.bls.gov/oco/ocos156.htm).

The entire process is typically expensive for the state and federal correctional systems. Thus, they try to weed out unsuitable candidates early on in the process to prevent the expenditure of additional costs of hiring (Conover, 2001). Unlike most police departments, some correctional agencies will have their new hires go directly to the job, and after a probationary period working on a tier or cellblock will then send them to the training academy. This is because many DOCs have been in the awkward position of putting people through the expense of the academy only to have the recruit quit after they discover the monotony and fear attendant on the job.

Most DOCs separate recruits into different groups, give them specialized training, and then move on to the next group of new hires. This approach relies on the understanding that the majority of the new employees will learn the bulk of their job through experience and not in a classroom setting. The administration hopes "that

> ### EXHIBIT 11.1
>
> ## Classics in Corrections
>
> ### *Newjack: Guarding Sing Sing*
>
> This book, published in 2001 by Ted Conover, a nationally known investigative reporter, tells the story of the process he went through in order to become a CO. It takes us from the academy where he was tear-gassed to working in different sections of Sing Sing, the infamous New York State maximum-security prison, including rotations in solitary confinement, the gym, and the psych ward. Conover wrote about some of the deviant folks in the system, both other COs and inmates. He also told of how his family and he were affected by his job; in particular he was disproportionately short-tempered around them. Conover was basically thrown into the experience and had to rely on his own instincts to do the job. Conover, and his fellow officers, appeared to be totally unprepared for their new work experience. He discovered that every correctional professional in Sing Sing worked in a different manner; there was little uniformity among the people enforcing the rules in the facility. This caused Conover and his colleagues a lot of frustration.

recruits will learn general job responsibilities, procedures for carrying out these responsibilities, practical skills for task performance, and something about the expectations of supervisors. But many recruits" feel that these training sessions did not properly prepare them for their jobs (Champion: 488). At the very least, there are basically two types of training for recruits: preservice and in-service.

Preservice

Based on the 1995 ACA *Vital Statistics*, COs at "more than half of the agencies surveyed had to complete at least five weeks of pre-service training before they could begin working as officers. In many systems the combined length of time spent in basic and on the job training exceeded 25 weeks."

Preservice training "consists of both classroom instruction and on-the-job experiences. Probationary periods for correctional staff averaged 9.5 months, with a low of 3.8 months in Wisconsin to a high of 18 months in Utah. Most programs had 12 month training programs. In 1988, the training hours for most new correctional officers averaged 232 with 42 in-service hours. Vermont had the lowest number of required training hours with 40; Michigan required 640 training hours. . . . During the 1990s, the average probationary periods for state and federal correctional officers increased from 8 months to 9.5 months" (Champion: 493). A lot of this depends on supply and demand conditions.

What these figures neglect is the content of the courses, including the subjects covered, the method of instruction, exercises the recruits are trained in or educated in, and the instructors' qualifications and abilities. Subjects include first aid, the law, policies and procedures, and conducting proper searches.

There is no empirical evidence which suggests that more education makes better COs (Burke, Rizzo, and O'Rear, 1992: 174). "Generally, more education for officers is instrumental in gaining them managerial positions. Thus, those officers who aspire to middle-level or upper-level management in prison settings would probably benefit from acquiring an advanced degree. Some officers have reported that having a higher level of education enables them to understand inmate culture better and to resolve inmate-officer conflicts more effectively" (Burke, Rizzo, and O'Rear, 1992). When top-level prison managers seek additional educational training, it underscores the importance of training as well as improves the image of COs in their respective institutions.

Part of the need for training correctional personnel has been taken up by colleges and universities (Stinchcomb, 2000). An increasing number of brick-and-mortar institutions of higher learning and online educational institutions are offering two-year associate degrees in corrections. Some of these require internships or practicums working in actual or simulated jail or prison facilities.

In-Service

In addition to the formal training that recruits may receive in advance of their job, when they are actually working as COs, they may get some sort of in-service training, the frequency of which can vary from correctional institution to institution, and from state to state. This also includes periodic instruction in new rules and regulations. Many skills need to be periodically updated like cardiopulmonary resuscitation, first aid techniques, and cell search procedures. And when new developments occur, like the threat of HIV/AIDS, new methods are implemented in the care and treatment of inmates suffering from these ailments (Freeman, 2000: 316–320).

Extracurricular Education

Many COs attend community colleges and universities in pursuit of a diploma or a degree. They typically enroll in programs in criminology or criminal justice, and may take classes in psychology and sociology, or even a foreign language. As in the case of convicts, it is not necessary to attend a formal class somewhere. Because of their flexibility, there are several correspondence and/or online courses offered by universities and associations like the ACA that are available to COs. Another strategy is what is called "cross-training—temporally working in correctional fields that are not your own" (ACA: 63). Alternatively an officer may be seconded to another correctional institution where they will pick up additional job-related skills and experience that they can utilize when they return to their original facility. Employees can find out about these through their work network or through organizations such as the American Correctional Association (ACA), American Jails Association (AJA), and American Probation and Parole Association (APPA).

Regardless, like many fields, much of learning to be a CO is done on the job, by observing more senior officers and modeling their behavior after them.

PROFESSIONALISM

Closely connected to the issue of training is that of professionalism. Over the past 80 years, corrections much like the fields of law and medicine have adopted rigorous standards for training and certification of workers. This change is largely a reflection of the recognition that in order for COs to do their job properly they need specialized knowledge, skills, and training. These aspects generally include conducting searches, controlling and restraining convicts, writing and speaking effectively, providing proper medical and emergency care, transporting prisoners, self-defense, and using a variety of weapons (e.g., firearms and chemical weapons). Many of these policies and practices are contained in standards, which are specified by state DOCs, and national accrediting bodies like the ACA.

CERTIFICATION

As mentioned earlier, a handful of membership organizations (e.g., ACA) have started to certify COs and DOCs. "A fundamental concomitant of accreditation is certification, which involves a review and evaluation of an individual's credentials and capabilities as they relate to his or her current correctional functions" (Champion, 2004: 529). This means that the members will have to know a specific body of knowledge, adhere to certain moral and ethical standards, and be tested on a periodic basis to maintain their certification. Other options are for individual states to develop a certification process and have COs be licensed by these entities.

CONCLUSION

Entry requirements to the field of corrections are similar to those found in other types of criminal justice and law enforcement jobs. The demand for qualified correctional personnel is high, but the competition is not as stiff as that found in other law enforcement positions. In general, working in a correctional facility is less desirable than parole or probation, municipal police, or state patrol. For the amount of education required, however, the pay is respectable.

Other issues need to be taken into consideration. These include the current and future needs amongst COs. Given changes in demographics in the United States, there is a strong need for bilingual officers, particularly those who can speak Spanish. Criminals who come to prison these days are also probably better educated or knowledgeable in the ways of the institution. Some of these people can be quite dangerous. For example, if a convict has a trade (e.g., electricity and plumbing), knows a lot about this aspect of institutional structure, and gets a job in the facility, they could wreak havoc with the day-to-day operations of the institution.

It is difficult to make the job of a CO more attractive. Certainly, paying candidates more money would be a step in the right direction. Treating COs better, properly training recruits and those who are on the job, and educating the public might minimize turnover and attract suitable candidates to the profession. Additionally, trying to better educate the public (as alluded to in Chapter 2) about the realities of corrections would minimize the myths and might prevent individuals from quitting shortly after being hired.

There is considerable variability with respect to the educational and work history background required for suitable recruits. Each state and the federal system have their own requirements for COs. Some mandate a high school education. Others require that applicants not have a criminal record, including misdemeanor convictions. Some DOCs are more lax and are willing to accept recruits who have been convicted of some misdemeanors.

Many people enter the field of corrections with only a GED, while others come in with a community college diploma. Still some recruits possess a university degree. Although initially resistant to recruits who have advanced education, as more members among their ranks have bachelors and higher degrees, correctional administrators are now requiring this kind of advanced education at least for middle management positions.

Finally, jail and prison personnel receive training through a wide spectrum of programs. These include courses offered by a centralized state correctional facility, on-the-job classes, and in-service courses. Multiple opportunities exist for entrance into the profession and new methods for training recruits are experimented with on a regular basis.

KEY TERMS

certification   preservice training
cross-training demographics   professionalism
extracurricular education   secondment
in-service training   turnover
job corps

REVIEW QUESTIONS

PART 1: MULTIPLE-CHOICE QUESTIONS

1. Why is it difficult to recruit suitable personnel as correctional officers?
   a. public has a less than favorable attitude to corrections
   b. too many people in the general public have criminal records
   c. all prisons are located in rural areas
   d. all of the above
   e. none of the above

2. What is/are the fastest growing segment/s of uniformed correctional officers in the United States?
   a. females
   b. males

    c. nonwhites

    d. some of the above

    e. none of the above

3. Amongst the following options, why is working as a correctional officer most attractive to prospective candidates?

    a. excitement

    b. chance to improve one's verbal skills

    c. for the amount of education the person has, the pay is reasonable

    d. chance to interact with real-life criminals who are mentioned in the daily paper

    e. none of the above

4. In the hiring process, state and federal correctional systems try to

    a. place their decisions disproportionately on face-to-face interviews

    b. weed out candidates early in the selection process

    c. fire recruits after a probationary period

    d. turn back most candidates as unsuitable

    e. all of the above

5. What is one of the special problems regarding new correctional officers?

    a. immature applicants and insufficient training

    b. educational requirements are too strict for the position

    c. too many applicants for number of positions open

    d. training is too long

    e. none of the above

6. Which of the following is one of the organizational role conflicts faced by correctional officers?

    a. supervising violent inmates

    b. inability to organize a union for like-minded individuals

    c. being both a supervisor and a worker

    d. the quality of life in prisons

    e. all of the above

7. If you were a correctional officer and you wanted to join a professional association, which one is the most appropriate?

    a. Academy of Criminal Justice Sciences

    b. American Correctional Association

    c. American Society of Criminology

    d. American Probation and Parole Association

    e. American Prison Guard Association

8. What is the term applied when a person temporarily works in a correctional position that is NOT their own?

    a. preservice training

    b. in-service training

    c. cross-training

    d. diversity training

    e. none of the above

9. What typically follows most preservice training of correctional officers?

    a. they quit

    b. they work in a maximum-security prison

    c. they work in solitary confinement

    d. probationary period

    e. graduate is offered a long-term contract

10. What is the term used for "specialized knowledge and training?"

    a. accreditation

    b. education

    c. professionalization

    d. standardization

    e. unionization

11. In most state DOCs and the FBOP, how valuable is a university education for correctional officers?

    a. necessary

    b. advised

    c. not necessary

    d. an entry-level requirement

    e. only in special subjects

12. Which of the following is NOT a skill that correctional officers learn during training/ probationary period?

    a. conducting searches of the yard

    b. surveillance

    c. transporting inmates

    d. using weapons

    e. conducting cell searches

PART 2: SHORT-ANSWER QUESTIONS

1. What are two types of training for recruits?

2. List five things correctional officers find problematic about their jobs.

3. What are six steps to getting a job as a correctional officer?

4. What are three skills that are improved by correctional officers taking classes?

5. List three ways that training of correctional officers can be improved.

6. What factors do you suspect stand in the way of improving training for correctional officers?

7. What is the typical educational requirement for a correctional officer?

PART 3: ESSAY QUESTIONS

1. Why is it difficult to recruit people to corrections? How can these problems be overcome?

2. Is it easier or more difficult to be hired as a police officer or a correctional officer?

3. Some argue that the profession of a correctional officer is an overstatement. Do you agree with this or disagree? Provide examples for your position.

4. Some analysts suggest that requiring correctional officers to earn bachelors degrees would only make them bored and thus ill-suited to the job. Do you agree or disagree with this statement and why?

NOTES

1. Texas has approximately 125 prisons units.
2. Personal conversation with Cheeseman, Gary Training Center, San Marcos, TX, June 23, 2006.

Chapter 12

Working Conditions

INTRODUCTION

Many correctional officers (COs) are unhappy with their jobs. This is largely because of perceived and actual poor working conditions and the low status accorded to their profession by the wider public. Most people do not plan to have a career in corrections (Commission on Safety and Abuse, 2006: 65–75). They start working in jails and prisons through a various channels including having long bouts of unemployment, having poorly paid service jobs, or their unions going on strike with no hope in the immediate future that matters will be resolved in a expeditious manner (Lombardo, 1989).

Many officers also feel that they cannot leave to find better paying jobs—a situation often referred to as *golden handcuffs*. Although a correctional worker may dislike their current job, the relative pay (compared to other occupations the individual is qualified for) is typically good enough to rule out the option of quitting. Meanwhile, other semiattractive jobs do not offer competitive pay, seniority, or similar working conditions, and so the officer stays put. These working conditions can lead to stress, cynicism, burnout, and CO deviance. The following chapter is a review of these problems and some suggested solutions.

THE PROBLEMS

Correctional workers cite numerous issues about their working conditions that cause them difficulties (National Commission on Safety and Abuse in Prison, 2006: Chapter 4). These problems include boredom, shift work, understaffing, dealing with prisoners' bad attitudes, catching a disease, and violence.

Boredom

One of the chief complaints COs cite is boredom. This is one of the reasons why many do not like to talk about their work with their family or friends. Some suggest that the unchanging routine of their jobs (e.g., standing around, observing inmates, filling out forms, doing count at specified times) makes COs lazy. Some observers have even argued that a considerable amount of the abuse that took place against Iraqis detained at Iraq's Abu Ghraib prison (2004) can be attributed to the officers' boredom. On the other hand, working as a correctional professional does offer more variety than, say, working on an assembly line.

Rotating Shift Work

Corrections, like many other criminal justice careers or first responder jobs (such as firefighters and emergency medical technicians), usually involves rotating shift work. This kind of schedule can take its toll on a person's physical and mental health. Individuals nearly always feel deprived of sleep, which often leads to irritability, poor eating habits, weight gain, and stomach ulcers. Scheduling quality time with a spouse or significant other and children is difficult, as is making time for a routine visit with the doctor or dentist. It also means that, for some people, regular exercise is not easily manageable, as most gyms are not open 24–7. This complaint is by no means universal as some COs actually look forward to the fact that every few weeks they will be rotating the time that they work. It also breaks up the monotony or boredom incumbent in the job, and this may psychologically help correctional workers get through the week.

Understaffing

Due to a lack of funding and/or budget deficits, many correctional facilities are forced to operate with a less-than-ideal number of officers. Some individuals work more than one post doing two different tasks. Although this can break up the monotony, it can equally result in inefficiency and a tendency to take shortcuts to get the job done. Sure, many officers are able to work doubles and earn time-and-a-half pay, thereby paying off the loans for their house or car earlier—but this comes at a price. Officers who push themselves in this way frequently suffer psychological and physical consequences and are often tired and irritable. Another aspect is compromised safety when inmates become unruly and a limited number of officers need to respond. Officers need to be mentally alert to the changing dynamics of the institution and be able to make split-second decisions, all of which is hampered if the officer is overtired.

Inmates' Bad Attitudes

Although inmates may not threaten or use violence against correctional workers, many, regardless of the consequences, frequently harass, insult (using condescending language or gestures), and verbally abuse COs. Moreover, correctional workers are always under the watchful eye of the inmates, and every mistake is pointed out to them. This is especially true during count, the practice which ensures that the correctional facility has the requisite number of inmates it was assigned. If an officer or group of officers miscounts the number of prisoners, they are likely to be berated by the inmates. Sometimes as an ultimate act of disrespect convicts will toss urine and feces at COs. At any given time, the number of inmates for which a CO is responsible can be overwhelming. Such treatment and working conditions frustrate most conscientious workers and contribute to high levels of stress, fatigue, and burnout.

Life-Threatening Illnesses

Jails and prisons are notoriously unhealthy places in which both prisoners and COs have been known to develop serious medical illnesses. Those who spend time in a correctional institution, whether as inmates, as COs, or as administrative personnel, must be concerned about the reality of contracting a serious—and possibly fatal—disease or illness (e.g., TB, AIDS, and hepatitis). Not only is this because correctional workers may unnecessarily come into contact with inmates' blood, saliva, or other bodily secretions, but there is also the potential of contracting lung cancer from secondhand smoke and hearing loss for the constant racket, which takes place on the cellblocks and tiers. It is not simply correctional officers and administrators who are in danger of catching a disease themselves, but also they risk spreading it among family members and other loved ones. Prisoners' medical records are confidential, and the prison's medical staff may not take the time to do the appropriate tests to isolate the problem and implement a medical plan. A significant problem with many contagious diseases, however, is that a cure depends on early detection—which becomes more difficult in a correctional setting, where medical services are usually rationed out (Murphy, 2003).

If, in fact, a convict tests positive for serious illnesses, their condition is likely to be kept a secret because the prison authorities do not want convict to be attacked by fearful prisoners or improperly handled by COs. Also, unless the convict is in the infirmary or hospital under treatment, the prison administrators do not want COs to treat them any differently. In most facilities, individuals suffering from highly contagious diseases are terminally ill and placed in segregation.

The Threat of Violence

The threat of physical violence from inmates is always present. Not only does this occur on a daily basis, but the possibility of being assaulted or killed is heightened in the context of strikes, riots, and disturbances. There are many opportunities for aggression to occur, and inmates can be quite creative with respect to the places and things they can use as weapons. Riots, strikes, and disturbances can and may break out at any time, and the atmosphere is continuously unsafe (e.g., Hallinan, 2003: 105–113) (see Exhibit 12.1).

EXHIBIT 12.1

Classics in Corrections

Lombardo's *Guards Imprisoned*

During the 1970s, Lucien Lombardo, a former prison teacher at New York State's Auburn Correctional Facility and now a professor at Old Dominion University, had his book *Guards Imprisoned* published. The study is the product of a series of interviews Lombardo conducted with COs at the Auburn prison. While dated, the book outlines the numerous roles that correctional officers take on in managing and running a typical prison. He explains, in limited detail, some of the problems that each type of officer encounters in their ability to do the job.

Lombardo concluded that "[p]eople become correctional officers because they want stable jobs with steady pay and good benefits. Indeed, 60 percent of the officers interviewed reported that the pay and job security are the 'best' things about the job 'for the work we do' or 'for the education [level] we have attained' " (pp. 177–178). It wasn't the nature of the work that attracted them; it was avoiding less attractive work, or they took the job when the place where they were working at went on strike.

Lombardo's interviews found that most officers were dissatisfied with their jobs. Approximately 25 percent said that there was absolutely nothing satisfying about their jobs. Many even compared their jobs to prison sentences.

SOLUTIONS

Numerous solutions can be implemented to improve COs' working conditions including overcoming boredom, battling the negative effects of shift work, overcoming understaffing, dealing with inmates' bad attitudes, precautions against diseases, and avoiding becoming a victim of violence. The forming of correctional unions, an additional solution, will be discussed in Chapter 13.

Overcoming Boredom

Correctional workers who can "think outside of the box" often look for more exciting positions within the institution or create additional tasks for themselves in an effort to make their days go by more quickly and/or strengthening their resume for the possibility of job promotion. Volunteering for special assignments is also another option. Some COs try to work as many night shifts as possible in order to avoid the boredom of the days, sneak in time to do schoolwork, and, when they have to work the day shift, they will volunteer for escort details (i.e., transporting prisoners around or out of the institution) in order to get out of the facility as much as possible.

Battling the Negative Effects of Shift Work

For those who are married, cohabitating, have children and/or others they must care for (e.g., elderly or sick relatives) it always helps to have a spouse or significant other who has the same routine. This is why sometimes COs are married to partners who work shift work (e.g., nurses). Nevertheless, over time, because of seniority, it is easier for correctional workers to get the shifts that work best for them. Certainly, good communication with one's spouse (or significant other) will minimize the constant stress that always crops up.

Overcoming Understaffing

Not having enough officers to work a tier or cellblock can be most properly addressed by the correctional union. It is in the best interests of the union to have as many workers as possible. That way more dues are collected from each and every worker. If a grievance is filed in connection with understaffing, and no remediation is in store, the situation may lead to possible lawsuits and a court battle between the department of corrections (DOC) and the union.

Dealing with Inmates' Bad Attitudes

Although COs have the power to write up inmates who violate institutional rules, seasoned correctional professionals learn to ignore or not take seriously convicts' provocative communications and behavior. Alternatively, they have developed strategies to deflect threats or challenges through a combination of tough talk and humor.

Precautions Against Diseases

Prison staff take a number of precautions to minimize their exposure to contagious diseases. Many COs spend a lot of time worrying about and doing things to prevent themselves from being infected. The prison staff has better access to information, memos/directives, procedures, training, and protective equipment than convicts. Most correctional personnel avoid coming into contact with blood and bodily fluids at all costs, as it could carry any number of infectious organisms. Typically, they just tell an inmate to clean up the mess if they discover it. Otherwise, most COs now wear plastic gloves when handling inmates and surgical masks while cleaning up blood or physically handling prisoners. A common precaution is also to practice good personal hygiene by frequently washing hands with antibacterial soap.

In this environment, it is especially necessary to take the appropriate amount of time to properly screen inmates during classification or intake. Some experts have argued that COs should be made aware of the health status of all inmates they supervise, rather than having a blanket or universal caution against all prisoners. Advocates of this position suggest the officers' lives could be in jeopardy at any time, or that it could affect their health and safety. Moreover, infected officers might unknowingly spread the disease among their family members and loved ones. It is also understood that, once sentenced to prison, arrestees lose a considerable measure of their privacy and that these critical health issues should be made public—at least to the COs and administrators. Administrators, on the other hand, might argue that once COs know this kind of information, they may consciously or unconsciously refuse to assist infected inmates or give preferential treatment to noninfected convicts. It may also serve to stigmatize the infected convicts among the other inmates. The debate about revealing the health status of prisoners and who specifically should know is not easily resolved; no matter which side prevails, few people will be happy.

In a more general sense, departments of corrections should, to the extent possible, abolish the contracting out of medical facilities. Approximately 18 states use private Health Maintenance Organizations (HMOs) that are relatively unaccountable to the public. If these were eliminated, then it might go a long way in improving the health not only of inmates but of correctional officers too (National Commission on Safety and Abuse in Prison, 2006).

Avoiding Becoming a Victim of Violence

In terms of violence, COs take many precautions. Most become constantly aware, even hypervigilant, of their surroundings in their workplace. They learn to be on guard for any swift atmosphere changes on the tiers, which often signals that something serious is about to occur. The most common precaution used by COs to maintain or even improve their health, work off stress, and lose weight is regular exercise: walking, jogging, weightlifting, or playing sports like basketball, handball, or softball. Not only will exercise, plenty of sleep, and a proper diet help keep a correctional worker alert and deal better with potential attacks, it may also help minimize stress.

Increasingly, state DOCs are requiring or enabling (financially) officers to purchase stab-resistant vests. This kind of protective gear minimizes the damage of an attack via a knife or sharp object to the body of the CO. The vests do not, however, protect the officer's face, neck, or legs.

Correctional officers also need to avoid defining their lives singularly by their role at the workplace. Regular doctor visits are a must to keep their health in check and to make sure that their panels of immunizations are up-to-date.

BURNOUT

Introduction

Most helping professions (e.g., social workers and educators) and those involving shift work lead to some sort of burnout. Burnout includes most of the following attributes:

> emotional exhaustion, depersonalization, and reduced personal accomplishment that can occur among individuals who do "people work" of some kind;
>
> a progressive loss of idealism, energy, and purpose experienced by people in the helping professions as a result of the conditions of their work;

a state of physical, emotional, and mental exhaustion marked by physical depletion and chronic fatigue, feelings of helplessness and hopelessness, and the development of a negative self-concept and negative attitudes toward work, life, and other people (Champion, quoting Maslach, 1982).

Burnout "signifies a reduction in the quality or effectiveness of an officer's job performance. . . . Debilitating reductions in effectiveness are often accompanied by higher recidivism rates among probationers and parolees, more legal problems and case filings from officer/inmate interactions, and greater labor turnover among correctional officers" (Champion: 498).

Some of the factors that contribute to or mediate burnout are age, sex, years on the job, "self-esteem, marital status, and degree of autonomy and job satisfaction function. . . . The social support system is made up of others who perform similar tasks and the frequency of contact with these people for the purpose of sharing the frustrations of work. These factors form a mosaic from which stress stems. Stress is manifested by physiological, psychological, and/or emotional indicators. Burnout may result; one important consequence of burnout may be labor turnover" (Champion: 498).

It should be understood that although most criminal justice practitioners encounter stress and possible burnout, the amount varies based not only on the individual, but also on the situation. Probation and parole officers experience stress differently. "In contrast to probation-parole offices, state prisons are more austere, controlled, and stress-provoking environments" (Carlson, Anson, and Thomas, 2003: 279).

Stress

Stress "is a physical and mental reaction to a demanding situation or event. It is tension or excitement created by a particular situation. Stress can be either negative or positive. . . . Although positive stress is often called 'excitement' and negative tension is called 'stress' they are the same thing—the body's reaction is the same in either situation" (ACA: 78).

> Stress causes changes in a person's body, triggering what is often called a "flight or fight" reaction. The body readies itself to do whatever is necessary for survival (either fight or run away) by: increasing the heart rate, tensing muscles, dilating the pupils, making breathing faster and deeper, raising blood pressure. (ACA: 79)

For some people, the stresses of modern life are often insurmountable. Many households cannot get by financially without both husbands and wives working. This also means that some people find it difficult to balance the competing demands made upon their time and paycheck. Like in most helping professions, COs can work long hours, shifts, and be subjected to a considerable amount of stress.

Over time, stress takes its toll on their physical and mental health. If not addressed, it typically leads to serious medical problems like heart disease, high blood pressure, strokes, circulatory problems, stomach ulcers, urinary problems, and loss of interest in sexual activity. It can also lead to burnout, "loss of care and concern about one's profession that resulted from continued and unresolved stress" (ACA: 81). Moreover, "[s]uppressed anger or burnout may be expressed through: irritability, hopelessness, emotional over-reactions, intensely negative attitudes toward people, rigidity or 'going by the book' " (ACA: 81).

Sources of Stress

The sources of stress for COs are found in many shift work jobs including those that require workers to "rotate among various posts and duty hours, . . . come in early or stay late, drop what convict are doing to help out another officer, . . . called in on a day you weren't scheduled to work. These disrupt your sleep patterns and family life, often creating more tension" (ACA: 82).

> Doctors say that it is not the amount of stress that causes health problems; [i]t is the way a person deals with stress that really matters. Therefore, what COs need to learn to do is manage the stress they have in their lives. They need to find productive, socially acceptable ways of releasing it so that it doesn't harm them. (ACA: 82)

The subject matter of stress amongst COs has frequently been researched. The findings are complicated and somewhat contradictory (Brodsky, 1982; Honnold and Stinchcomb, 1985; Lasky and Strebalus, 1986; Lindquist and Whitehead, 1986; Cheek and Miller, 1993). One way that researchers have examined stress is through life expectancy and other quality-of-life measures. Cheek (1984), for example, said that COs have a life span of 59 years (whereas the national average is 75). They also have a divorce rate that is twice the national average and have higher rates of suicide, alcoholism, heart attacks, ulcers, and high blood pressure. These figures are now outdated and do not take into consideration the kinds of people who become COs. In other words, is it the working conditions or the individuals who want to work in the field that presents a selection bias? No one knows for sure.

It is also important to understand that the sources of stress differ between managers and workers (Weinberg et al., 1985). In sum, stress can manifest itself in constantly being late for work or meetings, calling in sick, absenteeism, prisoner abuse, irritability, and feelings of hopelessness. If stress is not minimized, not only does it have an effect on the individual employee, but it can affect the ability of the institution to operate effectively and efficiently.

The Federal Government Takes an Interest

Under Title XXI of the *Crime Act*, Congress established a Law Enforcement Family Support program. The funding of solicitations for research was handed over to the National Institute of Justice (NIJ). There were three objectives to this program.

> To develop, demonstrate, and test innovative stress prevention or treatment programs for State or local law enforcement and/or correctional personnel and their families.

To conduct research on the nature, extent, causes, and consequences of stress experienced by correctional officers and their families, or to evaluate the effectiveness of law enforcement and/or correctional officer prevention or treatment programs.

To develop, demonstrate, and test effective ways to change law enforcement or correctional agency policies practices, and organizational culture to ameliorate stress experienced by law enforcement and correctional officers and their families.

Although the majority of the research it inspired was directed toward police officers (e.g., Finn and Esselman Tomz, 1996), many of the findings were applicable to correctional workers too. Utilizing interviews with close to "100 people, including mental health practitioners, law enforcement administrators, union and association officials, and almost 50 line officers and family members from both large and small agencies," the report provides detailed information on initiatives including planning, structuring programs, staffing options, dealing with confidentiality, and a variety of different services to minimize stress.

Turnover

"Burnout and stress occur among correctional officers, especially during the first year of their duties." During this time "[t]urnover rates are as high as 38 percent in some juris-dictions, such as Arkansas." "Between 1990 and 1998, turnover among correctional officers ranged from a low of 9.6 percent in 1991 to a high of 14.9 percent in 1998 . . . 20 percent of all entry-level correctional officers left before completing their probationary period" (Champion: 498). In order to minimize job turnover, a number of suggestions have been advanced. One of them that apparently does not get used enough is using more senior officers as mentors. DOCs also need to hire the individuals who have the appropriate educational background and personality for the job. This is not an easy task.

SOLUTIONS TO BURNOUT AND STRESS

Correctional administrators must be vigilant about the sources of stress, how they are caused, and try to implement procedures to minimize the unsettling effects of stress (Champion: 499). One way to reduce stress is to allow correctional workers to contribute to the decision making of their unit through some kind of participatory management. COs "often say that their supervisors focus only on the negative aspects of work performed. When supervisors provide only criticisms of work improperly done and leave unrewarded work of good quality, the morale of personnel suffers greatly" (Champion: 499).

In sum, maintaining physical health through regular exercise, ample recreation, eating a healthy diet, sufficient rest, not smoking, restricting alcohol use, engaging in deep relaxation (e.g., yoga, transcendental meditation, tai chi, etc.), and taking vaca-tions on a regular basis can help alleviate burnout and stress. Some of these solutions would be aided if the correctional institution provided a well-equipped gym or discounts at a respectable nearby gym or health club.

CONCLUSION

Working conditions for COs are almost similar to living conditions for prisoners. Understanding how they operate and think in this unique environment may help them minimize stress, burnout, and turnover. COs must remain aware and vigilant to take responsibility for their own safety and health and not rely on the DOC to do it for them.

A number of practical solutions for minimizing burnout found in other law enforcement and helping professions can be applied to the field of corrections. If properly utilized by both corrections officers and administration, it can minimize health concerns, encourage better on the job performance of personnel, and reduce turnover.

KEY TERMS

burnout
escorts
golden handcuffs
helping profession
National Institute of Justice (NIJ)

rotating shift work
stab-resistant vest
stress
turnover

REVIEW QUESTIONS

PART 1: MULTIPLE-CHOICE QUESTIONS

1. Which of the following is not a good way for COs to deal with boredom on the job?
   a. create additional tasks for themselves
   b. more exciting positions within the institution
   c. volunteer for special assignments
   d. volunteer for escort details
   e. play board games with fellow COs

2. What percent of correctional officers are dissatisfied with their jobs?
   a. 10
   b. 15
   c. 20
   d. 25
   e. 30

3. What is the term that describes the situation of correctional officers who feel that they are stuck in their position based on their relative education and the steady pay they receive?

    a. posttraumatic stress disorder
    b. insane workplace syndrome
    c. golden handcuffs
    d. toxic workplace disorder
    e. none of the above

4. What precautions will not help correctional officers avoid becoming a victim of violence by inmates?

    a. buying a gun
    b. rest
    c. daily exercise
    d. being hypervigilant
    e. all of the above

5. Which of the following factors affect burnout?

    a. age
    b. sex
    c. years on the job
    d. marital status
    e. all of the above

6. In what year did the Department of Justice take an interest in stress amongst correctional officers?

    a. 1980
    b. 1994
    c. 2004
    d. 2005
    e. none of the above

7. Which of the following have been recommended to reduce correctional worker stress?

    a. allow probation and parole workers to contribute to the decision making of their unit
    b. maintaining physical health
    c. engaging in deep relaxation
    d. all of the above
    e. none of the above

8. Who wrote the book *Guards Imprisoned*?

    a. Cohen
    b. Lombardo
    c. Patterson
    d. Turner
    e. none of the above

PART 2: SHORT-ANSWER QUESTIONS

1. What are four things that correctional officers can do to prevent themselves from contracting a disease at the workplace?

2. In what ways are working conditions for correctional officers dissimilar to living conditions for prisoners?

3. List four factors that mediate correctional officer burnout.

4. What are four ways suppressed anger or burnout may be expressed?

5. What is meant by the term *organizational culture* in the context of corrections?

6. List four causes of correctional officer stress.

7. How can a correctional officer overcome the golden handcuffs problem?

PART 3: ESSAY QUESTIONS

1. Does it make sense to tell correctional officers the health status of prisoners who are under their supervision?

2. What is the effect of a lack of a sense of mission among correctional officers?

3. Burnout is endemic to all helping professions (e.g., social work). This has prompted some observers to suggest that because of the unique nature of COs' jobs, the term burnout is improperly used for this job classification. Do you agree or disagree with this statement and why?

4. Design a program for your fellow correctional workers that over the course of ten days would reduce their stress. And how would you demonstrate that it was effective?

Chapter 13

Correctional Officer Deviance

INTRODUCTION

Deviance can and does occur in all workplaces and throughout all professions. In the field of corrections deviance is generally considered to be inappropriate work-related activities that correctional workers may engage in (Kappeler, Sluder, and Alpert, 1994: 22). Although some correctional officers (COs) commit acts of deviant behavior, most introductory textbooks on corrections rarely tackle this subject at any great length, nor do the scholarly journals. Authors might briefly mention COs' violent acts, but rarely will they write anything about less visible behaviors such as theft, corruption, or sexual assault.

Before continuing, however, it is important to explain what we mean by the word *deviance*. Typically, this is an action or behavior that violates generally accepted norms (Adler, 2005). This is the foundation from which many of society's policies and laws are developed. Policies, and sometimes our laws, are written because entities (from organizations to countries) codify acts of deviance. Many agencies have codes of ethics or standards of conduct—"dos" and "don'ts"—which are taught to recruits and reinforced by veterans of the organization.

A closely related term is corruption. According to McCarthy (1996) this practice includes "the intentional violation of organizational norms (i.e., rules and regulations) by public employees for personal material gain" (p. 231). This would subsume theft, smuggling contraband, embezzlement of money from the correctional facility or inmates and theft of property, and misuse of authority (p. 232).

This chapter has benefited from the comments of David Curry.

Identifying and finding appropriate remedies to deviance gets tricky, however, when public officials (such as COs and administrators) engage in behavior that is morally reprehensible or ethically questionable (e.g., accepting free meals from contractors), but is rarely sanctioned. This type of action may even occur with a supervisor's knowledge and thus calls into question if, in fact, norms are actually being violated.

When a news story describing an incident of CO deviance is brought to the public's attention, an organization's legitimacy is typically called into question and can even prompt some sort of investigation. The behavior in question will typically be compared to existing norms and policies, and one of three things will commonly happen: The administration may publicly announce that they will no longer tolerate this behavior, they might increase enforcement against rule-breakers, or the rules and regulations will be changed to reflect current practices (Ross, 2000c).

Responding to CO deviance becomes challenging in cases in which nearly all of the workers have violated an existing policy and practice over a considerable period of time—with the knowledge of supervisors and administrators, who fail to take some sort of meaningful remedial action. This is a situation in which a norm hasn't been violated, but a policy has.

The discussion about deviance is intimately tied to the study of ethics. Clearly, COs face many temptations on the job, and deviant acts do take place. How often this happens, however, is generally a matter of speculation. Interest in this kind of deviant behavior has increased over the past decade, largely because of well-publicized inquiries that have taken place in the field of corrections, in addition to the allegations of abuse in connection with Baghdad's Abu Ghraib prison in 2004. In fact, the major National Commission on Safety and Abuse in Prisons (www.prisoncommission.org) (2005–2006) appeared to have selected aspects of CO deviance as one of its major areas that it investigated. Finally, because of the lack of attention scholars devote to the more general problem of deviance, and the difficulty obtaining reliable and comprehensive evidence, it is generally unknown just how much deviance takes place among COs and whether it is worse than among other law enforcement personnel or other professionals.

Bowker (1980) is known for producing perhaps the most thorough treatment of COs' deviant behavior. Though his research is outdated, he looked specifically at COs' victimization of prisoners. He noted, "The treatment of the subject is superficial in that incidents tend to be mentioned only in passing (or as part of a polemical piece of writing), and they are not presented or analyzed in any great detail" (p. 143). He also pointed out that incidents of deviance "tend to be recorded factually" and not placed into a theoretical context; "[the] quality of the reporting of incidents is often difficult to determine. Reports are almost always limited to the views of one of the participants or observers, with no corroboration from others. Even when reports are written by social scientists, they usually consist of second and third-person accounts derived from interviews rather than direct observation by the scientists" (p. 143). Finally, he had difficulty with the variable definitions of prior victimization. Bowker divided victimization into three types: physical, psychological, and sexual. Although this perspective is a beginning, the concept of deviance is more encompassing.

Regardless, there are two major types of deviance: the abuse of/violence toward prisoners and the corruption of COs. There is a considerable scholarly history on the abuse of prisoners. For example, Sykes' classic and controversial book *The Society of Captives* (1958) argued that, periodically, COs are susceptible to corruption. There are three major explanations: correctional workers develop friendships with prisoners; they engage in reciprocity; and simply default (which is a catch-all phrase to indicate that they may be either lazy or overcommitted and/or they can't spend the necessary time that is required to properly do their jobs). In its day, this was judged a relatively controversial finding; thus it inspired a lot of research about COs' working conditions and relationships with inmates. During the 1970s and 1980s, accumulated evidence on this subject called Sykes' conclusions into question.

THE PROBLEM OF DEVIANCE

There are approximately 12 primary types of deviance committed by correctional workers. These types of deviance include improper use of agency equipment and property, mishandling/theft of inmate property, drinking alcohol on the job, accepting gifts from inmates and contractors, discrimination, abuse of authority, sexual relationships with inmates, smuggling contraband, theft, unnecessary violence against prisoners, general boundary violations, and sexual harassment of fellow COs (see Exhibit 13.1). Most of these deviant behaviors are interrelated and self-explanatory, but the following reviews them in depth.

Improper Use/Misuse of Agency Equipment and Property

Multiple opportunities exist for COs and administrators to take advantage of their organizations' resources for personal benefit. This includes things as simple as using photocopy machines for personal reasons—like photocopying texts for classes—and borrowing equipment like vehicles for personal use. At other times—because of boredom, anger, or frustration COs may break equipment. Using corrections equipment in a manner in which it was not intended (including "monkey-wrenching," or purposely breaking equipment) is a frequent occurrence in factories and industry (Abbey, 1975). Many of these instances are acts of low-scale, unconscious rebellion, a reflection of frustration with poorly functioning or maintained equipment or difficulties with the management of the institution. Additionally, if the equipment does not work properly, there may be a tendency among workers to further damage it either as a demonstration of their frustration or to speed things up so that the administration will finally replace the tool or equipment.

Mishandling/Theft of Inmate Property

Inmates' possessions come in and out of the facility either when convicts are transferred to the institution or when friends and family mail items to the prison. Inmates routinely complain that COs steal or damage their possessions. Part of the reasons for these concerns is connected with the fact that, in the normal course of doing their jobs, officers must ensure the safety of the institution and prevent contraband from coming into the institution. That is why, for example, officers are typically required to rip off the covers of hardcover books or search inmates' personal effects at intake and during cell searches (Worley and Cheeseman, 2006).

Drinking on the Job

Correctional officers, who come to work under the influence of alcohol, drink on the job, use prescription or over-the-counter drugs in a manner in which they are not prescribed, or use soft or hard drugs that impair their judgment will not be able to properly respond to the demands of their job. They threaten not only their safety, but also that of their fellow COs. Alcohol use is often part of the CO subculture. Drinking is usually done for camaraderie, social bonding, and stress relief. Using illegal drugs typically sets the CO up for charges of corruption (i.e., they are the first to be suspected of smuggling contraband into the facility), regardless of where or how it was obtained.

Accepting Gifts from Inmates and Contractors

Occasionally, inmates (their friends, families, and associates), because of camaraderie or in hopes of ensuring a future favor, try to give some sort of gift, whether homemade or acquired, to COs. Likewise, sometimes contractors and suppliers to the facility give correctional workers gifts or discounts on purchases or services. The hope is that if their products or services are needed again, these vendors will be favored. These gratuities are typically frowned upon by more senior administrators and accrediting bodies.

Discrimination

Correctional workers, like most people, should also be cognizant about discriminating based on age, race, ethnicity, sexual preference, and national origin. This takes ugly forms when we periodically hear the occasional news media story about COs being members of radical right-wing organizations such as Aryan Nations or the Ku Klux Klan.

Abuse of Authority

Correctional officers have a considerable amount of power while on the job (Clemmer, 1958). They can write up (submit negative reports about) inmates they do not like and/or they can humiliate the convicts in front of others. These actions can be manifested in giving some inmates preferential housing or jobs, and access to entertainment and sports via television privileges. All combined, these kinds of actions are often referred to as abuse of authority. It "frequently involves one, or all, of the following activities: the acceptance of inmate payoffs for special consideration in receiving legitimate prison privileges . . . ; the acceptance of inmate payoffs for special consideration in obtaining or protecting illicit activities . . . and extortion" (Freeman, 2000: 350).

General Boundary Violations

Another issue is what is often referred to as boundary violations. These include "actions that blur, minimize, or disrupt the professional distance between correctional staff members and prisoners" (Marquart, Barnhill, and Balshaw-Biddle, 2001: 878), and fly in the face of the typical roles of COs as supervisors and guardians and inmates who are to follow orders. This kind of deviance can be further demarcated into *general* boundary violations which are " 'unserious' framebreaks committed by employees who accepted from inmates, or exchanged with inmates, . . . drinks, food, craft work or materials, or wrote letters to prisoners" (Marquart, Barnhil, and Balshaw-Biddle, 2001: 883).

Sexual Harassment of Fellow Correctional Workers

Both male and female officers and administrators can engage in sexual harassment toward each other. This can include constantly asking fellow workers for dates, inappropriate touching, and stalking. Sexual harassment can also border on making a hostile work environment by bringing pornographic magazines to work, displaying pornographic materials on the job, objectifying other individuals, and making comments about body parts (Stohr et al., 1998; Savicki, Cooley, and Gjesvold, 2003).

Sexual Relations with Inmates

There is a long history of male staff members who work in women's prisons sexually abusing the female convicts. In most states, it is understood that sexual relations or inappropriateness between prison staff and convicts is considered by law to be sexual assault or rape. In the institution, there's no such thing as consensual sex between the keepers and the kept. Over the past two decades, hundreds of COs have been fired and/or indicted on sexual assault charges.

Some state prison systems, like Georgia, have implemented tough "no touch, no contact" policies. In these situations, men are not allowed to supervise female convicts. If a male enters the unit, COs are instructed to announce "man [or] male on range." At some federal prisons for women, administrators have installed hotlines through which female prisoners can make complaints if they have been sexually abused. Sometimes this is a public relations exercise designed to garner support from the wider public to show them that something is being done about this problem. Still, today there are a number of states that have not outlawed staff–inmate sex.

Most commonly, sexual relations is more of a problem with male correctional employees than with female correctional workers. But occasionally, we hear news stories of male-on-male and female-on-female sexual relations. For example, in 2000 Garrett Cunningham, while incarcerated at the Luther Unit of the Texas Department of Criminal Justice, was repeatedly raped—this time not by a fellow inmate, but by a CO. Rarely do we hear about female officers abusing male inmates, as it is often perceived that male prisoners are the beneficiaries in this kind of behavior.

Smuggling Contraband

Contraband is brought into prisons with the help of a variety of individuals, including COs. Correctional workers may have been compromised (e.g., an inmate or group of convicts has some damaging information on the CO that they will use against them) and/or see these opportunities as additional ways to supplement their income.

Theft of Correctional Facility Property

Institutional food is not only of poor quality, but it may also disappear even before being served in the mess hall. In some penitentiaries, staff will occasionally eat or steal the better food, load it into their cars or pickup trucks, and take it home to feed their farm animals (as slop for pigs), feed their pets, or sell it on the black market. Other items of value may also mysteriously disappear and make their way into the correctional workers' possessions.

Violence Against Prisoners

The prison staff can and do use violence against convicts. They are allowed by law to use force when life and property are in peril. The question becomes, How frequently is force used and is it done in an indiscriminate manner? Most often, officers will avoid using violence if at all possible. It creates too much ill will that the prisoners are not likely to forget. Instead, the correctional workers will rely on threats and humor to motivate inmates to comply with directives. When officers do beat inmates (and here I am not talking about excessive force), it is quite often because the latter have initiated or followed through on an attack or have instigated work strikes, riots, or escape attempts.

Unlike the deadly violence that convicts often inflict on one another, most acts of violence committed by COs are psychological. If the officers want to remind a prisoner who's in charge, they might tear up that convict's mail, refuse to turn up the heat, deny telephone privileges, or toss (search) the prisoner's cell, more frequently than normal. In the middle of the night, while convicts are sleeping, COs may overturn a bed, dumping the convict on the floor. The COs are not going to take the time to politely wake up an inmate; rather, the officers might drag him to the floor, handcuff him, and rummage through his personal items to search for weapons, drugs, or other contraband items. An officer who wants to particularly anger an inmate might confiscate pictures of loved ones or take away sheets, clothing, food, and legal papers.

Strip searches, ostensibly used to detect drugs and weapons, are another form of intimidation and violence. If they want, COs can order an arrestee to go through this humiliating act numerous times a day on the cellblock, in the cafeteria, outdoors, or when the convict comes in and out of the visiting room. They can leave a prisoner standing naked outside in a snowstorm, regardless of the danger of frostbite. This can happen below the gun tower, with machine guns pointed in the prisoner's direction, all in the freezing weather.

EXHIBIT 13.1

Selected types of CO deviance

Improper use/misuse of agency equipment and property
Mishandling/theft of inmates' property and paperwork
Drinking on the job
Accepting gifts from inmates, their friends, family, and contractors
Sexual relationships with inmates
Discrimination
Violence against prisoners
Smuggling contraband General boundary violations
Sexual harassment of fellow correctional workers
Theft of correctional facility property
Abuse of authority

Sometimes, in medium- and maximum-security prisons, when the COs think an inmate may have contraband hidden inside his rectum, a strip search will include a finger wave. Similar to a doctor conducting a prostate examination, the guard will insert a gloved finger in the rectum—but the CO is much less likely to be as gentle as a doctor. It must also be remembered that staff do not necessarily have to inflict violence on an inmate themselves; they can get another prisoner to do it on their behalf.

SOLUTIONS

There are several methods by which COs' deviance can be minimized. These include conducting thorough background investigations on applicants, proper and thorough training, running periodic criminal investigation checks on all employees after they have been hired (e.g., they may have had a run-in with the law that needs to be evaluated), and performing random drug tests. Other options include having clearly articulated codes of conduct. The following section examines impediments to reporting deviance, and solutions such as total quality management (TQM), using power appropriately, reporting of malfunctioning and broken equipment, exposing waste and violation of policies and procedures, ombudsman and ethics committees, the creation and use of internal affairs departments, proper employee evaluation, better leadership and accreditation, certification, and sanctions.

Impediments to Reporting Deviance

Corruption, violence, or violations of rules should be reported. But this is easier said than done. COs, like police officers, have to deal with the powerful effects of the occupational subculture (Kauffman, 1988), especially the "blue wall of silence"—the idea that officers will not reveal potentially harmful information about a fellow correctional worker because it may result in a lack of teamwork or mutual protection from inmates while on the job. Clearly, no CO relishes the thought of being in a dangerous situation and not being able to count on having backup. Thus, both law enforcement officers and COs are very careful about reporting the deviance of their fellow officers.

Total Quality Management

During the 1980s and 1990s correctional facilities—inspired by the private sector—introduced new opportunities for the line staff to contribute to the formation of institutional policies and practices. This process called Total Quality Management (TQM) was followed up by a number of evaluations of selected experiments. Most suggested that TQM was in name only and that it had to compete with the paramilitary approach to managing correctional personnel. TQM is often no more than a buzzword or a phrase used to describe techniques used to get employees more involved in decision making. When it is properly utilized, it is not simply window-dressing (Freeman, 2000: Chapter 11). TQM circumvents this process by soliciting and acting on the input of workers.

Using Power Appropriately

The general public may think that correctional facilities, administrators, and officers are, by nature, authoritarian (Freeman, 2000: Chapter 9). This impression, largely influenced by the mass media, derives from the numerous rules that inmates must follow and from the fact that infractions will typically lead to some sort of administrative action—or even physical action on the part of the COs if their commands are not followed. Nothing could be farther from the truth. COs do not have the resources to sanction each inmate. They recognize that, in general, they are outnumbered (often at a ratio of 40: 1) and that forcing convicts to do things against their will most likely backfire.

In order to accomplish their jobs, COs must make appropriate use of their power. As mentioned earlier in this book, Hepburn (1985) determined that there were five kinds of power: legitimate, coercive, reward, expert, and referent. The most useful types are legitimate and expert power; the worst type is coercive.

By law, COs are empowered to do certain things. They know the policies and procedures of the institution better than anyone and can help guide inmates through the day. In terms of expertise, COs should know the institutional rules better than the prisoners; this creates a context in which the CO can work effectively. Hepburn concluded that effective COs manage to get prisoners' cooperation through a complicated set of rewards and punishments. Some of the privileges include not enforcing the rules, overlooking violations, choice job assignments, and writing favorable reports. The problem with this kind of exchange relationship is that it must not be taken to the extreme, where the CO starts smuggling in contraband or encourages illegal behavior on the part of the convict.

Reporting Malfunctioning or Broken Equipment

In order to minimize the likelihood of their being blamed for malfunctioning or broken equipment, COs should inform the proper individuals in their correctional institution in a timely fashion. This is especially important if it is safety-related equipment. If the administration is slow to fix or replace broken equipment, then correctional workers can file this type of report through a union representative (e.g., shop steward). Supervisors who are slow to fix or replace broken equipment can spark plenty of cynicism about the organization. This is something they should avoid creating at all costs.

Exposing Waste and Violations of Rules

Although the "blue wall of silence" among correctional workers is ever present, most training manuals will advise recruits to report infractions to their immediate supervisor. This is easier said than done because of the ramifications a correctional worker might experience if they report these instances. And certainly there are rational-sounding arguments for both reporting violations and remaining silent. It is easy for outsiders to take the moral high ground and to cite the whistleblower legislation that currently exists in some states and at the federal level. But consider the complications that arise when the deviant individual is a CO's immediate supervisor, or when the CO has skeletons in their own closet.

Correctional officers are naturally timid about reporting the deviance of others. Those who choose to remain silent often do so out of fear of retaliation from fellow officers and administrators. Once COs consider a colleague to be a snitch, as previously mentioned, that individual may find themselves without the necessary backup in dangerous situations. The litmus test is usually when COs predict that not reporting their colleagues' deviant behavior may later wind up implicating themselves; in such a case, the COs may feel a stronger obligation to inform appropriate-level superiors of an infraction.

From a strictly moral/ethical point of view, the failure to report an act of deviance can be almost as bad as committing the act in the first place. And most departments of corrections (DOCs) stress how employees have a duty to report infractions. Obviously, there are better and worse ways to report the violations of norms and policies. It does not have to be in a face-to-face or confrontational situation. The more experience COs have, the greater the odds will be that they discover or know ways to report wrongdoings so that they will not be caught in an undesirable situation in the future. Sometimes, this may mean talking to the offending person in private. Then again, once the deviant behavior has been reported, management frequently attempts to blame the incident (i.e., pass the buck) on the workers and not accept responsibility for its failure to manage or lead.

The Use of Ombudsmen and Ethics Committees

Occasionally, correctional facilities or DOCs have ombudsmen who on their own or with their staff investigate abuse and or cut through the red tape for prisoners, their loved ones and correctional workers. An additional mechanism to serve as a check on correctional work is the creation and use of ethical committees, which consist of a group of "every level of management, union representatives, and community representatives" that review complaints against COs (Freeman, 2000: 354). A similar function is conducted by an inspector general who acts as in-house quality control in large government organizations.

The Creation and Use of Internal Affairs Units

Most DOCs have developed a mechanism to investigate officer or administrator wrongdoing. They go by a variety of names including offices of inspector generals, offices of professional responsibility, and departments of internal affairs. Once a complaint is launched, they usually collect evidence that substantiates the complaint or exonerates the accused. In some DOCs, if they find evidence of wrongdoing, they will take this information to the commissioner of corrections for further action (i.e., dismissal, sanction, etc.). In other situations, the authorities have the power to arrest the culprit (Freeman, 2000: 356–357).

Proper Employee Evaluation

Most correctional facilities evaluate their employees' performance. These evaluations provide many benefits, including preventing COs from engaging in deviance or crime and discipline for employees who have engaged in periodic deviance. Performance evaluations can be as simple as a written report where the supervisor checks off the boxes or involve a complex process of negotiation between a boss and employee. Performance appraisals are also mediated by union regulations (Latham and Wexley, 1981).

Better Leadership

Better leadership is key to minimizing deviant behavior among COs. "Effective correctional leadership involves a set of practices that acknowledges both the internal and external environment of corrections" (e.g., Freeman, 2000: 237). It is wise to point out that a distinction exists between managers and leaders. Managers usually help workers perform their daily tasks, including processing the appropriate paperwork, whereas leaders see the bigger picture and plan for the organizational mission. The correctional field needs administrators who are not simply managers, but also leaders who help an organization move forward and deal both with planned and unanticipated changes. This field requires individuals who can act in a proactive rather than a reactive fashion.

Accreditation

In order to improve the working conditions at a prison, correctional managers and officials can seek accreditation by the American Correctional Association (ACA) that have developed standards that have been agreed upon by recognized experts. Accreditation helps ensure that an organization remains current and functioning to the best of its ability. The accreditation process requires jails and prisons to submit to voluntarily inspections by the ACA, representatives of the media, scholars, and possibly a board appointed by a governor; this is a complex relationship but typically leads to improvements in a facility's programs and infrastructure. COs do not like working in institutions that have practices and enforce rules and regulations that do not appear to make sense. These protocols may have made sense to previous administrations, but are inappropriate for current practices and conditions and seem silly, illogical, or antiquated.

Certification

Certification of COs, including requiring them to know a specific body of knowledge, adhere to certain moral and ethical standards, and be tested on a periodic basis to maintain their certification, may go a long way to decreasing the possibility of deviance. This can be done by the ACA or by a state regulatory agency. One suggestion is to "treat criminal justice professionals just like doctors and lawyers, by making their employment conditional upon a valid license or certification. Half of the states in the country, however, lack a formal process for certifying qualified corrections officers and decertifying those who violate the law or rules of professional conduct. Additionally, there is no national-level mechanism that exists to record and share such information among local jurisdictions and states. Thus, dangerous officers can find employment in different facilities and systems because their past behavior is not known to new employers" (National Commission on Safety and Abuse in Prison: 71–72). The commission also recommended a national CO data bank to prevent this kind of occurrence.

Sanctions

Depending on how severe the deviance, if uncovered, an internal investigation proceeds, and typically the CO appears in front of an in-house disciplinary board. This unit can recommend dismissal, transfer, docking of pay, or retraining. If the matter is of a criminal nature, then formal criminal charges can be made through the local district attorney. During these periods, the officer is allowed to be represented by a lawyer or a representative of their correctional union.

CONCLUSION

Correctional officers' and administrators' deviance leads to a breakdown in inmate–officer trust. This perception has a wider audience and may lead to a decrease in public confidence in correctional facilities' ability to do their jobs. When this trust is lost, it is rarely reasserted or takes an incredible amount of time to reestablish. When levels of deviance are high, the facility cannot work at an optimal level and cannot successfully implement meaningful rehabilitative programs. Both COs and managers must be astute to prevent themselves from participating in deviant behavior or insure that they deal with it in a timely fashion.

KEY TERMS

blue wall of silence
boundary violations
deviance
guard subculture
leader
manager

monkey wrenching
norm
power
retribution
Total Quality Management (TQM)

REVIEW QUESTIONS

PART 1: MULTIPLE-CHOICE QUESTIONS

1. What is deviance?

   a. an action or behavior that violates accepted norms
   b. something illegal
   c. it can't be defined
   d. behavior labeled as such by supervisors
   e. none of the above

2. What can happen when a story that alleges deviance by a correctional officer comes to the public's attention?

   a. There is some sort of investigation.
   b. The behavior will be compared to existing policies.
   c. The administration will crack down on the violations.
   d. The rules and regulations will be changed to reflect current practices.
   e. All of the above.

3. Who divided the victimization of prisoners into three types?

   a. Bowker
   b. Jones
   c. Lombardo
   d. Match
   e. Sykes

4. According to Hepburn, the two most useful kinds of power for a correctional officer to utilize are

   a. legitimate and neutral
   b. legitimate and expert
   c. expert and referent
   d. coercive and referent
   e. reward and expert

5. Which type of power do correctional officers feel will not get their jobs done?

   a. legitimate
   b. coercive
   c. expert
   d. referent
   e. reward

6. State departments of corrections can seek accreditation by the

   a. APPA
   b. ACA
   c. AARP
   d. NAACP
   e. all of the above

7. Why has there been a recent interest in prisoner abuse?

   a. statistics indicate that it has increased
   b. the Abu Ghraib scandal
   c. similar studies in the field of policing
   d. some of the above
   e. all of the above

8. What is the term used to describe correctional/police officers' unwillingness to report the deviance of others?

   a. blue flu
   b. the blue wall of silence
   c. the runaround
   d. all of the above
   e. none of the above

9. Why might correctional officers NOT want to report the deviance of others?

   a. retribution
   b. benevolence
   c. parsimony
   d. upbraiding
   e. lecturing

PART 2: SHORT-ANSWER QUESTIONS

1. What three things does the presence of the "guard subculture" provide for correctional officers?

2. Name five kinds of power that correctional officers possess.

3. Name two means of restructuring prison relations.

4. What are the three reasons Sykes suggested that lead to corruption among correctional officers?

5. List four primary types of deviance committed by correctional officers.

6. Define "correctional officer deviance."

PART 3: ESSAY QUESTIONS

1. What do you believe is the single most important problem within correctional organization management? What is the evidence supporting this position and what are some of the solutions offered to correct it?

2. Why should a discussion of correctional officer deviance and power be linked together?

Chapter 14

Officer Pay and Workload

INTRODUCTION

A considerable amount of research has been conducted on correctional officers (COs). Most findings suggest that they "are alienated, cynical, burned out, stressed but unable to admit it, suffering from role conflict of every kind and frustrated beyond imagining" (Welch, 1996: 137). It is not a profession that a lot of people choose as their lifelong career. Most individuals go into corrections seeing it as a temporary job, thinking that they will spend at the most one or two years in a correctional setting, but over time, it ends up being a career. Some correctional workers see their jobs as a sentence, much like one handed down to a person who is convicted of a crime. The only good thing about the CO's sentence is that they can go home at the end of their shift. Historically, COs have not been paid well, nor have they received many benefits. One of the biggest effects of this negativity is that there is approximately a 16 percent turnover of COs each year "and is higher where the pay is lower. Directors of systems remain on the job for no more than three years on average, and their rapid turnover destabilized entire systems" (National Commission on Safety and Abuse in Prison, 2006).

Over time, with the advent of unionization and professionalization, however, this situation has improved. There are discrepancies in salaries between states and between gender (Mallicoat, 2005). Another relevant issue is professionalization, which started with the requirement of wearing uniforms and possessing a specific body of knowledge. One of the most significant, if not symbolic changes, was the change during the nineteenth and twentieth centuries from using the job title guard to CO.

CORRECTIONAL OFFICERS WORK IN TRANSITION

Introduction

Crouch (1991) argues that over the past two decades the work of COs has changed largely because of "(1) an emphasis on rehabilitation, (2) changes in the size and composition of inmate populations, and (3) judicial intervention" (as cited in Welch: 137).

Guard Subculture

Crouch and Marquart (1980) suggest that the subculture developed by COs "is vital to the occupational socialization of the recruit. Rookies listen to, observe, and imitate ranking officers. Moreover, the presence of the guard subculture teaches rookies the following (1) how to perceive inmates, (2) how to anticipate trouble, (3) and how to manage inmates" (Welch: 139). The guard subculture idea is not without its critics. For example, Crouch and Marquart (1975) believe it exists, while others like Klofas and Toch (1982) and Klofas (1984) suggest that there is so much variability among COs, their superiors, and inmates that the guard subculture argument does not carry much weight.

Pay/Benefits

At an earlier point in time COs' pay was very poor. Over the past five decades, through the passage of labor laws and professionalization the salaries have improved. Nevertheless, wages vary based on region, state, the system (state or federal) a CO works in, and gender. In some states COs may not make much more than minimum wage. On the other hand, the best-paid COs work for the Federal Bureau of Prisons (FBOP). "As the workforce has become increasingly professionalized, with college-educated staff who claim to possess special expertise in the area of 'corrections,' salaries and status have increased correspondingly. Prison guards in a number of states, county jails, and the Federal Bureau of Prisons can earn $40,000 to $56,000 per year not including overtime" (Austin and Irwin, 2001: 98). "The average staring salary for a guard is $21,246, with twenty-three states offering a starting salary of $15,000 to $18,000." This does not include overtime. If you factor in overtime, this could mean that COs make what amounts to be a middle class income (Austin and Irwin, 2001: 98).

There are significant pay differentials between women and men. Male correctional workers are generally paid better than women. In 2002, according to the U.S. Bureau of Labor, female COs only made 78.6 percent of their male counterparts' salaries. Moreover, few management positions are held by women COs. True, you will see some women as captains, lieutenants, and wardens, but these ranks are typically reserved for men. This is even visible in female-controlled correctional institutions run by women wardens. Women are found working more in state facilities rather than in the FBOP. The compensation is increasing in prisons for COs—both male and female—and one of the most important reasons is unionization.

Unionization

Starting in the 1940s, COs have attempted to gain more control of their work environment. They have achieved this through the interrelated processes of seeking professionalization and unionization (Welch: 145). CO unions started in the mid-twentieth century. About 50–70 percent of all COs are now unionized. What do they do? Try to improve wages, benefits, and working conditions for their membership.

This makes sense as many criminal justice jobs have become either unionized or the workers are governed by rules established by professional associations. In addition to a desire for better pay and working conditions, one of the reasons why correctional workers have unionized is because they believe that both correctional administrators and the judicial system have abandoned them as a result of court decisions that have been passed in support of convicts' rights (Welch: 145). In addition to joining unions COs have joined professional organizations like the American Correctional Association (ACA). This entity "offers training and networking opportunities and speaks for the field in national forums" (ACA, Professionalism in Corrections: 10). The ACA also has a code of conduct that members must abide by if they want to be in good standing.

Unions can also minimize the turnover rates of COs. How can this be? If the workers get more money, benefits, and better working conditions, who wants to leave? There is not simply one union that represents state or federal correctional workers. There are many. In Maryland prisons, for example, some of the unions include the Communications Workers of America and the Maryland Correctional Law Enforcement Union. In some states, CO unions have become very powerful. One of the most powerful is the California Peace Officers Association. It is very successful in lobbying the legislature, putting into place a correctional building program, and having an effect on sentencing (i.e., making them longer and harsher, thereby ensuring jobs for all their membership). Even so, because COs' jobs, like law enforcement ones, are essential services, they are typically not allowed to strike. So what do they do to exert their will? They go on "job actions," sick-outs, or suffer "the blue flu."

Blue flu is when most of the COs call in sick. This means that the institution is short staffed and this typically puts the correctional facility into a state of crises. Meanwhile, inmates need to be supervised and fed. Unless noncustody personnel can be easily shifted around, management can rely on scab (nonunion) labor (and in most states thus violating labor laws), or recruits can be rushed through the corrections academy (all of which are poor options); the warden and senior personnel can no longer attend to their paperwork and must start working the tiers. Thus, correctional administrators grudgingly have to assume the responsibilities of directly caring for the inmates.

Convicts end up spending more time behind bars and get increasingly frustrated with the conditions. When they are out of cell, there may be a greater possibility of more interinmate violence and more contraband flowing around the institution because proper and/or frequent searches are not being conducted. No self-respecting warden, superintendent, or commissioner of corrections wants this to happen for a long time. This process forces management's hands to quickly conclude labor negotiations by making numerous concessions.

Professionalization

Correctional officers have responded to criticisms about their work through professionalization. This usually encompasses the development of a systematic theory, specialized knowledge, an occupational culture, a code of conduct, and the capability of sanction by the group (Vollmer and Mills, 1966). In short, this typically means increasing the educational and training requirements needed to work in correctional facilities. Many of these rules and regulations have been developed and promoted by the ACA. It is also important to have the correctional institution accredited. Policies that are present in an institution should not simply be there because of past practice, because many are no longer applicable or are simply a function of the whims of some administrator/s some 10–15 years ago. Most people who have been in the working world for a while realize that a considerable number of the rules and regulations in organizations are silly, irrelevant, antiquated, illogical, and this may be because one does not have enough experience with the rationale behind their origins, or it may be that no one has challenged their inclusion and use in the daily routines. In sum, there are countless ineffective rules that are still on the books.

Summary

Surveys of the American public consistently show that few people have considered working as COs. This is largely because correctional work is a low-prestige job. This can be explained by the company that they must keep, the paramilitary structure of the work place, and pay.

Correctional workers frequently complain that the rules are always changing so that neither they nor the convicts are certain. And COs are also frustrated about a number of significant supreme court cases that have curtailed their power. Some are nostalgic about "the good old days" when convicts were more respectful and CO's orders went unquestioned (Cole, 1994).

CONCLUSION

Being a CO is similar in some respects to being a dentist. Both dentists and COs perform a valuable service, but few people want to be under their care or supervision. Although paid reasonably well, or capable of making a respectable income, unless one is a masochist, no one really wants to visit the dentist.

Compared to many jobs, that of a CO is a good pay for the amount of education required. Most departments of corrections (DOCs) do not require recruits to have an education beyond high school. The better jobs in administration generally require candidates to have a minimum of a bachelor's degree. The higher up you go, however, the more the preference for higher education. Undoubtedly, unionization and professionalization have improved work conditions, salaries, and benefits for COs, but the fact remains that few people want to enter this profession.

KEY TERMS

blue flu   professionalization
guard subculture   unionization

REVIEW QUESTIONS

PART 1: MULTIPLE-CHOICE QUESTIONS

1. What percent of correctional officers have become unionized?
    a. 25
    b. 69
    c. 76
    d. 97
    e. none of the above

2. What is the name of the method by which correctional officers can force management to negotiate for higher wages, improved benefits, and improved working conditions?
    a. abuse prisoners
    b. blue flu
    c. strike
    d. destroy prison property
    e. riot

3. Which of the following is the largest state correctional officer union in the United States?
    a. Maryland Correctional Law Enforcement Union
    b. California Peace Officers Association
    c. Communications Workers of America
    d. FBOP union
    e. none of the above

4. In the United States male and female correctional officers are paid
    a. about the same
    b. males are paid more than women
    c. women are paid more than men
    d. only if women are in administrative position are they paid more than men
    e. none of the above

5. Crouch has argued that, over the years, correctional officers have changed because of
   a. an emphasis on rehabilitation
   b. changes in size and composition of inmates
   c. judicial intervention
   d. all of the above
   e. none of the above

6. What is the importance of guard subculture?
   a. It brings in contraband for the prisoners.
   b. It is vital to the occupational socialization of the recruit.
   c. It leads to correctional officers' abuse of prisoners.
   d. It shares many similarities with the criminal subculture.
   e. None of the above.

7. Which researcher has examined the transition of guard work over the past few decades?
   a. Irwin
   b. Crouch
   c. James
   d. Ross
   e. Sykes

PART 2: SHORT-ANSWER QUESTIONS

1. What does the guard subculture mean?

2. Are men and women correctional workers paid the same and why?

PART 3: ESSAY QUESTIONS

1. Are correctional officer unions too powerful? Justify your answer.

2. What have been the benefits of correctional officer unions? How can these organizations be made stronger?

Chapter 15

Management and Administration

INTRODUCTION

Although many correctional officers (COs) and correctional administrators believe that in any given correctional facility inmates are the biggest problem, in many institutions both inmates and COs think that the administration (particularly those at senior levels) are the bigger obstacles to effectively accomplishing their jobs. Partially because of the paramilitary nature of prisons, wardens and senior management are often seen as autocratic, poorly trained, and ineffective (Freeman, 2000).

The history of corrections is replete with stories of wardens making decisions with minimal consultation with their staff. For example, "To protect his authority, the autocratic warden created disunity in the prison community in that the formation of groups of either prisoners or guards was never permitted. The wardens' intelligence system ensured that neither guard nor prisoner could trust anyone. The paramilitary model of management, with its military terminology, downward flow of communication, rigid rules and regimentation, and impersonal relationships, further protected the wardens' absolute power and helped maintain an orderly, neat, and secure institution" (Bartollas, 2002: 259).

"Many wardens complain that they spend far too much time in their offices, coping with memoranda and urgently required reports. They say that they are too busy to inspect their cellblocks from one week to the next" (Bartollas: 259). But history is replete with examples of wardens who have been very hands on and made significant changes not only in the institutions that they managed, but in their state departments of corrections (DOCs) (e.g., DiIulio, 1987).

EXHIBIT 15.1

Classics in Corrections

John J. DiIulio's *Governing Prisons* (1987)

Governing Prisons is one of the first rigorous comparative studies of prison organization and management in the United States. It was performed by a conservative and controversial political scientist, John J. DiIulio, who examines the social science literature on corrections and finds it sadly lacking. He then identifies three different types of prison systems: Texas (a control model), Michigan (a responsibility model), and California (a combined model). He traces the history of these models and the advantages and disadvantages of each. DiIulio favors a mix between prisons run by inmates that have limited power and where prison administrators are skilled in monitoring convicts, are compassionate, and have earned the respect of the inmates.

Over time the way that wardens related to their subordinates has changed. "The majority of bureaucratic wardens of the 1970s used participatory management. Many wardens of the 1980s chose the control, consensual, or responsibility model to manage their correctional facilities. The wardens of the 1990s and first decade of the twenty-first century viewed themselves as professionals and team players dealing with institutional problems in innovative ways" (Bartollas, 2002: 261).

THE PROBLEMS

Introduction

Effectively managing correctional staff is frequently a challenge for most administrators. The biggest difficulties lie in the area of staff selection, developing COs and managers, and staff retention.

Selecting the Appropriate Staff

Corrections has always suffered from being able to attract and retain suitable officer candidates to do the job. "The problem is tied to the public's notion of penal institutions, as well as to the comparably less favorable aspects of the job" (Ford and Moore, 1992: 10). Managers typically rise up through the ranks from either the custody or programming sides of the institutions. Rarely do they come in from private industry and thus they often suffer from tunnel vision, an inability to think outside the box.

Development of COs and Managers

In most DOCs, rising up through the ranks usually is done through competitive exam. It also helps a candidate if they have at a minimum a bachelor's degree. Reaching

---

EXHIBIT 15.2

Classics in Corrections

Brubaker

Brubaker is a film (released in 1980) based on the real-life story of Tom Murton, the prison superintendent who between 1967 and 1968 confronted corruption and state-sanctioned murder and cover-ups in the Cummins Unit, one of Arkansas' most notorious prisons. Murton, played by actor Robert Redford, with the blessing of the state commissioner of corrections, enters Wakefield prison, undercover as a prisoner, to observe and experience the problems firsthand. He quickly learns how convict bosses (trustees) practically run the place, strike terror into the lives of prisoners, and the COs and warden appear thoroughly corrupt. He reveals himself to the prison authorities, is granted the position of warden, and constantly confronts a state prison administration that is unwilling to change the prisons under their control.

---

the level of warden usually requires a master's degree. Commissioners of DOCs are typically political appointees. They serve at the pleasure of the governor. In other words, they do not have civil service protection (i.e., job security). They do not need to have any expertise in the field or have even worked in the field of corrections. Most however do.

Retaining the Good Correctional Managers and Wardens

One of the biggest problems is turnover of management. According to the Commission on Safety and Abuse, "the average tenure for a top corrections administrator in a state system is just three years" (p. 73). Based on a survey of correctional managers, 29 percent only held their job for one year or less (Clem, 2003). There is a consensus that this is simply too short a time to improve or change things. Not only is it difficult to keep good managers but workers too.

SOLUTIONS

The most important solutions to address the previously mentioned management difficulties have been for correctional workers to stay out of the way of difficult bosses, and the attempt to give COs more power. These include avoiding autocratic supervisors, properly training managers, empowering employees, facilitating unions and collective bargaining, and total quality management and unit management.

Avoiding Autocratic Supervisors

Traditionally, wardens were political appointees. This meant that there was no necessity for them to have any practical experience in the field of corrections. They often ruled their organizations in an autocratic fashion. This philosophy and practice created a climate of fear and contributed to low worker morale and productivity. Over time, this situation has changed; although political connections cannot hurt, wardens typically have practical corrections experience working their way up the chain of command. In order to cope with problem superiors, many COs try to get jobs in the institution where they will not be in constant contact with supervisors. They volunteer to spend the lion's share of their time up in a watchtower, or spend a significant amount of their shifts transporting prisoners. An alternative, which ultimately has negative consequences for the CO, is using up as many of their sick days as possible. The downside here is that often they will come under the scrutiny of management and they may be subtly disciplined for this kind of behavior.

Properly Training Managers

Starting in the 1980s, states such as South Carolina and California began sending correctional managers to specialized training programs to improve many of their job-related skills including communication, leadership, handling grievances, and understanding new management practices, and the economy (Freeman, 2000: 322–329). A similar function has been provided by the Federal Bureau of Prisons' (FBOP) National Institute of Corrections that "provide[s] training, technical assistance, information services, and policy/program development assistance to federal, state, and local corrections agencies" (www.nicic.org/AboutUs).

Employee Empowerment

Allowing employees who previously had little or no ability for independent action to act with more autonomy is typically called employee empowerment (Freeman, 2000). Workers who are empowered are able to exert influence on organizational policy development and practices. In order to accomplish this, COs have formed unions, and some facilities have experimented with work groups, unit management, and the implementation of Total Quality Management (TQM) programs (Freeman, 2000: Chapter 11).

Unions and Collective Bargaining

The process of unionization and collective bargaining have been slow to come to American prisons. In the 1940s, the only state that had a union was Connecticut. The movement took off in the 1960s with New York and Washington entering the fray. "By the 1970s, more than twenty states had formally authorized collective bargaining by public employees, and by the end of the twentieth century, more than half of the states had collective bargaining for at least some correctional employees" (Seiter, 2005: 334). Essentially, collective bargaining refers to the contract entered into between management and the unions that represent the workers. It is understood that there is a mutually agreed upon process for negotiating different aspects of the contact that are connected to wages, benefits, working conditions, and grievance procedures.

Total Quality Management and Unit Management

During the 1970s, recognizing that the old style of managing COs would not work so well, DOCs started experimenting with and in some cases implementing both corporate and participatory methods for running their correctional facilities (Bartollas, 2002: 261).

The corporate management model "emphasizes modern management techniques and participant management. Lines of authority and accountability are clear; feedback and quantitative evaluations are widely used. It did not take long for correctional administrators to discover that the new management theory did not solve the problems they faced in American prisons. By the late 1980s, most of these correctional administrators saw that in spite of private-sector management theory, most prisons had more violence, worse conditions, and fewer programming opportunities than they had had under the autocrats of old" (Bartollas, 2002: 261–262).

During the 1980s, many DOCs abandoned the shared-powers model. They started moving toward a system where inmates yielded considerable power. The problem with this state of affairs was that prison gangs made up the power vacuum (Bartollas: 262).

Started in 1966 by the FBOP, unit management is designed to break the correctional facility into small parts, push decision-making downward, and try to increase contact between correctional workers and prisoners (Seiter, 2005: 317–318). In general, this approach is intended to improve staff–inmate communication. This is fostered by having the staff offices located right on the tiers.

CONCLUSION

Typically, programs that are designed to empower correctional employees in the management of correctional facilities are simply public relations exercises designed to temporarily pacify the COs until another fad or gimmick comes along. Most seasoned correctional workers are quick to realize this, which in turn creates bad morale, and impedes sincere efforts to change and forces the institution to carry on with maladaptive polices and practices and hostility by COs to their supervisors.

KEY TERMS

autocratic management   unit management
collective bargaining   union
Total Quality Management (TQM)

REVIEW QUESTIONS

PART 1: MULTIPLE-CHOICE QUESTIONS

1. What is considered the greatest challenge in managing change in correctional organizations?

    a. changing employee attitudes and behavior

    b. finding things to change

    c. time constraints

    d. budgetary concerns

    e. none of the above

2. Who argued in favor of participative management by suggesting that control rests not on force, but on peer-group formulation and enforcement of norms?

    a. Donald Clemmer

    b. Richard McCleary

    c. Gresham Sykes

    d. George Bento

    e. Max Weber

3. Traditionally, wardens were

    a. political appointees

    b. elected

    c. civil servants

    d. holders of Ph.D.s

    e. none of the above

PART 2: SHORT-ANSWER QUESTIONS

1. What is Total Quality Management?

2. Define unit management.

3. How can correctional officers avoid dealing with supervisors who are uncaring?

PART 3: ESSAY QUESTIONS

1. What do you believe is the single most important problem of correctional organization management? What is the evidence supporting this position and what are some of the solutions offered to correct it?

2. Some observers of prisons suggest that management skills of a correctional administrator are not that different than those of a hotel or restaurant manager. Do you agree or disagree? And why?

Chapter 16

The Future of Corrections

INTRODUCTION

In order to conclude this book, perhaps the most important question to ask is what the future holds for corrections in the United States. After careful reflection, internal debate, and considerable agonizing, I struggled about whether to end the book on an optimistic or pessimistic note. Unfortunately, I could not come to a decision which option was best. Some of the reforms I list are certainly things to celebrate, while others will be questioned by scholars, practitioners, inmates, ex-cons, and activists. Some suggestions may also work for a short period of time, while others may look good on paper, but are not effective once put into practice.

Indeed, in order to improve conditions, a comprehensive strategy must be taken. When I say this, I'm not referring to the fact that we need better cooperation among the different branches of the criminal justice system, although this might be helpful. A more holistic approach, incorporating labor unions, foundations, social welfare organizations, social work agencies, and criminal justice actors, is preferable. This emphasis should involve people and organizations at the interlocking individual, community, legal, and political levels.

Regardless, this concluding chapter provides a glimpse of the future of corrections in the United States, and in doing so answers a number of questions. These include what types of criminals one might expect to find in correctional institutions, what problems will jails and prisons encounter, and what are some emerging ideas

This chapter has benefited from the comments of Angela West Crews and Miguel Zaldivar.

that have been proposed? This chapter also outlines what sorts of scenarios we might expect in the future, and given the multiplicity of theories and types of crimes, how can we realistically reduce the number of people behind bars and orient the criminal justice and correctional systems more toward rehabilitation and less toward retribution.

PESSIMISM OR OPTIMISM?

There are two basic and opposing perspectives toward interpreting the future: pessimistic and optimistic. In the pessimistic alternative, which can be as simple as maintaining the status quo, things will only get worse. Jail and prison populations will continue to grow, those behind bars will age, their health problems will increase, and there will be less money for suitable living conditions and programming. In a more drastic scenario, crime will increase, real and alleged perpetrators will continue to be incarcerated, and things will go from bad to worse (JFA Institute, 2007).

In an optimistic and somewhat utopian scenario, the frequency, intensity, and lethality of crime will subside until crime becomes a thing of the past. Those who were sentenced to long prison terms will be rehabilitated, and eventually be released into society. Those who are first-time drug offenders will also be released, get appropriate treatment in the community, and they will cease and desist committing crimes to support their drug habits. Let's, however, take a closer look at these contrasting perspectives.

THE PESSIMISTIC SCENARIO EXAMINED

Introduction

The criminal justice system, and corrections in particular, is running out of options that would help improve the current state of affairs. The future does not look bright; most of the problems reviewed in this book are likely to affect jails and prisons, convicts, and correctional officers in the decades to come. At a minimum, these issues include a desensitized public, obedience/deference to authority, distrust of the criminal justice system, apathy, policy ignorance and confusion, the graying prison population, the growing number of women in prison, and lack of funding. Resolving these problems will keep researchers, practitioners, consultants, and activists busy for the foreseeable future.

Desensitized Public

Americans are becoming more desensitized to the problems that do not immediately impact their lives. This is attributable to a number of factors. For instance, we are now barraged with numerous communications—including the proliferation of direct mail, cable television, e-mail, the World Wide Web, and now satellite radio—that reach Americans on a daily basis. Given the amount of information that any one person receives, they may simply not have the time or interest to find out what goes on in jails and prisons. In a similar fashion, many Americans feel they know everything about criminal justice and corrections because they regularly watch popular television shows like *CSI* or *Law and Order*. As outlined in Chapter 2, this mitigates against proper understanding of realistic solutions toward crime and those who commit crimes.

Obedience/Deference to Authority

Many individuals are all too willing to accept, believe in the infallibility of, and/or act obedient or deferent to authority (Milgram, 1974). According to Piven and Cloward,

> people usually remain acquiescent, conforming to the accustomed patterns of daily life in their community and believing those patterns to be both inevitable and just . . . most of the time people conform to the institutional arrangements which enmesh them, which regulate the rewards and penalties of daily life, and which appear to be the only possible reality. Those for whom the rewards are most meager, who are the most oppressed by inequality, are also acquiescent. Sometimes they are the most acquiescent. (1977: 6)

One of the reasons why people are deferent or obedient to authority structures is that "they have little defense against the penalties that can be imposed for defiance" (Piven and Cloward, 1977: 6). Obedience to authority may also be a result of cost–benefit calculations that citizens have made. They conclude that they have more to lose than to gain from criticizing (i.e., protesting against) large powerful organizations like prisons, departments of corrections (DOCs), and governmental bodies. It may also be a result of strong and hidden pressures to conform.

Distrust of the Criminal Justice System

It is popularly assumed that communities that are disproportionately affected by crime or in which a greater number of individuals are imprisoned (i.e., in the United States this would primarily include African Americans and Hispanics) will complain or protest against this pattern and in some way try to alter existing economic, political, or social conditions. Most members of the affected communities have a collective memory of repression, powerlessness, and isolation in the political sphere. Many segments of society are very distrustful of the criminal justice system. And thus they are reluctant to participate in the political process.

Newly arrived immigrants, for example, particularly those from underdeveloped and developing countries, especially those who may have entered the country illegally, may fear that their status can be easily revoked. Immigrants may also have language problems, have a deep distrust of the criminal justice system, and are less knowledgeable about their constitutional rights—all of which make them shy away from political participation.

Apathy

Many people are apathetic about participating in the political process (Ricci, 1984: 154). Political participation is not simply voting. It can include working on behalf of a politician, signing a petition, or writing letters to the editor of a newspaper. The public may have a feeling that "if it does not affect me personally, why get involved?" (e.g., Lamb, 1975). Participating involves a series of cost–benefit calculations. Many people who are bothered by political or social conditions rationalize that they stand to lose more (i.e., police harassment, absenteeism from work, and lost wages) than to gain in criticizing the criminal justice system. In particular, they cannot afford time off from their jobs or school to complain about social injustices that occur in their lives or community.

Some researchers (e.g., Grodzins, 1956; Converse, 1964; McClosky, 1964) have suggested that apathy can be prosocial. Why? Because you probably don't want an uninformed population suddenly participating in politics. The results may be poorly informed decision making. Finally, apathy often leads to individuals' failure to assist in criminal investigations and prosecutions—in particular, the reluctance to become witnesses or to report offenses, both because of a fear of reprisal and a hatred and/or distrust of the police.

Applying this reasoning to the overreliance on corrections as a solution, and reactions to it, we might be witnessing a process in which concerned communities are socialized into apathy because of previous failed attempts to change the political system.

Policy Ignorance and Confusion

One of the perpetual problems of corrections is the "pendulum of politics," which is the tendency for policies and practices to come in and out of fashion. This phenomenon may frustrate corrections policies and practices because it constantly fluctuates between liberal and conservative initiatives. Also definitions of social problems often shift, which leads to confusion among policy alternatives. This includes not only the political parties that are in power, but also the individuals who are tasked with implementing the new courses of action. In situations like this, neither of the competing goals of rehabilitation and punitiveness are totally achieved. Perhaps this is not what is intended in the first place. Changing policies and practices can lead to anger, cynicism, and apathy on the part of inmates and correctional professionals alike (e.g., Fleisher, 1996; Fabelo, 1997). Also because corrections is not a simple subject, many people are unwilling to appropriately educate themselves on this subject matter.

The Graying Prison Population

One of the biggest problems is the graying of the prison population. One of the reasons for this pattern is the high number of individuals who were sentenced to life in prison in state and federal institutions. The graying of the prison population continues unabated, with more convicts serving life sentences and dying of old age or natural causes behind bars. Some prison systems allow elderly prisoners or younger convicts who are diagnosed to die in a few months to apply for "compassionate release." This may allow the convict to go home and die in the company of their loved ones. The problem is that few prisoners ever make it out the door before dying, as the application process may take many months to be officially approved. The graying prison population means that prison systems will need to spend even more money on special medical treatments to keep these individuals alive and to build specially designed facilities that allow for an expanded population of older inmates.

Women in Prison

It is generally understood that the rate of crimes committed by females is increasing, which causes unique problems to the correctional facilities in which women convicts are housed. Almost 15 percent of all correctional populations consist of females. Unfortunately, the building rate for women's facilities has not increased like it has with men. Additionally, female convicts suffer qualitatively different problems than men, including having a history of being a victim of sexual abuse, and guilt surrounding their separation from their children. When a mother is incarcerated, there may not always be a spouse or relative who can care for her children. In a best-case scenario, the children may end up under the supervision of the inmate's mother, sister, or grandmother. Too often, however, the children are under the care of a distant relative or the Department of Social Services (Ross and Richards, 2003: Chapter 11).

Lack of Funding

Without adequate funding all other problems of the correctional enterprise are exacerbated and this contributes to the revolving-door syndrome (i.e., no sooner than prisoners are released, they commit a crime, and/or violate the conditions of their probation or parole, and return to prison). Frequently, even the best-laid plans fail because the state either does not have enough money or squanders it with needless stopgap measures.

THE OPTIMISTIC SCENARIO EXAMINED

Introduction

When we look to the field of corrections, few truly new solutions are being proposed. A handful of promising initiatives recently singled out include new technologies, a CompStat-like initiative for correctional personnel, selective release, and DNA testing.

New Technologies

Over time, advances in forensic/detection and communication technologies have made work-related equipment smaller, more portable, cheaper, and more widely available to criminal justice personnel. This may mean that possibilities for monitoring those convicted of a crime are easier in the community than behind bars. To a limited extent, the introduction of new technologies may be of some aid to the corrections field (see Chapter 9). Here, I am not referring to weaponry such as pepper spray, or restraints like stun belts, but specifically to electronic monitoring (EM) or chemical castration. Although their connection to rehabilitation is questionable, these mechanisms and procedures can lead to cost savings only after correctional systems make an initial investment of money and properly train personnel to effectively use the equipment. Also, they are not flawless, as some individuals out on community corrections who know how to use the technology may find ways to circumvent devices. They may simply deactivate or modify them for their own benefit (Fabelo, 2000).

CompStat-like Programs for the Corrections Industry

In 1994 New York City Police Commissioner William Bratton introduced a new management philosophy and practice that attempted to use timely statistics on crime rates and regular follow-up with senior command staff in order to better marshal the New York City Police Department's (NYPD's) resources to combat crime. He called this CompStat (Bratton, 1998). The use of CompStat-like programs, similar to those currently used in large American police departments to increase middle management accountability, and using scarce resources may be beneficial for corrections and community corrections in particular. In the spring 2003 issue of *City Magazine*, a well-known, New York City-based policy magazine, Heather Mac Donald argued that the reason for so many failures from prison is an unaccountable corrections system. She wrote that we should hold corrections professionals accountable just like we are now making the police accountable through CompStat procedures (Mac Donald, 2003). Mac Donald argues that there are plenty of rehabilitation programs, and—although her data is anecdotal—there may be some truth to Mac Donald's argument that not requiring probationers and parolees to finish such programs is not helping them to succeed after release.

Selective Release

Some states, like Illinois and Kentucky, have realized that the last two decades of skyrocketing expenditures for corrections have had a minimal positive impact on the safety and well-being of their citizens. That is why they have implemented significant changes by releasing nonviolent inmates near the end of their sentences (Austin, Richards, and Jones, 2003). Incarceration has also proved once again to have little rehabilitative results on those sentenced to jail or prison.

DNA Testing

The revelations of wrongful convictions as demonstrated in high-profile cases, such as the 1989 New York City Central Park jogger incident, have questioned the rush to judgment attitude of some criminal justice systems (Huff, Rattner, and Sagarin, 1996). The incident involved a young white female investment banker who was brutally attacked and raped. Almost immediately, the police and prosecutors, who were later accused of being overzealous, arrested, charged, and convicted five Puerto Rican youths. They spent upward of five years in a New York State prison. In 2002, the actual perpetrator, who was doing time, confessed to the crime, and this was supported by DNA evidence that linked the real attacker/rapist, and the wrongfully convicted men were set free.

This incident and others have led to an increased willingness of judges and juries to consider DNA evidence and have convinced some governors in death penalty states to temporarily suspend this practice. DNA testing of individuals who are on death row (or in general population) can lead in some situations to the release of convicts who otherwise require constant monitoring and vigilance (Scheck, Neufeld, and Dwyer, 2000). It can also reduce the expenditure involved in putting a person to death. When you factor in not only the corrections cost, but also any expenses related to appeals, this could mean millions of dollars saved. Why is the criminal justice system not doing this in every case? DNA investigations are very resource intensive. There is a considerable amount of legal work in each of these situations, and many people are exonerated mainly through the pro bono work of criminal lawyers. These attorneys typically work for major law firms that, for public relations purposes, take on cases they believe have merit for reversal. As a result of the work of entities like the Innocence Project, led by well known defense attorney Barry Scheck, some governors have asked their sentencing commissions to review guidelines, to make recommendations for the shortening of sentences, for the release of convicted felons, for official moratoria, or for the elimination of the death penalty.

In all fairness, there is probably a happy medium (i.e., a realistic perspective) that lies between the extremes of optimism and pessimism. Nevertheless, outlining the complexities of what these could be as I have just done should help correctional planners, politicians, activists, and students get a sense of what the range of alternative possibilities can be.

FUTURE CHALLENGES

How much do current events affect corrections in the United States? This is a difficult question to answer. The future is ultimately unknown, but there are developments on the horizon that can and may affect our country's jails and prisons, particularly the kinds of people who may be incarcerated in America's correctional facilities.

Consequences of the War in Iraq

The United States' military and political efforts in Iraq and Afghanistan could have several effects. If and when the troops finally pull out, there is the strong likelihood that violent crime in the United States may increase. If the history of other conflicts is similar, after major wars domestic crimes in the United States typically increase. In particular, there have been significant periods in American history during which violent crime peaked, particularly after the Civil War, during Prohibition, the Great Depression, after World War II, and during the 1970s after the war in Vietnam (Monkkonen, 1981; Archer and Gartner, 1984; Gurr, 1989).

Future Causes of Crime

Crime has numerous causes. Around the world, small civil wars, population growth, natural disasters, conflicting values, and limited or unequal access to food, employment, and natural resources (through destruction and depletion) are prime motivators for mass migrations, refugee problems, and unaddressed grievances. Over time, these factors will place a greater burden on governments, and as we have learned, individuals and groups whose needs are not met may resort to crime as both protest and for survival. Indeed the future will bring new challenges to the criminal justice system like cybercrime and environmental crime, and eventually, the legal system will need to better deal with individuals and organizations who have committed these offences.

The Effects of 9/11

The terrorist attacks of 9/11 have had a dramatic effect on the practice of criminal justice in the United States. This reaction has been felt in the field of corrections, particularly through a lack of funding, which continues to be one of the most important problems. More money has been spent on other branches of the criminal justice system and on homeland security (not to mention the war in Iraq), and corrections has come up short. The corrections field is always trying to do more with less. This includes keeping costs low by outsourcing and constantly renegotiating contracts. The new set of domestic terrorism laws embedded in the PATRIOT Act has already resulted in an increase in Middle Eastern males and Muslims entering the criminal justice system. The corrections profession may also suffer from a tendency to profile members of certain ethnic groups (especially Arabic and Muslim males), and many will undoubtedly be sent to maximum-security facilities.

But after the events of 9/11, the passage of the PATRIOT Act, and the creation of the Department of Homeland Security, in a strictly economic sense, there should be an increase in the number of individuals being sent to jail and prison. Simply stated, it means that law enforcement will now be stopping, questioning, searching, and arresting more people. And the likelihood that the police will discover some sort of criminal law violation will increase. These unlucky individuals will share the already crowded jails and prisons throughout our states and at the federal level. Some have been imprisoned in places like Guantanamo Bay, while others have been held in military brigs or Supermax prisons.

SOLUTIONS TO DEALING WITH CURRENT CHALLENGES

The future is ultimately unpredictable, and coming up with appropriate solutions is not easy. After reading this book the student should understand that a number of current approaches will not help. Poorly thought-out or designed policies or technological fixes, like facial recognition systems derived from biometric screening, will probably not help much in deterring or detecting possible criminals. There are still too many problems with these tools to make them as useful as their inventors currently claim they are. Similarly, target hardening will not deter the most dedicated individuals from committing crimes.

What is going to win the day in the fight against crime and the appropriate use and management of jails and prisons? Clearly, a multipronged approach is most beneficial, some of which is reviewed below.

International resolutions. A catalyst for speeding up the process of change might include resolutions (backed up by sanctions) passed by international government bodies such as the Council of Europe, or the United Nations Human Rights Committee. Alternatively, federalization (e.g., consent decrees) or the threat of this process may at least temporarily improve the level of safety and services in correctional facilities.

Demands for more accountability. Perhaps the recent revelations of abuse that took place in Iraq's infamous Abu Ghraib prison (Hersh, 2004) will force Americans to demand more accountability, along with institutional and programmatic changes—not only in the foreign detention centers they operate but also in those at home. In many respects some have argued that the National Commission on Safety and Abuse in Prisons (2005–2006) was a direct outgrowth of this incident.

More transparency. More transparency has to occur. Increased and regular inspections of correctional institutions by outside parties like the media, scholars, and politicians needs to happen. Too often, inspections are simply public relations gestures, designed to pacify a less-than-informed public and politicians.

Increased resources. More money needs to be spent specifically on rehabilitative programs that have been proved to reduce recidivism. Once the jail and prison populations come down to a manageable size, COs should be encouraged, through educational and salary incentives, to switch from their current roles—in which they basically function as parking lot and hotel attendants—to becoming true "Rehabilitation Officers," implementing and managing meaningful rehabilitation programs. This also means hiring more individuals whose sole purpose would be to rehabilitate convicts. Additional funding would also make the profession more attractive in terms of salary and benefits.

Sentencing reform. In an effort to minimize prisoner despair and reinforce the focus on rehabilitation, legislators should work hard to pass discretionary sentencing and indeterminate sentences for most if not all felonies. Although this approach has its downsides, the merits override the drawbacks. Over the past decade, the number of people sentenced to life in prison has doubled. This kind of sanction has contributed to the overcrowded conditions in American jails and prisons.

According to a relatively recent *New York Times* survey (Liptak, 2005), about one in ten prisoners in the United States is doing a life sentence. Most "lifers" are behind bars because they have been convicted of crimes other than murder, burglary, and drug-related offences. This would be fine if there was some hope of eventual release, but only about 30 percent of lifers have the possibility of parole. What has caused this surge of sentencing individuals to life without parole? Part of the reason can be traced to the reluctance of judges to hand down death penalties, because of both the recent exonerations based on DNA evidence and the growing strength of the anti-death penalty lobby. Surely, it is important that lawyers counsel their clients to plead to charges where life without parole is the better alternative to the death penalty. But why is it that so many lifers remain behind bars even if there is a possibility of parole? In short, parole boards are reluctant to grant these individuals parole and governors have cut back on the number of individuals to whom they have granted clemency. Over the past ten years, because of the horror stories connected to individuals who were granted parole and then committed heinous crimes (e.g., the incidents which led up to the passage of Aimee's Law), governors seeking reelection or wanting to leave the office with an untarnished record have been hesitant to use this power to their advantage.

It must be understood that, for one reason or another, some people who are given a criminal sanction do change, while others—no matter how long the sentence or how severe the punishment—may never mend their ways. Moreover, as individuals age and mature, they present less of a threat to society. Notwithstanding, over the past two decades, our state and federal prison populations have grown at exponential rates. This makes it difficult to implement rehabilitative programs. It also means that the job of a correctional officer (CO) is more dangerous. A recent study by the Sentencing Project, based in Washington, D.C., concluded that the recidivism rate for lifers is considerably lower than that for the average person who is released from jail or prison. Thus, policies and practices in connection with life sentences should be reexamined. Parole boards and sentencing commissions must reexamine the purpose, intent, and effects of life sentences and governors should begin reviewing cases for executive clemency, particularly for cases that deserve merit.

INDIVIDUAL LEVEL

In order to comprehensively combat crime, we must deal with the social and emotional health of prisoners and their families, correctional personnel, and victims. This means investing a greater amount of resources into improving children's lives including Head Start and after-school programs that emphasize prosocial activities like creative (e.g., art and music) or physical (e.g., sports) pursuits. Society should also heavily invest in parenting skills and mentorship programs.

COMMUNITY LEVEL

The government must also provide more infrastructure in poorer neighborhoods, including safe parks, playgrounds, and schools. There must also be better training of criminal justice personnel to be more than law enforcers and adopt more of a social work approach. Daycare workers and public school teachers should be better trained and paid and not treat their job as simply a paycheck. Some people commit crimes because it is a cry for help or they need more attention. Free counseling by competent therapists should be provided to all who need it, and our society should work to reduce or eliminate the stigma related to participating in counseling.

ORGANIZATIONAL LEVEL[1]

We can reduce prison populations by transferring many nonviolent inmates to community corrections programs. Traditionally, this has meant probation or parole. But, more recently, these programs have also come to rely on EM devices, house arrest, chemical castration, and intensive supervision, all of which have generally proved to keep inmates in check. In December 2003, for example, in order to deal with budget deficits, Kentucky started releasing numerous short-timers (those with less than a year on their sentence) who had been convicted of nonviolent crimes. This action had minimal effect on recidivism rates (Richards, Austin, and Jones, 2004).

Once the jail and prison populations come down to a manageable size, COs should be encouraged through educational and monetary incentives, to become true "rehabilitation officers," implementing and managing meaningful rehabilitation programs rather than functioning as mere "hotel attendants." Prison systems should be rewarded for their ability to rehabilitate inmates, not for simply preventing inmates from escaping. State DOCs should be given more money if their released inmates prove to commit fewer crimes. This also presupposes that an accurate measure of rehabilitation can be settled on.

Of course, it must be understood that some individuals will never be appropriate for release into society. These people must be housed in secure facilities, but jails and prisons should really be reserved only for the most violent criminals.

Our correctional facilities should be smaller, too. Large jails and prisons are costly to run, unnecessarily bureaucratic, and impersonal. Cost–benefit analyses must be conducted in order to determine what kinds of savings can truly be achieved by increasing scale. Smaller physical structures go a long way in minimizing the alienation of prisoners and COs alike. The older facilities can be torn down, or alternative uses found for them like homeless shelters, or as tourist attractions for the public to see "the way things used to be."

Within the remaining prisons and jails, we need to rethink the way prisoners are housed. Older, more experienced prisoners typically prey on younger prisoners. This leads to both physical and sexual violence. Over time, younger prisoners become socialized to prison life (i.e., "prisonization"), making it more difficult for them to reenter society. Violent prisoners who have committed felonies should never be mixed with first-time offenders or people convicted of nonviolent crimes.

Over the past two centuries, American jails and prisons have adopted a fortress mentality. Wardens and correctional administrators should be more amenable to continuous inspection, and should even allow the public to take a regular look at what goes on behind bars. This may simultaneously serve as a deterrent against abuse of inmates, and might help "scare straight" juveniles at risk of a life of crime, providing them with a wake-up call to mend their ways.[2]

LEGAL SYSTEM LEVEL

The legal system should be reformed. In particular, we should seriously consider legalizing many soft drugs or decriminalizing them, recognizing their use as a medical need rather than as a criminal activity. Hopefully this means that the prices will fall and be more affordable and be within the reach of those who use drugs; thus their proclivity to commit crimes to support their habits will decrease.

Additionally, we should ban the sale of personal handguns or at the very least tighten up restrictions on their use, and fight the powerful lobbies that support their manufacture, sale, and use. Laws about handgun use should be revised so that only police and the military carry a gun and no one else should be allowed to own or use one. Taking a page out of one of Chris Rock's (the comedian) stand-up routine as an alternative, the government should find a way to make bullets very expensive.

The federal government should also implement a "No Prisoner Left Behind" program, which requires state correctional departments to ensure that all prisoners pass their GEDs and complete one or more practical technical training courses. Moreover, community college and university education should be facilitated for any prisoner upon request. We know that most inmates have few marketable skills to rely on when they get out of jail or prison. It is incumbent on the correctional system to ensure that these individuals have at least a high school education, a trade, and/or a university education.

CONCLUSION

I began this book with an ambitious goal of outlining the most important problems and potential and realistic solutions facing the field of corrections. I also pointed out, where appropriate, that many of our "solutions" have had unintended consequences, have exacerbated existing difficulties, or have created new ones. This is only natural because corrections is a system, and tinkering with one aspect can be expected to have an effect somewhere else in the process. We also need to be cognizant of doing more with less. There are some changes taking place in a piecemeal fashion, but nothing radical is happening in the field of corrections. Hopefully, many of the suggestions outlined in this book will pave the way to meaningful reform and minimizing problems in corrections for the next decade and beyond.

Although crime creates a considerable amount of pain, heartache, controversy, and costs individuals, families, communities, governments, and corporations substantial resources, perhaps there is a tolerable level of crime with which a society can live (Durkheim, 1895/1982). For example, during the 1960s and 1970s, citizens in advanced industrialized countries were constantly reminded through the media, educators, and personal experience that street crime was increasing. This created a furor of public indignation and governmental responses that manifested in a "war on crime." While the rate of crime has increased and decreased in a cyclical fashion since those times, and the methods by which we gather and interpret crime data have been debated and improved, the crisis of *response* seems to have abated, or has been replaced by "the war on terrorism." Crime is disruptive to the normal functioning of the government's, businesses' and individuals' daily lives. However, policymakers and practitioners, as much as possible, need to avoid simplistic responses that can create a more dangerous environment or lead to needless expenditure of resources.

Hopefully, the methodology, analysis, and suggestions outlined in this book will allow us to minimize the pain and suffering caused by incarceration, the danger, frustration, and boredom faced by correctional workers, and convicts alike, and prevent researchers, policymakers, and practitioners from going down blind alleys. Needless to say, we must recognize that neither understanding the root causes of crime, nor locking up everyone who breaks the law will entirely eliminate illegal behavior. About the best we can do in this scenario is to use our power and knowledge to be informed, to seek out reliable information, and to question that which seems confusing or is based on faulty reasoning.

Although the aforementioned ideas are probably utopian in tone and objective, the amount and types of crime will not be impacted unless we engage in a radical rethinking of how we approach human relations. Unfortunately, this will probably not happen anytime soon.

Perhaps we can expect no more from research, policies and practices that are sponsored by bureaucracies that are exceptionally rule-bound, government with such limited vision, and legislators who cannot see past the next election. At best, the research will result in policy review that merely tinkers with how prisoners are treated and managed. And so it goes, across the country, millions of Americans live in cages, academics conduct studies that do little more than rearrange the deck chairs on the Titanic, state DOCs talk of policy reforms, jail and prison conditions worsen, and the taxpayers drown in red ink. Maybe it is time to close some correctional facilities and, instead of transferring the inmates, send them home to their families and communities, and spend those saved public dollars on economic and community development (Clear and Cadora, 2003). Researchers, policymakers, and prison activists clearly need to explore these wider contexts and implications and not be afraid of failure. Prison change often takes place as a result of some sort of crisis, including underfunded budgets, failed privatization programs like convict leasing, failures of segregation, and class action lawsuits. Let's not wait until the next major crisis for thoughtful change to occur.

Until American jails, prisons, and community corrections are reinvented in a proactive manner, and rationally thought-out policies and practices are implemented, especially those that have controlled for unintended consequences, the number of people wasting away behind the razor wire and high walls will continue to grow. They represent the worst of a failed system that foreigners constantly point to as a lack of American ingenuity.

In the end, researching and writing this book has been a journey of sorts. I do not expect every reader to agree will the evidence I marshaled, my interpretations, and conclusions; however, this book should be the beginning (and not the end) of a serious and thoughtful dialogue, one which is necessary and long overdue.

KEY TERMS

alienation
apathy
biometric screening
CompStat
cybercrime
deference to authority
DNA testing

graying prison population
Innocence Project
optimistic view
pendulum of politics
pessimistic view
target hardening

REVIEW QUESTIONS

PART 1: MULTIPLE-CHOICE QUESTIONS

1. When budgets are tight, on what issues do correctional institutions mainly focus?
   a. rehabilitation
   b. punishment
   c. protecting the community
   d. mediation
   e. none of the above

2. In the future, which of the following will continue to be problems with the correctional system in the United States?
   a. overcrowding
   b. classification of prisoners
   c. lack of adequate facilities
   d. all of the above
   e. none of the above

3. Which perspectives is probably the best for analyzing the future in the field of corrections?
   a. optimistic
   b. pessimistic
   c. rational
   d. mixed
   e. intermediate

PART 2: SHORT-ANSWER QUESTIONS

1. What is the pendulum of politics?
2. List six problems that will plague corrections in the future.
3. What is CompStat?

PART 3: ESSAY QUESTIONS

1. How does the pendulum of politics contribute to the difficulties in implementing changes in corrections?
2. What suggestion will probably not help corrections in the future and why?

NOTES

1. This section builds upon Ross (2006b).
2. As mentioned earlier the scared straight program had questionable findings (Finckenauer and Gavin, 1999). That is why I use the word *may* in this sentence.

Answers to Multiple-Choice Questions

Chapter 1: "What Is Corrections and What Are Its Problems?

1.	e	7.	a	13.	a
2.	b	8.	e	14.	c
3.	b	9.	a	15.	d
4.	b	10.	c	16.	b
5.	d	11.	c	17.	e
6.	c	12.	a	18.	e

Chapter 2: "Myths of Corrections"

1.	e	4.	c	7.	b
2.	a	5.	b	8.	d
3.	b	6.	e		

Chapter 3: "Misuse of Jails"

1.	d	10.	a	19.	e
2.	a	11.	c	20.	c
3.	d	12.	d	21.	b
4.	e	13.	b	22.	a
5.	c	14.	b	23.	d
6.	e	15.	d	24.	b
7.	d	16.	a	25.	c
8.	c	17.	e	26.	b
9.	d	18.	e		

Chapter 4: "Underfunding"

1.	d	5.	d	9.	b
2.	e	6.	b	10.	b
3.	d	7.	d	11.	d
4.	b	8.	a	12.	d

Chapter 5: "Prison Conditions"

1. a	5. a	9. c
2. d	6. e	10. d
3. b	7. a	
4. d	8. b	

Chapter 6: "Classification/Proper Assessment"

1. a	3. b	5. d
2. b	4. d	

Chapter 7: "Special Populations"

1. e	3. d
2. a	4. b

Chapter 8: "Rehabilitation"

1. b	4. b	7. d
2. c	5. d	8. b
3. b	6. d	9. c

Chapter 9: "Overburdened Community Corrections System"

1. d	5. b	9. a
2. d	6. d	10. d
3. e	7. c	11. c
4. d	8. e	

Chapter 10: "Crowding/Overcrowding"

1. b	3. b	5. d
2. c	4. a	

Chapter 11: "Hiring Standards, Requirements, Practices, and Training"

1. a	5. a	9. d
2. d	6. c	10. c
3. c	7. b	11. c
4. b	8. c	12. b

Chapter 12: "Working Conditions"

1. e	4. a	7. d
2. d	5. e	8. b
3. c	6. b	

Chapter 13: "Correctional Officer Deviance"

1. a	4. b	7. b
2. e	5. b	8. b
3. a	6. b	9. a

Chapter 14: "Officer Pay and Workload"

1.	b	4.	b	7.	b
2.	b	5.	b		
3.	b	6.	b		

Chapter 15: "Management and Administration"

1.	a	2.	d	3.	a

Chapter 16: "The Future of Corrections"

1.	c	2.	a	3.	c

Bibliography

ABBEY, EDWARD. 1975. *The Monkey Wrench Gang*. New York: Harper.

ABBOT, HENRY JACK. 1981. *In the Belly of the Beast*. New York: Random House.

ABU-JAMAL, MUMIA. 1996. *Live from Death Row*. New York: Avon Books.

ADAY, R. 1994. "Golden Years Behind Bars: Special Programs and Facilities for Elderly Inmates," *Federal Probation*, Vol. 58, No. 2, pp. 47–54.

ADLER, PATRICIA. 2005. *Constructions of Deviance*. Belmont, CA: Wadsworth.

ALLEMAN, TED. 2002. "Correctional Philosophies: Varying Ideologies of Punishment," in Rosemary Gido and Ted Alleman (eds.) *Turnstile Justice: Issues in American Corrections*. Upper Saddle, NJ: Prentice Hall, pp. 18–37.

ALLEN, HARRY and CLIFFORD E. SIMONSEN. 2001. *Corrections in America: An Introduction*. Ninth Edition. Upper Saddle, NJ: Prentice Hall.

American Correctional Association. 1993. *Gangs in Correctional Facilities: A National Assessment*. Washington, D.C.: U.S. Department of Justice.

American Correctional Association. 2004. "Correctional Officers: Survey Summary," *Corrections Compendium*, Vol. 29, No. 5, pp. 10–17.

Amnesty International. 2001. *Abuse of Women in Custody: Sexual Misconduct and Shackling of Pregnant Women*. New York: Amnesty International. www.amnestyusa.org/women/custody/ (accessed August 28, 2007).

ANDERSON, ELIJAH. 1980. *Streetwise: Race, Class, and Change in an Urban Community*. Chicago: University of Chicago Press.

ANDERSON, ELIJAH. 2000. *Code of the Street*. New York: W. W. Norton & Company.

ANDREWS, DON A. and JAMES BONTA. 2006. *The Psychology of Criminal Conduct*. Fourth Edition. Cincinnati, OH: Anderson/LexisNexis.

ANDREWS, D., A. ZINGER, R. D. HOGE, J. P. BONTA, P. GENDREAU, and F. T. CULLEN. 1990. "Does Correctional Treatment Work? A Clinically Relevant and Psychologically Informed Meta Analysis?" *Criminology*, Vol. 28, No. 3, pp. 369–404.

ANONYMOUS. 1989. "Corrections and the Media," *Corrections Today*, Vol. 51, February.

ANONYMOUS. 1992. "Prison Envelope Art: Imagery in Motion," *Artpaper*, Vol. 12, pp. 16–17.

ANONYMOUS. 1997. *America's Prisons: Opposing Viewpoints*. San Diego, CA: Greenhaven Press.

ANONYMOUS. 1998a. "Access Prisons," *The Quill*, Vol. 86, No. 4, p. 4.

ANONYMOUS. 1998b. "Freedom of Information," *The Quill*, Vol. 86, p. 29.

ANONYMOUS. 1998c. "Pot Noodle Uses Hard Cell in Latest TV Work," *Marketing*, January 22, p. 3.

ANONYMOUS. 1999. "Common Myths and Misconceptions About Prisons and Prison Life," www.patrickcrusade.org/myths.htm.

ARCHAMBEAULT, WILLIAM. 2003. "Soar Like an Eagle and Dive Like a Loon," in Jeffrey Ian Ross and Stephen C. Richards (eds.) *Convict Criminology*. Belmont, CA: Wadsworth, pp. 287–308.

ARCHAMBEAULT, WILLIAM. 2006. "Imprisonment and American Indian Medicine Ways: A Comparative Analysis of Conflicting Cultural Beliefs, Values, and Practices," in Jeffrey Ian Ross and Larry Gould (eds.) *Native Americans and the Criminal Justice System: Theoretical and Policy Perspectives*. Boulder, CO: Paradigm Publishers, pp. 143–160.

ARCHER, D. and R. GARTNER. 1984. *Violence and Crime in a Cross-National Perspective*. New Haven, CT: Yale University Press.

ARMSTRONG, GAYLENE STYVE, ANGELA R. GOVER, and DORRIS MACKENZIE. 2002. "The Development and Diversity of Correctional Boot Camps," in Rosemary Gido and Ted Alleman (eds.) *Turnstile Justice: Issues in American Corrections*. Upper Saddle, NJ: Prentice Hall, pp. 115–130.

ARRIGO, BRUCE (ed.). 1998. *Social Justice/Criminal Justice*. Belmont, CA: Wadsworth.

ARRIGO, BRUCE. 2005. "Mental Health," in Mary Bosworth (ed.) *Encyclopedia of Prisons & Correctional Facilities*. Thousand Oaks, CA: Sage Publications, pp. 593–596.

AUSTIN, JAMES. 1998. "The Limits of Prison Drug Treatment," *Corrections Management Quarterly*, Vol. 2, No. 4, pp. 66–74.

AUSTIN, JAMES. 2003. "The Use of Science to Justify the Imprisonment Binge," in Jeffrey Ian Ross and Stephen C. Richards (eds.) *Convict Criminology*. Belmont, CA: Wadsworth, pp. 17–36.

AUSTIN, JAMES, MARINO A. BRUCE, LEO CARROLL, PATRICIA L. MCCALL, and STEPHEN C. RICHARDS. 2001. "The Use of Incarceration in the United States," American Society of Criminology National Policy Committee. *Critical Criminology: An International Journal*, Vol. 10, No. 1, pp. 17–41.

AUSTIN, JAMES and JOHN IRWIN. 2001. *It's About Time*. Belmont, CA: Wadsworth.

AUSTIN, JAMES and BARRY KRISBERG. 1981. "Wider, Stronger and Different Nets: The Dialectics of Criminal Justice Reform," *Journal of Research on Crime and Delinquency*, Vol. 18, No. 1, pp. 165–196.

AUSTIN, JAMES, STEPHEN C. RICHARDS, and RICHARD S. JONES. 2003. "Prison Release in Kentucky: A Convict Perspective on Policy Recommendations," *Offender Programs Report*, Vol. 7, No. 1, pp. 1, 13–16.

BACA, JIMMY SANTIAGO. 2001. *A Place to Stand*. New York: Grove Press.

BARAK, GREGG. 1995. "Media, Crime and Justice: A Case for Constitutive Criminology," in Jeff Ferrell and Clinton R. Sanders (eds.) *Cultural Criminology*. Boston: Northeastern University Press, pp. 142–168.

BARAK-GLANTZ, ISRAEL. 1983. "Who's in the Hole?" *Criminal Justice Review*, Vol. 8, pp. 29–37.

BARTOLLAS, CLEMENS. 2002. *Invitation to Corrections*. Boston: Allyn & Bacon.

BAYENS, GEORGE, JIMMY J. WILLIAMS, and JOHN ORTIZ SMYKLA. 1997. "Jail Types Makes a Difference," *American Jails*, Vol. 11, No. 2, pp. 32–39.

BECK, ALLEN J. and LAURA M. MARUSCHAK. 2001. "Mental Health Treatment in State Prisons, 2000," *Bureau of Justice Statistics*, NCJ 188215.

BECKETT, KATHERINE and THEODORE SASSON. 2003. *The Politics of Injustice*. Second Edition. Thousand Oaks, CA: Sage Publications.

BELKNAP, J. 1995. "Women in Conflict: An Analysis of Women Correctional Officers," in Barbara R. Price and Natalie J. Sokoloff (eds.) *The Criminal Justice System and Women: Offenders, Victims and Workers*. Second Edition. New York: McGraw-Hill, pp. 195–227.

Bell v. Wolfish 441 U.S. 520 (1979).

BELLIN, E. Y., D. D. FLETCHER, and S. M. SAFER. 1993. "Association of Tuberculosis Infection with Increased time in or Admission to the New York City Jail System," *Journal of the American Medical Association*, Vol. 269, No. 17, pp. 2228–2231.

BENDER, DAVID. 1997. *America's Prisons: Opposing Viewpoints*. San Diego, CA: Greenhaven Press.

BERGER, PETER and THOMAS LUCKMANN. 1966. *The Social Construction of Reality*. New York: Anchor.

BERK, RICHARD A., HEATHER LADD, HEIDI GRAZIANO, and JONG-HO BAEK. 2003. "A Randomized Experiment Testing Inmate Classification Systems," *Criminology & Public Policy*, Vol. 2, No. 2, pp. 215–242.

BLAKELY, CURTIS R. 2003. "Innovations in Prison and Inmate Classification: Gill Revisited," *The Prison Service Journal*, March, pp. 6–9.

BLAKELY, CURTIS R. 2004a. "Prison Privatization and Neo-Liberalism: Ill-Effects for the Poor and Minority?" *The Prison Service Journal*, January, pp. 23–25.

BLAKELY, CURTIS R. 2004b. "Private and State Run US Prisons Compared," *Probation Journal*, Vol. 51, No. 3, pp. 254–256.

BLAKELY, CURTIS R. and VIC BUMPHUS. 2005. "An Analysis of Civil Suits Filed Against Private and Public Prisons: A Comparison of Title 42: Section 1983 Litigation Filed Against Both Private and Public Prison Sectors since 1992," *Probation Journal*, Vol. 52, No. 1, pp. 6–75.

BLUMSTEIN, A., J. COHEN, S. MORITA, and D. NAGIN. 1981. "On Testing the Stability of Punishment Hypothesis: A Reply," *Journal of Criminal Law and Criminology*, Vol. 72, pp. 1799–1808.

BLUMSTEIN, A., J. COHEN, and D. NAGIN. 1977. "The Dynamics of a Homeostatic Punishment Process," *Journal of Criminal Law and Criminology*, Vol. 67, pp. 317–334.

BOHM, ROBERT M. 2003. *Deathquest II: An Introduction to the Theory and Practice of Capital Punishment in the United States*. Second Edition. Cincinnati, OH: Anderson.

BOTTOMS, ANTHONY E. 1999. "Interpersonal Violence and Social Order in Prisons," in Michael Tonry and Joan Petersilia (eds.) *Prisons*. Chicago: University of Chicago Press, Vol. 26, pp. 205–281.

BOURGOIS, PHILPPE. 2002. *In Search of Respect: Selling Crack in El Barrio*. Second Edition. New York: Cambridge University Press.

BOWKER, LEE H. 1978. *Prison Subcultures*. Lexington, MA: Lexington Books.

BOWKER, LEE H. 1980. *Prison Victimization*. New York: Elsevier Science.

BRAITHWAITE, JOHN. 1989. *Crime, Shame and Reintegration*. Cambridge: Cambridge University Press.

BRATTON, WILLIAM. 1998. *The Turnaround: How America's Top Cop Reversed the Crime Epidemic*. New York: Random House.

BRIGGS, CHAD S., JODY L. SUNDT, and THOMAS C. CASTELLANO. 2003. "The Effect of Supermaximum Security Prisons on Aggregate Levels of Institutional Violence," *Criminology*, Vol. 41, No. 4, pp. 1341–1376.

BRITTON, D. 1997. "Perceptions of the Work Environment Among Correctional Officers: Do Race and Sex Matter?" *Criminology*, Vol. 35, No. 1, pp. 85–105.

BRODER, JOHN M. 2003. "No Hard Time for Prison Budgets," *New York Times*, January 19, p. 5.

BRODSKY, C. M. 1982. "Work Stress in Correctional Institutions," *Journal of Prison Jail Health*, Vol. 2, No. 2, pp. 74–102.

BROWN, J. R. 2002. "Drug Diversion Courts: Are They Needed and Will They Succeed in Breaking the Cycle of Drug-Related Crime?" in L. Stolzenberg and S. J. D'Alessio (eds.) *Criminal Courts for the 21st Century*. Second Edition. Upper Saddle, NJ: Prentice Hall, pp. 5–37.

BROWN, P. 1986. "Probation Officer Burnout," *Federal Probation*, Vol. 50, No. 1, pp. 4–7.

BROWNSTEIN, HENRY. 1995. "The Media and the Construction of Random Drug Violence," in Jeff Ferrell and Clinton R. Sanders (eds.) *Cultural Criminology*. Boston: Northeastern University Press, pp. 45–65.

BRUTON, JIM. 2004. *The Big House: Life Inside a Supermax Security Prison*. Minneapolis, MN: Voyageur Press.

BUENTELLO, SAM and R. S. FONG. 1991. "The Detection of Prison Gang Development: An Empirical Assessment," *Federal Probation*, Vol. 55, pp. 66–69.

BURKE, T. W., E. RIZZO, and C. E. O'REAR. 1992. "Do Officers Need College Degrees," *Corrections Today*, Vol. 54, pp. 174–176.

BYNUM, TIM. 1982. "Release on Recognizance: Substantive or Superficial Reform," *Criminology*, Vol. 20, pp. 67–82.

BYRNE, JAMES, FAYE TAXMAN, and DON HUMMER. 2005. "Examining the Impact of Institutional Culture (and Cultural Change) on Prison Violence and Disorder: A Review of the Evidence on Both Causes and Solutions." Paper presented at the 14th World Congress of Criminology, Philadelphia, August 11.

CAMP, G. and C. CAMP. 1985. *Prison Gangs: Their Extent, Nature, and Impact in Prisons*. Washington, D.C.: U.S. Department of Justice.

CAMP, GRAHAM and GEORGE CAMP. 1999. *Corrections Yearbook 1999*. Middletown, CT: Criminal Justice Institute.

CAMP, C. G., G. CAMP, and B. MAY. 2003. *The 2002 Corrections Yearbook*. Middletown, CT: Criminal Justice Institute.

CAMP, S. D., W. G. SAYLOR, and K. N. WRIGHT. 2001. "Racial Diversity of correctional workers and inmates: Organizational Commitment, Teamwork and Workers' Efficiency in Prisons," *Justice Quarterly*, Vol. 18, No. 2, pp. 411–427.

CAMPBELL, CURTIS, CANDACE MCCOY, and CHIMEZIE A. B. OSIGWEH. 1990. "The Influence of Probation Recommendations on Sentencing Decisions and Their Predictive Accuracy," *Federal Probation*, Vol. 54, pp. 13–20.

CARLSON, JOSEPH R., RICHARD H. ANSON, and GEORGE THOMAS. 2003. "Correctional Officer Burnout and Stress: Does Gender Matter? *The Prison Journal*, Vol. 83, No. 3, pp. 277–288.

CARROLL, LEO. 1988. *Hacks, Blacks, and Cons: Race Relations in a Maximum Security Prison*. Prospect Heights, IL: Waveland Press.

CAUCHON, DENNIS. 1994. "The Alcatraz of the Rockies," *USA Today*, November 16, p. 6A.

CHAMPION, DEAN J. 1999. *Probation, Parole, and Community Corrections*. Third Edition. Upper Saddle River, NJ: Prentice Hall.

CHAMPION, DEAN J. 2002. *Probation, Parole, and Community Corrections*. Fourth Edition. Upper Saddle River, NJ: Prentice Hall.

CHAMPION, DEAN J. 2004. *Corrections in the United States: A Contemporary Perspective*. Fourth Edition. Upper Saddle, NJ: Prentice Hall.

CHAMPION, DEAN J. 2005. *Corrections in the United States: Contemporary Perspectives*. Fourth Edition. Upper Saddle River, NJ: Prentice Hall.

CHEATWOOD, DARRYL. 1998. "Prison Movies: Films About Adult, Male, Civilian Prisons: 1929–1995," in Frankie Bayley and Donna Hale (eds.) *Popular Culture, Crime & Justice*. Belmont, CA: Wadsworth, pp. 209–231.

CHEEK, F. E. 1984. *Stress Management for Correctional Officers and Their Families*. College Park, MD: American Correctional Association.

CHEEK, F. E. and M. D. S. MILLER. 1983. "The Experience of Stress for Corrections Officers: A Double-Blind Theory of Correctional Stress," *Journal of Criminal Justice*, Vol. 11, No. 2, pp. 105–120.

CHERKIS, JASON. 2007. "Hard Time: Federal Judge Slams the District for Overdetaining Inmates," *Washington City Paper*, April 6, pp. 6–7.

CHERMACK, STEPHEN. 1998. "Police, Courts, Corrections in the Media," in Frankie Bailey and Donna Hale (eds.) *Popular Culture, Crime and Justice*. Belmont, CA: Wadsworth, pp. 87–99.

CHILTON, BRADLEY S. 1991. *Prisons Under the Gavel: The Federal Takeover of Georgia Prisons*. Columbus: Ohio State University Press.

CHRISTIAN, J. 1999. *Conflict Resolution and Conflict Management in Corrections*. Lanham, MD: American Correctional Association.

CHRISTIANSON, SCOTT. 2004. *Innocent: Inside Wrongful Conviction Cases*. New York: New York University Press.

CHRISTIE, NILS. 1993. *Crime Control as Industry*. London: Routledge.

CLEAR, TODD. 1994. *Harm in American Penology*. Albany: State University of New York Press.

CLEAR, TODD. 2001. "Ten Unintended Consequences of the Growth in Imprisonment," in E. J. Latessa, A. Holsinger, J. W. Marquart, and J. R. Sorensen (eds.) *Correctional Contexts: Contemporary and Classical Readings*. Los Angeles: Roxbury Publishing Company, pp. 497–505.

CLEAR, TODD and ERIC CADORA. 2003. *Community Justice*. Belmont, CA: Wadsworth.

CLEM, CONNIE. 2003. "Results of Data Analysis: NIC Needs Assessment on Correctional Management and Executive Leadership Development," *National Institute of Corrections*, www.nicic.org/library/018898 (accessed August 15, 2007).

CLEMMER, DONALD. 1958. *The Prison Community*. New York: Holt, Rinehart.

COHEN, JACQUELINE. 1983. "Incapacitating Criminals: Recent Research Findings," *Research in Brief*. Washington, D.C.: National Institute of Justice.

COHEN, LAURIE P. 2006a. "A Law's Fallout: Women in Prison Fight for Custody," *Wall Street Journal*, February 27, p. 1.

COHEN, LAURIE P. 2006b. "U.S. Custody Law Is the Exception," *Wall Street Journal*, February 27.

COHEN, STAN. 1985. *Visions of Social Control: Crime, Punishment and Classification*. Cambridge: Polity Press.

COHEN, A. K., G. F. COLE, and R. G. BAILEY. 1976. *Prison Violence*. Lexington, MA: Lexington Books.

COLE, GEORGE. 1994. *The American Criminal Justice System*. Belmont, CA: Wasdworth.

COLE, GEORGE. 1995. *The American System of Criminal Justice*. Seventh Edition. Belmont, CA: Wadsworth.

COLEMAN, R. J. 1998. "A Cooperative Corrections Arrangement: A Blueprint for Criminal Justice in the 21st Century," *Corrections Now*, Vol. 3, No. 1, p. 1.

COLVIN, MARK. 1992. *From Accommodation to Riot: The Penitentiary of New Mexico in Crisis*. Albany: State University of New York Press.

CONOVER, TED. 2001. *Newjack: Guarding Sing Sing*. New York: Vintage Books.

CONVERSE, PHILIP. 1964. "The Nature of Belief Systems in Mass Publics," in David Apter (ed.) *Ideology and Discontent*. New York: Free Press, pp. 206–261.

COOLEY, DENNIS. 1993. "Criminal Victimization in Male Federal Prisons," *Canadian Journal of Criminology*, Vol. 35, pp. 479–495.

CORBET, RONALD and GARY T. MARX. 1991. "Critique: No Soul in the New Machine: Technofallacies in the Electronic Monitoring Movement," *Justice Quarterly*, Vol. 8, No. 3, pp. 399–414.

COYLE, ANDREW. 2003. *Humanity in Prison. Questions of Definition and Audit*. London: International Centre for Prison Studies.

CRAWLEY, ELAINE. 2005. "Institutional Thoughtlessness in Prisons and Its impacts on the Day-to-Day Lives of Elderly Men," *Journal of Contemporary Criminal Justice*, Vol. 21, No. 4, pp. 350–363.

CROMWELL, PAUL F., ROLANDO V. DEL CARMEN, and LEANNE F. ALAIRD. 2002. *Community-Based Corrections.* Belmont, CA: Wadsworth.

CROUCH, BEN. 1991. "Guard Word in Transition," in Kenneth C. Haas and Geoffrey P. Alpert (eds.) *The Dilemmas of Corrections: Contemporary Readings.* Second Edition. Prospect Heights, IL: Waveland.

CROUCH, BEN M. and JAMES W. MARQUART. 1980. "On Becoming a Prison Guard," in B. M. Crouch (ed.) *The Keepers: Prison Guards and Contemporary Corrections.* Springfield, IL: W. I. Thomas, pp. 63–106.

CROWTHER, BRUCE. 1989. *Captured on Film: The Prison Movie.* London: B. T. Batsford.

CULLEN, FRANCIS T. 2002. "Rehabilitation and Treatment Programs," in James Q. Wilson and Joan Petersilia (eds.) *Crime: Public Policies for Crime Control.* Second Edition. Oakland, CA: ICS Press, pp. 253–289.

CULLEN, FRANCIS. 2006. "It's Time to Reaffirm Rehabilitation," *Criminology & Public Policy,* Vol. 5, No. 4, pp. 665–672.

CULLEN, FRANCIS, J. CULLEN, and J. WOZNIAK. 1988. "Is Rehabilitation Dead? The Myth of the Punitive Public," *Journal of Criminal Justice,* Vol. 16, pp. 303–317.

CULLEN, FRANCIS T., BONNIE S. FISHER, and BRANDON K. APPLEGATE. 2000. "Public Opinion About Punishment and Corrections," *Crime and Justice,* Vol. 27, pp. 1–79.

CULLEN, FRANCIS T. and PAUL GENDREAU. 1989. "The Effectiveness of Correctional Rehabilitation: Reconsidering the 'Nothing Works' Debate," in Lynne Goodstein and Doris MacKenzie (eds.) *American Prisons: Issues in Research and Policy.* New York: Plenum Publishing Company, pp. 23–44.

CULLEN, FRANCIS T. and PAUL GENDREAU. 2000. "Assessing Correctional Rehabilitation: Policy, Practice, and Prospects," in Julie Horney (ed.) *Criminal Justice 2000: Volume 3 Policies, Processes, and Decisions of the Criminal Justice System.* Washington, D.C.: U.S. Department of Justice, National Institute of Justice, pp. 109–175.

CULLEN, FRANCIS and K. E. GILBERT. 1982. *Reaffirming Rehabilitation.* Cincinnati, OH: Anderson Publishing.

CULLEN, FRANCIS, E. J. LATESSA, V. S. BURTON, and L. X. LOMBARDO. 1993a. "Correctional Orientation of Prison Wardens: Is the Rehabilitation Ideal Supported?" *Criminology,* Vol. 31, No. 1, pp. 69–92.

CULLEN, FRANCIS, E. LATESSA, R. KOPACHE, L. LOMBARDO, and V. BURTON. 1993b. "Prison Warden Job Satisfaction," *The Prison Journal,* Vol. 73, No. 2, pp. 141–161.

CULLEN, FRANCIS, B. LINK, N. WOLFE, and J. FRANK. 1985. "The Social Dimensions of Correctional Officer Stress," *Justice Quarterly,* Vol. 2, No. 4, pp. 505–533.

CZAJKOSKI, EUGENE H. 1973. "Exposing the Quasi-Judicial Role of the Probation Officer," *Federal Probation,* Vol. 37, pp. 9–13.

DAVIS, CHARLES N. 1988 or 1998. "Access to Prisons," *The Quill,* Vol. 86, pp. 19–29.

DAVIS, RYAN. 2005. "At Jail, a 'Systems Overload,' " *Baltimore Sun,* April 21.

DAVIS, M. S. and D. J. FLANNERY. 2002. "The Institutional Treatment of Gang Members," *Correctional Management Quarterly,* Vol. 5, No. 1, pp. 37–46.

Delancey Street Foundation. www.eisenhowerfoundation.org/grassroots/delancey/index.html (accessed August 15, 2007).

DENNIS, NORMAN (ed.). 1997. *Zero Tolerance: Policing in a Free Society.* London: IEA Health and Welfare Unit.

DIIULIO, JOHN D. 1988. "What's Wrong with Private Prisons," *The Public Interest,* No. 92, Summer, pp. 66–83.

DIIULIO, JOHN J. 1987. *Governing Prisons.* New York: Free Press.

DITTON, PAULA M. 1999. "Mental Health and Treatment of Inmates and Probationers," *Bureau of Justice Statistics*, NCJ 174463.

DOMURAND, FRANK. 2000. "Who is Killing Our Probation Officers: The Performance Crisis in Community Corrections," *Corrections Management Quarterly*, Vol. 4, No. 2, pp. 41–51.

DOW, MARK. 2004. *American Gulag*. Berkeley: University of California Press.

DOWKER, FAY and GLEN GOOD. 1993. "The Proliferation of Control Unit Prisons in the United States," *Journal of Prisoners on Prisons*, Vol. 4, pp. 95–110.

DUNCAN, MARTHA GRACE. 1996. *Romantic Outlaws, Beloved Prisons*. New York: New York University Press.

DURHAM, ALEXIS M., III. 1993. "The Future of Correctional Privatization: Lessons from the Past," in G. Bowman, S. Hakim, and P. Seidenstat (eds.) *Privatizing Correctional Institutions*. New Brunswick, NJ: Transaction Publishers, pp. 33–50.

DURKHEIM, EMILE. 1895/1982. *The Rules of the Sociological Method*. Translated by W. D. Halls. New York: Free Press.

DYER, JOEL. 1999. *The Perpetual Incarceration Machine: How America Profits from Crime*. Boulder, CO: Westview Press.

ELLESWORTH, THOMAS (ed.). 1996. *Contemporary Community Corrections*. Second Edition. Prospect Heights, IL: Waveland Press.

ELROD, PRESTON and MICHAEL T. BROOKS. 2003. "I Mean You Ain't Really Learning Nothing [Productive]," in Jeffrey Ian Ross and Stephen C. Richards (eds.) *Convict Criminology*. Belmont, CA: Wadsworth, pp. 325–346.

Estelle v. Gamble 429 U.S. 97 (1976).

EVANS, MALCOLM and ROD MORGAN. 1998. *Preventing Torture: A Study of the European Convention for the Prevention of Torture and Inhumane or Degrading Treatment or Punishment*. London: Oxford University Press.

FABELO, TONY. 1997. "The Critical Role of Policy Research in Developing Effective Correctional Policies," *Corrections Management Quarterly*, Vol. 1, No. 1, pp. 25–31.

FABELO, TONY. 2000. "Technocorrections: The Promises, the Uncertain Threats," *Sentencing and Corrections: Issues for the 21st Century*. Washington, D.C.: U.S. Department of Justice.

FAITH, KARLENE. 1997. "Media, Myths and Masculinization: Images of Women in Prison," in Ellen Adelberg and Claudia Currie (eds.) *Too Few to Count: Canadian Women in Conflict with the Law*. Vancouver, BC: Press Gang Publishers, pp. 181–219.

FARKAS, MARY ANN. 1990. "Professionalization: Is It the Cure-All for What 'Ails' the Corrections Officer," *Journal of Crime and Justice*, Vol. 13, No. 2, pp. 29–54.

FARKAS, MARY ANN. 1999. "Correctional Officer Attitudes Toward Inmates and Working with Inmates in a 'Get Tough' Era," *Journal of Criminal Justice*, Vol. 27, No. 6, pp. 495–506.

FEELEY, MALCOLM M. 2002. "Entrepreneurs of Punishment: The Legacy of Privatization," *Punishment & Society*, Vol. 4, No. 3, pp. 321–344.

FEELEY, MALCOLM M. and JONATHAN SIMON. 1992. "The New Penology: Notes on the Emerging Strategy of Corrections and Its Implications," *Criminology*, Vol. 30, No. 4, pp. 449–474.

FEELEY, MALCOLM M. and VAN SWEARINGEN. 2004. "The Prison Conditions Cases and the Bureaucratization of American Corrections: Influences, Impacts and Implications," *Pace Law Review*, Vol. 24, No. 2, pp. 433–476.

FERRELL, JEFF. 1993. *Crimes of Style*. Boston: Northeastern University Press.

FERRELL, JEFF and CLINTON R. SANDERS (eds.). 1995. *Cultural Criminology*. Boston: Northeastern University Press.

FINCKENAUER, JAMES O. and PATRICIA W. GAVIN. 1999. *Scared Straight: The Panacea Phenomenon Revisited*. Springfield, IL: Waveland Press.

FINN, M. and S. MUIRHEAD-STEVES. 2002. "Effectiveness of Electronic Monitoring with Violent Male Parolees," *Justice Quarterly*, Vol. 19, pp. 293–312.

FINN, PETER. 2000. *Addressing Correctional Officer Stress: Programs and Strategies.* Washington, D.C.: U.S. Department of Justice Programs.

FINN, PETER and SARAH KUCK. 2005. "Stress Among Probation and Parole Officers and What Can Be Done About It," *National Institute of Justice, Research in Practice*, June, NCJ 205620.

FINN, PETER and JULIE ESSELMAN TOMZ. 1996. *Developing a Law Enforcement Stress Program for Officers and Their Families.* U.S. Department of Justice. NCJ 163175.

FISHER-GIORLANDO, MARIANNE. 1987. "Prison Culture: Using Music as Data," Ph.D. Dissertation, Ohio State University.

FISHER-GIORLANDO, MARIANNE. 2003. "Why I Study Prisons: My Twenty-Year Personal and Professional Odyssey and an Understanding of Southern Prisons," in Jeffrey Ian Ross and Stephen C. Richards (eds.) *Convict Criminology*. Belmont, CA: Wadsworth, pp. 59–76.

FLANAGAN, TIMOTHY J. FLANAGAN and SUSAN L. CAULFIELD. 1984. "Public Opinion and Prison Policy: A Review," *The Prison Journal*, Vol. 64, No. 2, 31–46.

FLEISHER, MARK S. 1989. *Warehousing Violence*. Newbury Park, CA: Sage Publications.

FLEISHER, MARK S. 1996. "Management Assessment and Policy Dissemination in Federal Prisons," *Prison Journal*, Vol. 76, No. 1, pp. 81–92.

FLEISHER, MARK S. 1997. "Health Care in the Federal Bureau of Prisons," in J. M. Marquart and J. R. Stevenson (eds.) *Correctional Contexts: Contemporary and Classical Readings.* Los Angeles: Roxbury Press, pp. 327–334.

FLYNN, E. E. 1992. "The Graying of America's Prison Population," *Prison Journal*, Vol. 72, Nos. 1 and 2, pp. 77–98.

FONG, ROBERT and RONALD E. VOGEL. 1992. "Prison Gang Dynamics: A Look Inside the Texas Department of Corrections," in P. J. Benekos and A. V. Merlo (eds.) *Corrections: Dilemmas and Directions.* Cincinnati, OH: Anderson Publishing, pp. 57–78.

FORD, MARILYN CHANDLER and FRANCIS T. MOORE. 1992. "Fiscal Challenges Facing Local Correctional Facilities," in Peter Benekos and Alida V. Merlo (eds.) *Corrections: Dilemmas and Directions.* Cincinnati, OH: Anderson Publishing, pp. 1–22.

FOUCAULT, MICHEL. 1977. *Discipline and Punish: The Birth of the Prison.* New York: Vintage Books.

FRANKLIN, H. Bruce. 1978. *The Victim as Criminal and Artist.* New York: Oxford University Press.

FRANKLIN, H. Bruce. 1982. *Prison Literature in America: The Victim as Criminal and Artist.* Westport, CT: Lawrence Hill and Company.

FRANKLIN, RICHARD H. 1998. "Assessing Supermax Operations," *Corrections Today*, Vol. 60, pp. 126–128.

FREEMAN, ROBERT M. 1998. "Public Perception and Corrections: Correctional Officers as Smug Hacks," in Frankie Bailey and Donna Hale (eds.) *Popular Culture, Crime & Justice.* Belmont, CA: Wadsworth, pp. 196–208.

FREEMAN, ROBERT M. 1999. *Popular Culture and Corrections.* Latham, MD: American Correctional Association.

FREEMAN, ROBERT. 2000. Burlington, MA: *Correctional Organization and Management* Butterworth–Heinemann.

FRY, L. and W. FREEZE. 1992. "Bringing the Convict Back In: An Ecological Approach to Inmate Adaptations," *Journal of Criminal Justice*, Vol. 20, No. 4, pp. 355–365.

GAES, GERALD G. and SCOTT D. Camp. 2004. *Measuring Prison Performance: Government Privatization and Accountability.* Walnut Creek, CA: Alta Mira Press.

GARLAND, GREG. 2005. "Contraband Floods Maryland Prisons: Officials Struggle to Stem Inflow of Drugs, Tobacco," *Baltimore Sun*, July 6.

GASTON, A. 1996. "Controlling Gangs Through Teamwork and Technology," *Large Jail Network Bulletin*. Washington, D.C.: U.S. Department of Justice, National Institute of Corrections.

GENDREAU, PAUL and JAMES BONTA. 1984. "Solitary Confinement is Not Cruel and Unusual Punishment: People Sometimes Are!" *Canadian Journal of Criminology*, Vol. 26, pp. 467–478.

General Accounting Office. 2005. *Adult Drug Courts: Evidence Indicates Recidivism Reductions and Mixed Results for Other Outcomes*. Washington, D.C.: General Accounting Office.

GERBER, J. and E. J. FRITSCH. 1994. "The Effects of Academic and Vocational Program Participation on Inmate Misconduct and Reincarceration," *Prison Education Research Report: Final Report*. Huntsville, TX: Sam Houston State University.

GERBER, J. and E. J. FRITSCH. 2001. "Adult Academic and Vocational Correctional Programs: A Review of Recent Research," in E. J. Latessa, A. Holsinger, J. W. Marquart, and J. R. Sorensen (eds.) *Correctional Contexts: Contemporary and Classical Readings*. Second Edition. Los Angeles: Roxbury Publishing Company, pp. 268–290.

GIDO, ROSEMARY L. and TED ALLEMAN (eds.). 2002. *Turnstile Justice: Issues in American Corrections*. Second Edition. Upper Saddle, NJ: Prentice Hall.

GILLIARD, D. 1999. *Prison and Jail Inmates at Midyear 1998 (BJS, USDOJ)*. Washington, D.C.: U.S. Department of Justice.

GLANTZ, LAUREN and THOMAS P. BONCZAR. 2006. "Probation and Parole in the United States, 2005," *Bureau of Justice Statistics*, NCJ 215091.

GLAZE, LAUREN E. and THOMAS P. BONCZAR. 2006. "Probation and Parole in the United States, 2005," *Bureau of Justice Statistics*, November, NCJ 215091.

GOFFMAN, ERVING. 1959. *The Presentation of Self in Everyday Life*. Garden City, NY: Doubleday.

GOFFMAN, ERVING. 1961. *Asylums: Essays on the Social Situation of Mental Patients and Other Inmates*. Garden City, NY: Doubleday.

GONDLES, JAMES A. 1999. "Foreword," in Robert M. Freeman (ed.) *Correctional Organization and Management*. Burlington, MA: Butterworth–Heinemann, p. v.

GRASSIAN, STUART. 1983. "Psychopathological Effects of Solitary Confinement," *American Journal of Psychiatry*, Vol. 140, pp. 1450–1454.

GRASSIAN, STUART and NANCY FRIEDMAN. 1986. "Effects of Sensory Deprivation in Psychiatric Seclusion and Solitary Confinement," *International Journal of Law and Psychiatry*, Vol. 8, pp. 49–65.

GREENBERG, DAVID. 1975. "The Incapacitative Effect of Imprisonment, Some Estimates," *Law and Society Review*, Vol. 9, pp. 541–580.

GREENE, DANA. 2005. "Abolition," in Mary Bosworth (ed.) *Encyclopedia of Prisons & Correctional Facilities*. Thousand Oaks, CA: Sage Publications, pp. 2–5.

GRODZINS, MORTON. 1956. *The Loyal and the Disloyal: Social Boundaries of Patriotism and Treason*. Chicago: University of Chicago Press.

GURR, TED ROBERT (ed.). 1989. *Violence in America, Vol. 1: The History of Crime*. Thousand Oaks, CA: Sage Publications.

HAGEDORN, J. 1988. *People and Folks: Gangs, Crime and Underclass in a Rustbelt City*. Chicago, IL: Lakeview.

HALL, ANDY. 1987. *Systemwide Strategies to Alleviate Jail Crowding*. Washington, D.C.: National Institute of Justice.

HALL, A., D. HENRY, J. PERLSTEIN, and W. F. SMITH. 1985. *Alleviating Jail Crowding: A Systems Perspective*. Washington, D.C.: National Institute of Justice.

HALLINAN, JOSEPH T. 2003. *Going Up the River*. New York: Random House.

HAMM, MARK S. 1995. *The Abandoned Ones: The Imprisonment and Uprising of the Mariel Boat People*. Boston: Northeastern University Press.

HAMM, MARK S. and JEFF FERRELL. 1994. "Rap, Cops, and Crime: Clarifying the Cop Killer Controversy," *ACJS Today*, Vol. 13, pp. 1, 3, 29.

HAMMETT, T. M., J. EPSTEIN, J. GROSS, M. SIFRE, and T. ENOR. 1995. *Update: HIV/AIDS and STDs in Correctional Facilities*. Washington, D.C.: Department of Justice, December.

HAMMETT, T., P. HARMON, and L. MARUSCHAK. 1999. *1996–1997 Update: HIV/AIDS, STDs, and TB in Correctional Facilities*. Washington, D.C.: National Institute of Justice.

HANEY, CRAIG. 1993. " 'Infamous' punishment: The Psychological Consequences of Isolation," *National Prison Project Journal*, Vol. 8, pp. 3–7, 21.

HANEY, CRAIG and M. LYNCH. 1997. "Regulating Prisons of the Future: A Psychological Analysis of Supermax and Solitary Confinement," *New York University Review of Law and Social Change*, Vol. 23, pp. 477–570.

HARRISON, PAIGE M. and ALLEN J. BECK. 2006. "Prisoners in 2005," *Bureau of Justice Statistics*, NCJ 215092.

HASSINE, VICTOR. 2002. "Prison Violence: From Where I Stand," in Rosemary Gido and Ted Alleman (eds.) *Turnstile Justice: Issues in American Corrections*. Upper Saddle, NJ: Prentice Hall, pp. 38–56.

HASSINE, VICTOR. 2004. *Life Without Parole*. Third Edition. Los Angeles: Roxbury.

HEATER, MARY LOU. 2000. "Age Sensitivity Training for Corrections Personnel," *Corrections Compendium*, Vol. 25, No. 6, June.

HEINER, ROBERT. 2001. *Social Problems: An Introduction to Critical Constructionism*. New York: Oxford University Press.

HEMMENS, CRAIG and E. ATHERTON. 2000. *Use of Force: Current Practice and Policy*. Lanham, MD: American Correctional Association.

HEMMENS, CRAIG and MARY K. STOHR. 2001. "Correctional Staff Attitudes Regarding the Use of Force in Corrections," *Corrections Management Quarterly*, Vol. 5, pp. 26–39.

HEMMENS, CRAIG, MARY STOHR, M. SCHOELER, and B. MILLER. 2002. "One Step Up, Two Steps Back: The Progression of Perceptions of Women's Work in Prisons and Jails," *Journal of Criminal Justice*, Vol. 30, No. 6, pp. 473–489.

HENDERSON, MARTHA, FRANCIS T. CULLEN, LEO CARROLL, and WILLIAM FEINBERG. 2000. "Race, Rights, and Order in Prison: A National Survey of Wardens on the Racial Integration of Prison Cells," *Prison Journal*, Vol. 18, No. 3, pp. 295–308.

HENRIQUES, DIANA B. and ANDREW W. LEHREN. 2006. "Religion for Captive Audiences, with Taxpayers Footing the Bill," *New York Times*, December 10, pp. 1, 32.

HENSLEY, C., M. KOSCHESKI, and R. TEWKSBURY. 2002. "Does the Participation in Conjugal Visitations Reduce Prison Violence in Mississippi? An Exploratory Study," *Criminal Justice Review*, Vol. 27, No. 1, pp. 52–65.

HENSLEY, PETER, SANDRA RUTLAND, and PHYLLIS GRAY-RAY. 2002. "Conjugal Visitation Programs: The Logical Conclusion," in Peter Hensley and Christopher Hensley (eds.) *Prison Sex: Practice and Policy*. Boulder, CO: Lynne Rienner, pp. 143–156.

HEPBURN, JOHN. 1985. "The Exercise of Power in Coercive Organizations: A Study of Prison Guards," *Criminology*, Vol. 23, No. 1, pp. 145–164.

HERMAN, EDWARD and NOAM CHOMSKY. 1988. *Manufacturing Consent: The Political Economy of the Mass Media*. New York: Pantheon.

HERSH, SEYMOUR M. 2004. *Chain of Command: The Road from 9/11 to Abu Ghraib*. New York: HarperCollins.

HINCLE, PIA. 1996. "Prisons to Journalists: Drop Dead," *Extra! Newsletter of FAIR*, July 1, Vol. 9, No. 4, p. 13.

HONNOLD, J. A. and J. B. STINCHCOMB. 1985. "Officer Stress," *Corrections Today*, December, pp. 46–51.

HOPPER, COLUMBUS B. 1970. *Sex in Prison: The Mississippi Experiment with Conjugal Visiting.* Baton Rouge: Louisiana State University Press.

HOSHEN, JOSEPH, JIM SENNOTT, and MAX WINKLER. 1995. "Keeping Tabs on Criminals," *IEEE Spectrum*, February, pp. 26–32.

HUFF, RONALD, AYRE RATTNER, and EDWARD SAGARIN. 1996. *Convicted by Innocent: Wrongful Conviction and Public Policy.* Thousand Oaks, CA: Sage Publications.

Human Rights Watch. 1996. *All Too Familiar: Sexual Abuse of Women in U.S. Prisons.* New York: Human Rights Watch.

Human Rights Watch. 2001. *No Escape: Male Rape in U.S. Prisons.* New York: Human Rights Watch.

HYLTON, WILL S. 2003. "Sick on the Inside," *Harpers*, August, pp. 43–54.

INNES, CHRISTOPHER A. and VICKI D. VERDEYEN. 1997. "Conceptualizing the Management of Violent Inmates," *Corrections Management Quarterly*, Vol. 1, No. 4, pp. 1–9.

IRWIN, JOHN. 1985. *The Jail.* Berkeley: University of California Press.

IRWIN, JOHN. 2005. *The Warehouse Prison: Disposal of the New Dangerous Class.* Los Angeles: Roxbury Company.

IRWIN, JOHN and JAMES AUSTIN. 1997. *It's About Time. America's Imprisonment Binge.* Belmont, CA: Wadsworth.

IRWIN, JOHN and DONALD CRESSEY. 1962. "Thieves, Convicts and Inmate Culture," *Social Problems*, Vol. 10, pp. 142–155.

JACKSON, GEORGE. 1970. *Soledad Brother: The Prison Letters of George Jackson.* Chicago, IL: Lawrence Hill Books.

JACKSON, S. and C. MASLACH. 1982. "After-Effects of Job Related Stress: Families as Victims," *Journal of Occupational Behavior*, Vol. 3, pp. 63–77.

JACOBS, JAMES. 1977. *Stateville.* Chicago: University of Chicago Press.

JACOBS, JAMES B. and HELEN A. BROOKS. 1983. "The Mass Media and Prison News," in James B. Jacobs (ed.) *New Perspectives on Prisons and Imprisonment.* Ithaca, NY: Cornell University Press, pp. 106–114.

JACOBSON, C. A., J. T. JACOBSON, and T. A. CROWE. 1989. "Hearing Loss in Inmates," *Ear and Hearing*, Vol. 10, No. 3, pp. 178–183.

JACOBY, J. E. 2002. "The Endurance of Failing Correctional Institutions: A Worst Case Scenario," *The Prison Journal*, Vol. 82, No. 2, pp. 168–188.

JAMES, DORIS J. and LAUREN E. GLAZE. 2006. "Mental Health Problems of Prisons and Jail Inmates," *Bureau of Justice Statistics*, NCJ 213600.

JFA Institute. 2007. *Public Safety, Public Spending: Forecasting America's Prison Population, 2007–2011.* The Pew Charitable Trusts. www.pewtrusts.org/pdf/PSPP_prison_projections_0207.pdf (accessed August 28, 2007).

JOHNSON, BYRON. 1994. "Exploring Direct Supervision: A Research Note," *American Jails*, March/April, pp. 63–64.

JOHNSON, ROBERT. 2002. *Hard Time: Understanding and Reforming the Prison.* Third Edition. Belmont, CA: Wadsworth.

JONES, RICHARD and THOMAS SCHMID. 2000. *Doing Time: Prison Experience and Identity Among First Time Inmates.* Stanford, CT: JAI Press.

KALINICH, DAVID B. 1986. *Power, Stability, and Contraband: The Inmate Economy.* Prospect Heights, IL: Waveland Press.

KAPPELER, VICTOR E., MARK BLUMBERG, and GARY W. POTTER. 1996. *The Mythology of Crime and Criminal Justice.* Prospect Heights, IL: Waveland Press.

KAPPELER, VICTOR E., RICHARD D. SLUDER, and GEOFFREY P. ALPERT. 1994. *Forces of Deviance: Understanding the Dark Side of Policing*. Prospect Heights, IL: Waveland Press.

KAUFFMAN, KELSEY. 1988. *Prison Officers and Their World*. Cambridge, MA: Harvard University Press.

KERNESS, BONNIE and MASAI EHEHOSI. 2001. *Torture in U.S. Prisons: Evidence of U.S. Human Rights Violations*. Philadelphia: American Friends Service Committee.

KIEKBUSCH, R., W. PRICE, and J. THEIS. 2003. "Turnover Predictors: Causes of Employee Turnover in Sheriff-Operated Jails," *Criminal Justice Studies*, Vol. 16, No. 2, pp. 67–76.

KIFER, M., CRAIG HEMMENS, and MARY STOHR. 2003. "The Goals of Corrections: Perspectives from the Line," *Criminal Justice Review*, Vol. 28, No. 1, pp. 47–69.

KINDEL, TIP. 1998. "Media Access: Where Should You Draw the Line," *Corrections Today*, Vol. 59, pp. 22–24.

KING, ROY. 1999. "The Rise and Rise of Supermax: An American Solution in Search of a Problem," *Punishment and Society*, Vol. 1, pp. 163–185.

KING, ROY. 2001. "Symposium, Conducted at the Conference Best Practices and Human Rights in Supermax Prisons: A Dialogue," Seattle, Washington, September.

KLEIMAN, MARK A. R. 2003. "Faith-Based Fudging: How a Bush-Promoted Christian Prison Program Fakes Success by Massaging the Data," www.slate.com/toolbar.aspx?action=print&id=2086617 (accessed August 15, 2007).

KLEIN, MALCOLM. 1997. *The American Street Gang*. New York: Oxford University Press.

KLEIN, NAOMI. 2000. *No Logo: Taking Aim at the Brand Bullies*. Toronto: Vintage Canada.

KLOFAS, JOHN M. 1984. "Reconsidering Prison Personnel: New Views of the Correctional Officer Subculture," *International Journal of Offender Therapy and Comparative Criminology*, Vol. 28, No. 3, pp. 169–175.

KLOFAS, JOHN and HANS TOCH. 1982. "The Guard Subculture Myth," *Journal of Research in Crime and Delinquency*, Vol. 19, No. 2, pp. 238–254.

KORN, R. 1988. "The Effects of Confinement in the High Security Unit at Lexington," *Social Justice*, Vol. 15, No. 1, pp. 8–19.

KRATCOSKI, P. and GEORGE POWNELL. 1992. "Federal Bureau of Prisons Programming for Older Inmates," *Federal Probation*, Vol. 31, No. 1, pp. 28–35.

KRIPPENDORF, KLAUS. 1981. *Content Analysis: An Introduction to Its Methodology*. Beverly Hills, CA: Sage Publications.

KURKI, LEENA and NORVAL MORRIS. 2001. "The Purpose, Practices, and Problems of Supermax Prisons," in Michael Tonry (ed.) *Crime and Justice, an Annual Edition*. Chicago, IL: University of Chicago Press, pp. 385–424.

LAMB, CURT. 1975. *Political Power in Poor Neighborhoods*. New York: John Wiley & Sons.

LAMBERT, E. 2004. "The Impact of Job Characteristics on Correctional Officer Staff Members," *The Prison Journal*, Vol. 84, pp. 208–227.

LASKY, G. L. and D. J. STREBALUS. 1986. "Occupational Stressors Among Federal Correctional Officers Working in Different Security Levels," *Criminal Justice Behavior*, Vol. 13, No. 3, pp. 317–327.

LATESSA, EDWARD J. and HARRY E. ALLEN. 1999. *Corrections in the Community*. Second Edition. Cincinnati, OH: Anderson Publishing.

LATESSA, EDWARD J., FRANCIS T. CULLEN, and PAUL GENDREAU. 2002. "Beyond Correctional Quackery: Professionalism and the Possibility of Effective Treatment," *Federal Probation*, Vol. 66, pp. 43–49.

LATHAM, G. P. and K. N. WEXLEY. 1981. *Increasing Productivity Through Performance Appraisal*. Menlo Park, CA: Addison-Wesley Publishing Company.

LAVIGNE, YVES. 1989. *Hell's Angels: Three Can Keep a Secret If Two Are Dead*. Toronto: Lyle Stuart.

LAWRENCE, R. and S. MAHAN. 1998. "Women Corrections Officer's in Men's Prisons: Acceptance and Perceived Job Performance," *Women and Criminal Justice*, Vol. 9, No. 3, pp. 63–86.

LEMERT, E. M. 1993. "Visions of Social Control: Probation Considered," *Crime & Delinquency*, Vol. 39, pp. 447–461.

LERNER, JIMMY A. 2002. *You Got Nothing Coming: Notes of a Prison Fish*. New York: Broadway.

LEVINSON, ROBERT B., JEANNE B. STINCHCOMB, and JOHN J. GREENE III. 2001. "Correctional Certification: First Step Toward Professionalization," *Corrections Today*, Vol. 63, No. 5, pp. 125–138.

LICHTER, ROBERT S., STANLEY ROTHMAN, and LINDA S. LICHTER. 1986. *The Media Elite*. Bethesda, MD: Adler and Adler.

LIEBLING, ALISON. 1999. "Doing Research in Prison: Breaking the Silence?" *Theoretical Criminology*, Vol. 3, No. 2, pp. 147–173.

LINDQUIST, CHARLES A. and JONATHEN T. WHITEHEAD. 1986. "Burnout, Job Stress, and Job Satisfaction Among Southern Correctional Officers: Perceptions and Causal Factors," *Journal of Criminal Justice*, Vol. 10, No. 4, pp. 5–26.

LIPTAK, ADAM. 2005. "To More Inmates, Life Term Means Dying Behind Bars," *New York Times*, October 2, pp. 1, A18–A19.

LOCKWOOD, DANIEL. 1980. "Reducing Prison Sexual Violence," in Robert Johnson and Hans Toch (eds.) *The Pains of Imprisonment*. Beverley Hills, CA: Sage Publications, pp. 257–265.

LOGAN, CHARLES H. 1993. "Criminal Justice Performance Measures for Prisons," in John J. DiIulio Jr. (ed.) *Performance Measures for the Criminal Justice System*. Washington, D.C.: Office of Justice Programs, pp. 19–41. USDOJ OJP NCJ-143505.

LOGAN, CHARLES H. and BILL W. McGRIFF. 1989. "Comparing Costs of Public and Private Prisons," *Research in Action*. Washington, D.C.: National Institute of Justice.

LOMBARDO, LUCIEN X. 1981/1989. *Guards Imprisoned*. Second Edition. Cincinnati, OH: Anderson Publishing.

LOPIANO-MISDOM, JANINE and JOANNE DE LUCA. 1997. *Street Trends: Today's Alternative Youth Cultures Are Creating Tomorrow's Mainstream Markets*. New York: HarperCollins Business.

LOVELL, DAVID, KRISTIN CLOYES, DAVID ALLEN, and LORNA RHODES. 2000. "Who Lives in Super-Maximum Custody?" *Federal Probation*, Vol. 64, pp. 33–38.

LUCKEN, KAROL. 1998. "Contemporary Penal Trends: Modern or Post Modern?" *British Journal of Criminology*, Vol. 38, No. 1, pp. 106–123.

LYNCH, MICHAEL and W. BYRON GROVES. 1986/1989. *A Primer in Radical Criminology*. Albany: Harrow and Heston.

LYNCH, MONA. 1998. "Waste Managers? New Penology, Crime Fighting and Parole Agent Identity," *Law and Society Review*, Vol. 32, pp. 839–869.

LYND, STAUNTON. 2004. *Lucasville: The Untold Story of a Prison Uprising*. Philadelphia: Temple University Press.

MAC DONALD, HEATHER. 2003. "How to Straighten Out Ex-Cons," *City Journal*, Spring, Vol. 13, No. 2, pp. 24–37.

MACKENZIE, DORIS. 2000. "Evidence-Based Corrections: Identifying What Works," *Crime and Delinquency*, Vol. 46, No. 4, pp. 457–472.

MACKENZIE, DORIS LAYTON. 2006. *What Works in Corrections: Reducing the Criminal Activities of Offenders and Delinquents*. New York: Cambridge University Press.

MACKENZIE, DORIS L. and CLAIRE SOURYAL. 1991. "Boot Camp Survey: Rehabilitation, Recidivism Reduction Outrank Punishment as Main Goals," *Corrections Today*, Vol. 53, pp. 90–96.

MAHAN, S. and R. LAWRENCE. 1996. "Media and Mayhem in Corrections: The Role of the Media in Prison Riots," *Prison Journal*, Vol. 76, No. 4, pp. 1–18.

MALLICOAT, STACEY. 2005. "Correctional Officer Pay," in Mary Bosworth (ed.) *Encyclopedia of Prisons & Correctional Facilities*. Thousand Oaks, CA: Sage Publications, pp. 185–187.

MARQUART, JAMES W. 1986. "The Use of Physical Force by Prison Guards: Individuals, Situations, and Organizations," *Criminology*, Vol. 24, pp. 347–366.

MARQUART, JAMES W., M. B. BARNHILL, and K. BALSHAW-BIDDLE. 2001. "Fatal Attraction: An Analysis of Employee Boundary Violations in a Southern Prison System, 1995–1998," *Justice Quarterly*, Vol. 18, No. 4, pp. 877–910.

MARQUART, JAMES W., D. E. MERIANOS, J. L. HEBERT, and L. CARROLL. 1997. "Health Condition and Prisoners: A Review of Research and Emerging Areas of Inquiry," *Prison Journal*, Vol. 77, pp. 184–208.

MARQUEZ, JEREMIAH and DON THOMPSON. 2006. "Prison 'Peacekeeper' Wielded Influence," *Associated Press*, January 22, www.nctimes.com/articles/2006/01/23/news/state/12206193342.txt (accessed August 15, 2007).

MARTINSON, ROBERT. 1974. "What Works—Questions and Answers About Prison Reform," *Public Interest*, Vol. 35, Spring, pp. 22–54.

MARTINSON, ROBERT. 1979. "New Findings, New Views, a Note of Caution Regarding Sentencing Reform," *Hofstra Law Review*, Vol. 7, pp. 243–258.

MARUSCHAK, LAURA M. 2005. "HIV in Prisons, 2003," *Bureau of Justice Statistics*, September.

MASSEY, DENNIS. 1989. *Doing Time in American Prisons: A Study of Modern Novels*. New York: Greenwood Press.

MATHIESEN, THOMAS. 1974. *The Politics of Abolition*. New York: John Wiley.

MAUER, MARC. 1996. "Tales of a Criminal Justice Reformer," *Criminal Justice Ethics*, Vol. 15, pp. 2–6.

MAUER, MARC and MEDA CHESNEY-LIN. 2003. *Invisible Punishment*. New York: New Press.

MAUR, MARC. 2006. *The Race to Incarcerate*. Revised Edition. New York: New Press.

MAY, JOHN P. and KHALID R. PITTS (eds.). 2000. *Building Violence: How America's Rush to Incarcerate Creates More Violence*. Thousand Oaks, CA: Sage Publications.

MCAULEY, L. 1994. "Exploding Myths About Correctional Industries," *Corrections Today*, Vol. 56, p. 8.

MCCARTHY, BELINDA and BERNARD J. MCCARTHY, JR. 1997. *Community-Based Corrections*. Third Edition. Belmont, CA: Wadsworth.

MCCARTHY, BELINDA, BERNARD J. MCCARTHY, JR., and MATTHEW C. LEONE. 2001. *Community-Based Corrections*. Fourth Edition. Belmont, CA: Wadsworth.

MCCARTHY, BERNARD J. 1996. "Keeping and Eye on the Keeper: Prison Corruption and Its Control," in Michael C. Braswell, Belinda R. McCarthy, and Bernard J. McCarthy (eds.) *Justice, Crime, and Ethics*. Second Edition. Cincinnati, OH: Anderson, pp. 229–241.

MCCLEARY, RICHARD. 1978/1992. *Dangerous Men: The Sociology of Parole*. New York: Harrow and Heston.

MCCLOSKY, HERBERT. 1964. "Consensus and Ideology in American Politics," *American Political Science Review*, Vol. 58, No. 2, June, pp. 361–382.

MCDONALD, DOUGLAS C. 1999. "Medical Care in Prisons," in Michael Tonry and Joan Petersilia (eds.) *Prisons*. Chicago: University of Chicago Press, pp. 427–478.

MCKINNON, KRISTI M. 2004. "Overcrowding," in Mary Bosworth (ed.) *Encyclopaedia of Prisons & Correctional Facilities*. Thousand Oaks, CA: Sage Publications, pp. 656–658.

MCLAUGHLIN, EUGENE and JOHN MUNCIE. 2002. *Controlling Crime*. Second Edition. Sage Publications.

MCSHANE, MARILYN and WESLEY KRAUSE. 1993. *Community Corrections*. New York: Macmillan.

MCVAY, D., VINCE SHIRALDI, and JASON ZIEDENBERG. 2004. "Treatment or Incarceration: National and State Findings in the Efficacy and Cost Savings of Drug Treatment versus Imprisonment," *Justice Policy*, Vol. 1, pp. 1–13.

MEARS, DANIEL P. 2006. *Evaluating the Effectiveness of Supermax*. Washington, D.C.: Urban Institute. www.urban.org/url.cfm?ID=411326 (accessed August 15, 2007).

MERLO, ALIDA. 1992. "Ethical Issues and the Private Sector," in Peter J. Benekos and Alida V. Merlo (eds.) *Corrections: Dilemmas and Directions*. Cincinnati, OH: Anderson/ACJS Monograph Series, pp. 23–36.

MERTON, ROBERT K. 1936. "The Unanticipated Consequences of Purposive Social Action," *American Sociological Review*, Vol. 1, No. 6, pp. 894–904.

MIESZKOWSKI, K. 1998. "She helps them help themselves," *Fast Company,* Vol. 15, p. 54.

MILGRAM, STANLEY. 1974. *Obedience to Authority*. London: Harper and Row.

MILLER, JEROME G. 1996. *Search and Destroy: African American Males and the Criminal Justice System*. New York: Cambridge University Press.

MILLER, JODY. 1995. "Struggles over the Symbolic: Gang Style and Meanings of Social Control," in Jeff Ferrell and Clinton R. Sanders (eds.) *Cultural Criminology*. Boston: Northeastern University Press, pp. 213–234.

MILLER, J. MITCHELL and LANCE H. SELVA. 1994. "Drug Enforcement's Double-Edged Sword: An Assessment of Asset Forfeiture Programs," *Justice Quarterly*, Vol. 11, No. 2, pp. 313–335.

MONKKONEN, ERIC H. 1981. *Police in Urban America, 1860–1920*. Cambridge: Cambridge University Press.

MOORE, J. W. 1978. *Homeboys: Gangs, Drugs and Prison in the Barrios of Los Angeles*. Philadelphia: Temple University Press.

MOREY, ANNE. 1995. "The Judge Called Me an Accessory: Women's Prison Films, 1950–1962," *Journal of Popular Film and Television*, Vol. 23, No. 2, pp. 80–87.

MORIARY, LAURA and CHARLES FIELDS. 1999. "Debating Correctional Controversies: Is the Segregation on HIV-Positive Inmates Ethical?" *The Prison Journal*, Vol. 78, No. 1, pp. 100–118.

MORRIS, NORVAL and MICHAEL TONRY. 1990. *Between Prison and Probation*. New York: Oxford University Press.

MUNRO-BJORKLUND, VICKY. 1991. "Popular Cultural Images of Criminals and Convicts since Attica," *Social Justice*, Vol. 18, No. 3, pp. 48–70.

MURPHY, DANIEL S. 2003. "Aspirin Ain't Gonna Help the Kind of Pain I'm in: Health Care in the Federal Bureau of Prisons," in Jeffrey Ian Ross and Stephen C. Richards (eds.) *Convict Criminology*. Belmont, CA: Wadsworth, pp. 247–266.

MURTON, T. O. 1976. *The Dilemma of Prison Reform*. New York: Praeger.

NAGEL, ROBERT. 1990. "The Myth of the General Right to Bail," *Public Interest*, Vol. 98, pp. 84–97.

National Advisory Commission on Criminal Justice Standards and Goals. 1973. *Task Force Report: Corrections*. Washington, D.C.: US Government Printing Office.

National Center for State Courts. 1975. *An Evaluation of Policy-Related Research on the Effectiveness of Pretrial Release Programs*. Denver, Co: National Center for State Courts.

National Commission on Safety and Abuse in Prison. 2006. www.prisoncommission.org.

National Institute of Corrections. 1997. *Supermax Housing: A Survey of Current Practice: Special Issues in Corrections*. Longmont, CO: U.S. Department of Justice, National Institute of Corrections.

NEAL, DONICE (ed.). 2002. *Supermax Prisons: Beyond the Rock*. Lanham, MD: American Correctional Association.

NELSON, W. RAYMOND and RUSSELL M. DAVIS. 1995. "Podular Direct Supervision: The First Twenty Years," *American Jails*, Vol. 9, No. 3, pp. 11–22.

NINK, C., C. B. JOHNSON, T. OLDBURY, G. CHEESEMAN, and R. RODRIGUEZ, 2005. "Job Corps: A Training Program Pipeline to the Corrections Profession," *Corrections Today*, Vol. 67, pp. 84–86.

ODO, JONATHAN, EMMANUEL C. ONYEOZILI, and IHEKWOABA D. ONWUDIWE. 2005. "Boot Camps," in Mary Bosworth (ed.) *Encyclopaedia of Prisons & Correctional Facilities*. Thousand Oaks, CA: Sage Publications, pp. 79–81.

OGDEN, AMY and PAUL REBEIN. 2001. "Do Prison Inmates Have a Right to Vegetarian Meals," *Vegetarian Journal*, March, www.vrg.org/journal/vj2001mar/2001marprison.htm (accessed August 15, 2007).

OGLE, ROBBIN. 1999. "Prison Privatization: An Environmental Catch 22," *Justice Quarterly*, Vol. 16, No. 3, pp. 579–600.

OJMARRH MITCHELL, DORIS LAYTON MACKENZIE, GAYLENE J. STYVE, and ANGELA R. GOVER. 2000. "The Impact of Individual, Organizational and Environmental Attributes on Voluntary Turnover Among Juvenile Correctional Staff," *Criminology*, Vol. 17, No. 2, pp. 333–353.

OWEN, BARBARA. 1988. *The Reproduction of Social Control: A Study of Prison Workers at San Quentin*. Greenwood, CT: Praeger.

OWEN, BARBARA. 1998. *In the Mix: Struggle and Survival in a Women's Prison*. Albany: State University of New York Press.

OWEN, BARBARA. 2005. "Women's Prisons," in Mary Bosworth (ed.) *Encyclopedia of Prisons & Correctional Facilities*. Thousand Oaks, CA: Sage Publications, Vol. 2, pp. 1051–1055.

PALMER, TED. 1975. "Martinson Revisited," *Journal of Research in Crime and Delinquency*, Vol. 12, pp. 133–152.

PARENTI, MICHAEL. 1995. *Democracy for the Few*. New York: St. Martin's Press.

PARISH, JAMES ROBERT. 1991. *Prison Pictures from Hollywood*. Jefferson, NC: McFarland.

PARSONAGE, WILLIAM H. 1990. "Worker Safety in Probation and Parole." Report supported by TA number 89C7002 from the National Institute of Corrections.

PARSONAGE, WILLIAM H. and W. CONWAY BUSHEY. 1989. "The Victimization of Probation and Parole Officers in the Line of Duty: An Exploratory Study," *Criminal Justice Policy Review*, Vol. 2, No. 4, pp. 372–391.

PATRICK, S. and R. MARSH. 2001. "Current Tobacco Policies in U.S. Adult Male Prisons," *The Social Science Journal*, Vol. 38, No. 1, pp. 27–37.

PATTILLO, MARY, DAVID WEIMAN, and BRUCE WESTERN (eds.). 2004. *Imprisoning America: The Social Effects of Mass Incarceration*. New York: Russell Sage.

PEDERSON, REBECCA D. and DENNIS J. PALUMBO. 1997. "The Social Construction of Intermediate Punishments," *The Prison Journal*, Vol. 77, No. 1, pp. 77–91.

Pell v. Procunier 4147 U.S. 817 (1974).

PEPINSKY, HAROLD and PAUL JESILOW. 1985. *Myths that Cause Crime*. Cabin John, MD: Seven Locks Press.

PEPINSKY, HAROLD E. and RICHARD QUINNEY (eds.). 1991. *Criminology as Peacemaking*. Bloomington: Indiana University Press.

PETERSILIA, JOAN. 2003. *When Prisoners Come: Parole and Prisoner Re-entry*. New York: Oxford University Press.

PETERSON, REBECCA D. and DENNIS J. PALUMBO. 1997. "The Social Construction of Intermediate Punishment," *Prison Journal*, Vol. 77, No. 1, pp. 77–91.

PIVEN, FRANCIS FOX and RICHARD CLOWARD. 1977. *Poor People's Movements*. New York: Pantheon.

POGREBIN, M. R. and ERIC D. POOLE. 1997. "The Sexualized Work Environment: A Look at Women Jail Officers," *Prison Journal*, Vol. 77, No. 1, pp. 41–57.

POLLOCK, J. M. 2004. *Prisons and Prison Life: Costs and Consequences*. Los Angeles: Roxbury Press.

POLLOCK-BYRNE, JOYCELYN. 1986. *Sex and Supervision: Guarding Male and Female Inmates*. Greenwood, CT: Greenwood Press.

POLLOCK-BYRNE, JOYCELYN. 1990. *Women, Prison and Crime*. Pacific Grove, CA: Brooks/Cole.

PRATT, TRAVIS C., JEFFREY MAAHS, and C. HEMMENS. 1999. "The History of the Use of Force in Corrections," in C. Hemmens and E. Atherton (eds.) *Use of Force: Current Practice and Policy*. Lanham, MD: American Correctional Association, pp. 13–22.

PRATT, TRAVIS C., JEFFREY MAAHS, and STEVEN D. STEHR. 1998. "The Symbolic Ownership of the Corrections 'Problem': A Framework for Understanding the Development of Corrections Policy in the United States," *The Prison Journal*, Vol. 4, No. 4, pp. 451–464.

PRESTON, FREDERICK W. and ROGER ROOTS. 2004. "Law and Its Unintended Consequences," Special issue of *American Behavioral Scientist*, Vol. 47, No. 11, pp. 371–375.

PRICE, MARY. 2005. "Compassionate Release," in Mary Bosworth (ed.) *Encyclopedia of Prisons and Correctional Facilities*. Thousand Oaks, CA: Sage Publications, Vol. 1, pp. 150–151.

QUINNEY, RICHARD. 1985. "Myth and the Art of Criminology," *Legal Studies Forum*, Vol. 9, No. 3, pp. 291–299.

RAFTER, NICOLE HAHN. 2000. *Shots in the Mirror: Crime Films and Society*. New York: Oxford University Press.

RALPH, P., R. J. HUNTER, J. W. MARQUART, S. J. CUVELIER, and D. MERIANO. 1996. "Exploring the Differences Between Gang and Nongang Prisoners," in C. R. Huff (ed.) *Gangs in America*. Thousand Oaks, CA: Sage Publications, pp. 123–138.

REIMAN, JEFFREY. 1979/2003. *The Rich Get Richer and the Poor Get Prison*. Seventh Edition. Boston: Allyn & Bacon.

REISIG, MICHAEL and NICHOLAS LOVRICH. 1998. "Job Attitudes Among Higher-Custody State Prison Management Personnel: A Cross-Sectional Comparative Assessment," *Journal of Criminal Justice*, Vol. 26, No. 3, pp. 213–226.

REISIG, MICHAEL D. and TRAVIS C. PRATT. 2000. "The Ethics of Correctional Privatization: A Critical Examination of the Delegation of Coercive Authority," *The Prison Journal*, Vol. 80, No. 2, pp. 210–222.

RHINE, EDWARD E., WILLIAM R. SMITH, RONALD W. JACKSON, with PEGGY B. BURKE and ROGER LABELLE. 1991. *Paroling Authorities: Recent History and Current Practice*. Laurel, MD: American Correctional Association.

RICCI, DAVID M. 1984. *The Tragedy of Political Science*. New Haven, CT: Yale University Press.

RICHARDS, STEPHEN C. 1998. "Critical and Radical Perspectives on Community Punishment: Lesson from the Darkness," in Jeffrey Ian Ross (ed.) *Cutting the Edge: Current Perspectives in Radical/Critical Criminology and Criminal Justice*. New York: Praeger, pp. 122–144.

RICHARDS, STEPHEN C. 2003. "Beating the Perpetual Incarceration Machine," in Shadd Maruna and Russ Immarigeon (eds.) *Ex-Convict Reentry and Desistance from Crime*. Albany, NY: SUNY Press, pp. 201–232.

RICHARDS, STEPHEN C. 2004. "Penitentiary Dreams: Books Will Take You Anywhere You Want to Go," *The Journal of Prisoners on Prisons*, Vol. 13, pp. 60–73.

RICHARDS, STEPHEN C., J. AUSTIN, and R. S. JONES. 2004. "Thinking About Prison Release and Budget Crisis in the Blue Grass State," *Critical Criminology: An International Journal*, Vol. 12, No. 3, pp. 243–263.

RICHARDS, STEPHEN C. and MICHAEL J. AVEY. 2000. "Controlling State Crime in the United States of America: What Can We Do About the Thug State?" in Jeffrey Ian Ross (ed.) *Varieties of State Crime and Its Control*. Monsey, NY: Criminal Justice Press, pp. 31–58.

RICHARDS, STEPHEN C. and RICHARD S. JONES. 1997. "Perpetual Incarceration Machine: Structural Impediments to Post-Prison Success," *The Journal of Contemporary Criminal Justice*, Vol. 13, No. 1, pp. 4–22.

RICHARDS, STEPHEN C., CHRIS D. ROSE, and SUSAN O. REED. 2006. "Inviting Convicts to College: Prison and University Partnership," in *The State of Corrections: 2005 Proceedings ACA Annual Conferences*. Lanham, MD: American Correctional Association, pp. 171–180.

RICHARDS, STEPHEN C. and JEFFREY IAN ROSS. 2003. "A Convict Perspective on the Classification of Prisoners," *Criminology & Public Policy*, Vol. 2, No. 2, pp. 242–251.

RICHARDS, S. C. and J. I. ROSS. 2007. "The New School of Convict Criminology: How Might Prison College Programs Rehabilitate Prisoners?" in Leanne F. Alarid and Philip Reichel (eds.) *Corrections: A Contemporary introduction*. Boston, MA: Allyn & Bacon, p. 330.

RIDEAU, WILBERT. 1992. "The Sexual Jungle," in Wilbert Rideau and Ron Wikberg (eds.) *Life Sentences: Rage and Survival Behind Bars*. New York: Times Books, pp. 73–107.

RIDEAU, WILBERT and RON WIKBERG. 1992. *Life Sentences: Rage and Survival Behind the Bars*. New York: Times Books.

RIVELAND, CHASE. 1997. "The Correctional Leader and Public Policy Skills," *Corrections Management Quarterly*, Vol. 1, No. 3, pp. 22–25.

RIVELAND, CHASE. 1998. *Supermax Prison: Overview and General Considerations*. Longmont, CO: National Institute of Corrections.

RIVELAND, CHASE. 1999. "Prison Management Trends: 1975–2025," in Michael Tonry and Joan Petersilia (eds.) *Prisons*. Chicago: University of Chicago Press, pp. 163–203.

ROBBINS, IRA P. 1986. "Privatization of Corrections: Defining the Issues," *Federal Probation*, Vol. 50, pp. 24–30.

ROBERTS, J. (ed.). 1994. *Escaping Prison Myths*. Washington, D.C.: The American University Press.

ROGERS, ROBERT. 1993. "Solitary Confinement," *International Journal of Offender Therapy and Comparative Criminology*, Vol. 37, No. 4, pp. 339–349.

ROLLAND, MIKE. 1997. *Descent into Madness: An Inmate's Experience of the New Mexico State Prison Riot*. Cincinnati, OH: Anderson Publishing.

ROMAN, J., W. TOWNSEND, and A. BHATI. 2003. *National Estimates of Drug Court Recidivism Rates*. Washington, D.C.: National Institute of Justice, U.S. Department of Justice, July.

ROOTS, ROGER. 2005. "New Generation Prisons," in Mary Bosworth (ed.) *Encyclopaedia of Prisons & Correctional Facilities*. Thousand Oaks, CA: Sage Publications.

ROSE, CHRIS D., SUSAN O. REED, and STEPHEN C. RICHARDS. 2005. "Inviting Convicts to College: A Free College Preparatory Program for Prisoners," *Offender Programs Report*, Vol. 8, No. 6, pp. 81, 91–93.

ROSS, JEFFREY IAN. 1983. "Jail Dehumanizing Say Abolitionists," *Now*, June 2–8, p. 5.

ROSS, JEFFREY IAN. 1998a. "The Role of the Media in the Creation of Public Police Violence," in Frankie Bayley and Donna Hale (eds.) *Popular Culture, Crime & Justice*. Belmont, CA: Wadsworth, pp. 100–110.

ROSS, JEFFREY IAN (ed.). 1998b. *Cutting the Edge: Current Perspectives in Radical/Critical Criminology and Criminal Justice*. New York: Praeger.

ROSS, JEFFREY IAN. 1999. "Content Analysis of the *Baltimore Sun*'s Coverage of Prison Issues," Unpublished.

ROSS, JEFFREY IAN (ed.). 2000a. *Controlling State Crime*. Second Edition. New Brunswick, NJ: Transaction Publishing.

Ross, Jeffrey Ian (ed.). 2000b. *Varieties of State Crime and Its Control*. Monsey, NJ: Criminal Justice Press.

Ross, Jeffrey Ian. 2000c. *Making News of Police Violence*. Westport, CT: Praeger.

Ross, Jeffrey Ian. 2003. "(Mis)representing Prisons: The Role of Our Cultural Industries," in Jeffrey Ian Ross and Stephen C. Richards (eds.) *Convict Criminology*. Belmont, CA: Wadsworth, pp. 37–56.

Ross, Jeffrey Ian. 2006a. "Is the End in Sight for Supermax," *Forbes,* On-line, April 18, www.forbes.com/blankslate/2006/04/15/prison-supermax-ross_cx_jr_06slate_0418super.html

Ross, Jeffrey Ian. 2006b. "Jailhouse Blues," *Forbes,* On-line, April 18, www.forbes.com/2006/04/15/prison-jeffrey-ross_cx_jr_06slate_0418ross.html.

Ross, Jeffrey Ian. 2006c. "Close Juvenile Boot Camps," *Tampa Tribune*, February 19.

Ross, Jeffrey Ian and Stephen C. Richards. 2002. *Behind Bars: Surviving Prison*. Indianapolis, IN: Alpha Books.

Ross, Jeffrey Ian and Stephen C. Richards (eds.). 2003. *Convict Criminology*. Belmont, CA: Wadsworth.

Rothman, David J. 1971/2002. *The Discovery of the Asylum: Social Order and Disorder in the New Republic*. Revised Edition. New York: Aldine.

Rothman, David J. 1980. *Conscience and Convenience: The Asylum and Its Alternatives in Progressive America*. Boston: Little, Brown and Company.

Ruiz, J. D., F. Molitor, R. K Sun, J. Mikanda, and M. Facer. 1999. "Prevalence and Correlates of Hepatitis C Virus Infections Among Inmates Entering the California Correctional System," *Western Journal of Medicine*, Vol. 170, No. 3, pp. 156–160.

Sanders, Clinton R. 1990. *Marginal Conventions: Popular Culture, Mass Media, and Social Deviance*. Bowling Green, OH: The Popular Press.

Sanders, Clinton R. and Elanor Lyon. 1995. "Repetitive Retribution: Media Images and the Cultural Construction of Criminal Justice," in Jeff Ferrell and Clinton Sanders (eds.) *Cultural Criminology*. Boston: Northeastern University Press, pp. 25–44.

Saum, C., H. Surratt, J. Inciardi, and R. Bennett. 1995. "Sex in Prison: Exploring the Myths and Realities," *Prison Journal*, Vol. 75, pp. 413–431.

Savicki, Vicktor, Eric Cooley, and Jennifer Gjesvold. 2003. "Harassment as a Predictor of Job Burnout in Correctional Officers," *Criminal Justice and Behavior*, Vol. 30, pp. 602–619.

Saxbe v. Washington Post 417 U.S. 843 (1974).

Scheck, Barry, Peter Neufeld, and Jim Dwyer. 2000. *Actual Innocence: Five Days to Execution, and Other Dispatches from the Wrongly Convicted*. New York: Doubleday.

Schicher, D. 1992. "Myths and Realities in Prison Setting," *Crime and Delinquency*, Vol. 38, pp. 70–88.

Schichor, David. 1999. "Privatizing Correctional Institutions. An Organizational Perspective," *The Prison Journal*, Vol. 79, No. 2, pp. 226–249.

Schiller, Herbert I. 1989. *Culture Inc. The Corporate Takeover of Public Expression*. New York: Oxford University Press.

Schmalleger, Frank. 1999. *Criminal Justice Today: An Introductory Text for the 21st Century*. Fifth Edition. Upper Saddle, NJ: Prentice Hall.

Schmalleger, Frank. 2006. *Criminology Today*. Upper Saddle, NJ: Prentice Hall.

Sechrest, D. K. and Don A. Josi. 1999. "A Pragmatic Approach to Parole Aftercare: Evaluation of a Community Reintegration Program for High-Risk Youthful Offenders," *Justice Quarterly*, Vol. 16, No. 1, pp. 51–80.

Seiter, Richard. 2005. *Corrections: An Introduction*. Upper Saddle, NJ: Prentice Hall.

Sentementes, Gus G. 2005. "City in Central Booking Lawsuit," *Baltimore Sun*, September 30.

SHADOIAN, JACK. 1979. *Dreams and Dead Ends: The American Gangster/Crime Film*. Cambridge, MA: MIT Press.

SIGLER, ROBERT and CHADWICK L. SHOOK. 1995. "The Federal Judiciary and Corrections: Breaking the 'Hands-Off' Doctrine," *Criminal Justice Policy Review*, Vol. 7, No. 3–4, pp. 245–254.

SLATE, RISDON and RONALD E. VOGEL. 1997. "Participative Management and Correctional Personnel: A Study of the Perceived Atmosphere for Participation in Correctional Decisions Making and Its Impact on Employees Stress and Thoughts About Quitting," *Journal of Criminal Justice*, Vol. 25, No. 5, pp. 397–408.

SLATE, R. N., R. E. VOGEL, and W. W. JOHNSON. 2001. "To Quit or Not to Quit: Perceptions of Participation in Correctional Decision Making and the Impact of Organizational Stress," *Corrections Management Quarterly*, Vol. 5, No. 2, pp. 68–78.

SLATER, DASHKA. 2003. "Lights, Camera, Lockdown," *Legal Affairs*, May/June, www.legalaffairs.org/issues/May-June-2003/review_slater_mayjun03.msp (accessed August 15, 2007).

SODERSTROM, IRINA R. and W. MICHAEL WHEELER. 1999. "Is It Still Practical to Incarcerate the Elderly Offender?" in Charles B. Fields (ed.) *Controversial Issues in Corrections*. Boston: Allyn & Bacon, pp. 72–89.

SPEED WEED, WILLIAM. 2001. "Incubating Disease. Prisons Are Rife with Infectious Illnesses—and Threaten to Spread Them to the Public," *Mother Jones*, July 10, www.motherjones.com/news/special_reports/prisons/print_disease.html.

STASTNY, C. and G. TYRNAUER. 1982. *Who Rules the Joint? The Changing Political Culture of Maximum-Security Prisons in America*. Lexington, MA: Lexington Books.

State of New York. 1972. *Attica: The Official Report of the New York State Special Commission on Attica*. New York: Praeger.

STEADMAN, H. J. and J. COCOZZA (eds.). 1993. *Mental Illness in America's Prisons*. Seattle, WA: National Coalition for the Mentally Ill in the Criminal Justice System.

STEPHAN, JAMES J. 2004. *State Prison Expenditures, 2001*. U.S. Department of Justice. Office of Justice Programs. Bureau of Justice Statistics. Special Report. June, NCJ 202949. www.ojp.usdoj.gov/bjs/abstract/spe01.htm (accessed August 27, 2007).

STINCHCOMB, JEANNE B. 1985. "Why Not the Best? Using Assessment Centers for Office Selection," *Corrections Today*, Vol. 47, p. 9.

STINCHCOMB, JEANNE B. 1998. "Quality Management in Corrections Implementation Issues and Potential Policy Implications," *Criminal Justice Policy Review*, Vol. 9, No. 1, pp. 123–136.

STINCHCOMB, JEANNE B. 1999. "Recovering from the Shocking Reality of Shock Incarceration—What Correctional Administration Can Learn from Boot Camp Failures," *Corrections Management Quarterly*, Vol. 2, No. 4, pp. 43–52.

STINCHCOMB, JEANNE B. 2000. "Developing Correctional Officer Professionalism: A Work in Progress," *Corrections Compendium*, Vol. 25, pp. 1–4, 18–19.

STOHR, M. K., G. L. MAYS, A. BECK, and T. KELLEY. 1998. "Sexual Harassment in Women's Jails," *Journal of Contemporary Criminal Justice*, Vol. 14, No. 2, pp. 135–155.

STOJKOVIC, S. and M. A. FARKAS. 2003. *Correctional Leadership: A Cultural Perspective*. Belmont, CA: Wadsworth.

STOLZ, BARBARA. 1997. "Privatizing Corrections: Changing the Corrections Policy-Making Subgovernment," *The Prison Journal*, Vol. 77, No. 1, pp. 92–111.

[STONE, JOSH. 2005. "Elmira Reformatory," in Mary Bosworth (ed.) *Encyclopedia of Prisons and Correctional Facilities*. Thousand Oaks, CA: Sage Publications, pp. 286–288].

STUEVER, HANK. 2000. "Radical Chic: Benetton Takes on the Death Penalty," *Washington Post*, January 25, p. C1.

SUEDFELD, PETER. 1974. "Solitary Confinement in the Correctional Setting: Goals, Problems, and Suggestions," *Corrective and Social Psychiatry*, Vol. 141, pp. 10–20.

SUEDFELD, PETER, CARMENZA RAMIREZ, JOHN DEATON, and GLORIA BAKER-BROWN. 1982. "Reactions and Attributes of Prisoners in Solitary Confinement," *Criminal Justice and Behavior*, Vol. 9, pp. 303–340.

SULLIVAN, LARRY E. 1990. *The Prison Reform Movement: Forlorn Hope*. Boston: Twayne Publishers.

SURETTE, RAY. 1998. "Prologue: Some Unpopular Thoughts About Popular Culture," in Frankie Bayley and Donna Hale (eds.) *Popular Culture, Crime & Justice*. Belmont, CA: Wadsworth, pp. viv–xxiv.

SURETTE, RAY. 1999. "Media Echoes: Systematic Effects of News Coverage," *Justice Quarterly*, Vol. 16, pp. 601–620.

SYKES, GRESHAM. 1958. *The Society of Captives*. Princeton, NJ: Princeton University Press.

SYKES, GRESHAM and SHELDON L. MESSINGER. 1960. "The Inmate Social System," in Richard A. Cloward et al. (eds.) *Theoretical Studies in the Social Organization of the Prison*. New York: Social Science Research Council, pp. 6–8.

TAFOYA, WILLIAM. 1996. "A Delphi Forecast of the Future of Law Enforcement," Ph.D. Dissertation, University of Maryland.

TAGGERT, WILLIAM A. 1997. "The Nationalization of Corrections Policy in the American States," *Justice Quarterly*, Vol. 14, No. 3, pp. 429–442.

TALBOTT, FREDERICK. 1988. "Reporting from Behind the Walls," *The Quill*, Vol. 76, pp. 16–20.

TALBOTT, FREDERICK. 1989. "Covering Prisons," *Editor & Publisher*, April 22, pp. 74–78.

TAYLOR, IAN, PAUL WALTON, and JOCK YOUNG. 1973. *The New Criminology*. London: Routledge and Kegan Paul.

TAYLOR, JON MARC and RICHARD TEWKSBURY. 2002. "Postsecondary Correctional Education: The Imprisoned University," in Rosemary Gido and Ted Alleman (eds.) *Turnstile Justice*. Upper Saddle, NJ: Prentice Hall, pp. 145–175.

TERRY, CHARLES. 2003. "From C-Block to Academia: You Can't Get There from Here," in Jeffrey Ian Ross and Stephen C. Richards (eds.) *Convict Criminology*. Belmont, CA: Wadsworth, pp. 95–119.

THOMAS, JIM. 1988. *Prisoner Litigation: The Paradox of the Jailhouse Lawyer*. Totowa, NJ: Rowman and Littlefield.

THOMAS, JIM. 2005. "Types of Clemency," in Mary Bosworth (ed.) *Encyclopedia of Prisons & Correctional Facilities*. Thousand Oaks, CA: Sage Publications, pp. 134–137.

THOMPSON, CHERYL W. 1998. "Prison Company Assailed: Report Slams Firm Hoping to Build D.C. Facility," *Washington Post*, October 8, pp. B1, B9.

THOMPSON, JOEL A. and G. LARRY MAYS (eds.). 1991. *American Jails: Public Policy Issues*. Chicago, IL: Nelson-Hall.

TOBERG, MARY. 1983. "Bail Bondsmen and Criminal Courts," *Justice System Journal*, Vol. 8, pp. 141–156.

TOCH, HANS. 2001. "The Future of Supermax Confinement," *The Prison Journal*, Vol. 81, pp. 376–388.

TOCH, HANS and JOHN KLOFAS. 1982. "Alienation and Desire for Job Enrichment Among Correctional Officers," *Federal Probation*, Vol. 46, pp. 35–44.

TOLLER, WILLIAM and BASIL TSAGARIS. 1996a. "A Comparison of Gang Members and Non-Gang Members in a Prison Setting. *The Prison Journal*, Vol. 81, No. 2, pp. 50–60.

TOLLER, WILLIAM and BASIL TSAGARIS. 1996b. "Managing Institutional Gangs: A Practical Approach, Combining Security and Human Services," *Corrections Today*, Vol. 58, No. 6, pp. 110–111, 115.

TONRY, MICHAEL. 2004. *Thinking About Crime: Sense and Sensibility in Penal Culture*. New York: Oxford University Press.

TORR, J. D. 1999. *Drug Abuse: Opposing Viewpoints*. San Diego, CA: Greenhaven Press.

TRAVISINO, A. P. 1980. "Brubaker: The Crusader Strikes Out," *On the Line*, Vol. 3, No. 6, p. 1.

TREGEA, WILLIAM S. 2003. "Twenty Years Teaching College in Prison," in Jeffrey Ian Ross and Stephen C. Richards (eds.) *Convict Criminology*. Belmont, CA: Wadsworth, pp. 59–76.

TRIPLE, H. R., J. Mullings, and K. Scarborough. 1996. "Work Related Stress and Coping Among Correctional Officers: Implications from Organizational Literature," *Journal of Criminal Justice*, Vol. 24, No. 4, pp. 291–308.

TUNNELL, KENNETH D. 1992. "99 Years Is Almost for Life: Punishment for Violent Crime in Bluegrass Music," *Journal of Popular Culture*, Vol. 26, pp. 165–181.

TUNNELL, KENNETH D. 1995. "A Cultural Approach to Crime and Punishment, Bluegrass Style," in Jeff Ferrell and Clinton R. Sanders (eds.) *Cultural Criminology*. Boston: Northeastern University Press, pp. 80–115.

TUNNELL, KENNETH D. 2000. *Living Off Crime*. Chicago, IL: Burnham Publishing.

USEEM, BERT. 1985. "Disorganization and the New Mexico Prison Riot of 1980," *American Sociological Review*, Vol. 50, pp. 677–688.

USEEM, BERT and PETER KIMBALL. 1989. *States of Siege: U.S. Prison Riots, 1971–1986*. New York: Oxford University Press.

USEEM, BERT, CAMILLE GRAHAM CAMP, GEORGE M. CAMP, and RENIE DUGAN. 1995. *Resolution of Prison Riots. National Institute of Justice Research in Brief*, October, NCJ 155283.

VALENTINE, BILL and ROBERT SCHOBER. 2000. *Gangs and Their Tattoos: Identifying Gangbangers on the Street and in Prison*. Boulder, CO: Paladin.

VALENTINE, GILL and BETH LONGSTAFF. 1998. "Doing Porridge: Food and Social Relations in a Male Prison," *Journal of Material Culture*, Vol. 3, No. 2, pp. 131–152.

VAUGHN, MICHAEL S. and L. CARROLL. 1998. "Separate and Unequal: Prison versus Free World Medical Care," *Justice Quarterly*, Vol. 15, pp. 3–40.

VOHRYZEK-BOLDEN, M. and T. CROISDALE. 1999. *Overview of Selected States' Academy and In-Service Training for Adult and Juvenile Correctional Employees*. Longmont, CO: National Institute of Corrections.

VOLLMER, HOWARD M. and DONALD L. MILLS. 1966. *Professional*. Englewood Cliffs, NJ: Prentice Hall.

VON ZIELBAUER, PAUL. 2005a. "As Health Care in Jails Goes Private, 10 Days Can Be a Death Sentence," *The New York Times*, February 27, pp. A1, A26–A29.

VON ZIELBAUER, PAUL. 2005b. "Inside City's Jails, Missed Signals Open Way to Season of Suicides," *The New York Times*, February 28, pp. A1, A18–A19.

WARD, D. 1994. "Alcatraz and Marion: Confinement in Super Maximum Custody," in J. Roberts (ed.) *Escaping Prison Myths*. Washington, D.C.: The American University Press, pp. 81–93.

WARR, MARK, R. F. MEIER, and M. L. ERICKSON. 1983. "Norms, Theories of Punishment, and Publicly Preferred Penalties for Crimes," *Sociological Quarterly*, Vol. 24, pp. 75–91.

WEBB, G. L. and D. G. MORRIS. 2002. "Working as a Prison Guard," in Tara Gray (ed.) *Exploring Corrections: A Book of Readings*. Boston: Allyn & Bacon, pp. 69–83.

WEINBERG, R. B., J. H. EVANS, C. A. OTTEN, and H. A. MARLOWE. 1985. "Managerial Stress in Corrections Personnel," *Corrective and Social Psychiatry and Journal of Behavior Technology Methods and Therapy*, Vol. 31, No. 2, pp. 9–95.

WEINSTEIN, COREY. 2000. "Even Dogs Confined to Cages for Long Periods of Time Go Berserk," in John P. May and Khalid R. Pitts (eds.) *Building Violence: How America's Rush to Incarcerate Creates More Violence*. Thousand Oaks, CA: Sage Publications, pp. 118–124.

WELCH, MICHAEL. 1994. "Jail Overcrowding: Social Sanitation and the Warehousing of the Urban Underclass," in A. R. Roberts (ed.) *Critical Issues in Crime and Justice*. Thousand Oaks, CA: Sage Publications, pp. 251–276.

WELCH, MICHAEL. 1996. *Corrections: A Critical Approach*. New York: McGraw-Hill.

WELCH, MICHAEL. 1998. "Critical Criminology, Social Control, and an Alternative View of Corrections," in Jeffrey Ian Ross (ed.) *Cutting the Edge: Current Perspectives in Radical/Critical Criminology and Criminal Justice*. New York: Praeger, pp. 107–121.

WELCH, MICHAEL. 2002. *Detained: Immigration Laws and the Expanding I.N.S. Jail Complex*. Philadelphia: Temple University Press.

WELCH, MICHAEL. 2004. *Corrections: A Critical Approach*. Second Edition. New York: McGraw-Hill.

WELSH, WAYNE N. 1992. "The Dynamics of Jail Reform Litigation: A Comparative Analysis of Litigation in California Counties," *Law & Society Review*, Vol. 26, No. 3, pp. 591–626.

WELSH, WAYNE N. 1995. *Counties in Court: Jail Overcrowding and Court Ordered Reform*. Philadelphia: Temple University Press.

WELSH, WAYNE N. and PHILLIP W. HARRIS. 2004. *Criminal Justice: Policy and Planning*. Second Edition. Cincinnati, OH: Anderson/LexisNexis.

WHITEHEAD, JONATHEN. 1985. "Job Burnout in Probation and Parole: Its Extent and Intervention Implications," *Criminal Justice & Behavior*, Vol. 12, pp. 91–110.

WHITEHEAD, JONATHEN. 1987. "Probation Officer Burnout: A Test of Two Theories," *Journal of Criminal Justice*, Vol. 15, No. 1, pp. 25–35.

WHITEHEAD, JONATHEN and CHARLES LINDQUIST. 1986. "Correctional Officer Job Burnout: A Path Model," *Journal of Crime & Delinquency*, Vol. 23, No. 1, pp. 23–42.

WICKER, TOM. 1980/1994. *A Time to Die: The Attica Riot*. Lincoln: University of Nebraska Press.

WILLIAMS, VERGIL L. and MARY FISH. 1974. *Convicts, Codes, and Contraband: The Prison Life of Men and Women*. Cambridge, MA: Ballinger.

WORLEY, ROBERT WORLEY and KELLY ANN CHEESEMAN. 2006. "Guards as Embezzlers: The Consequences of 'Nonshareable Problems' in Prison Settings," *Deviant Behavior*, Vol. 27, No. 2, pp. 203–222.

WRIGHT, ERIK OLIN. 1973. *The Politics of Punishment*. New York: HarperCollins.

WRIGHT, KEVIN N., W. G. SAYLOR, E. GILMAN, and S. CAMP. 1997. "Job Control and Occupational Outcomes Among Prison Workers," *Justice Quarterly*, Vol. 26, No. 3, pp. 213–226.

WRIGHT, THOMAS. 1993. "Correctional Employee Turnover: A Longitudinal Study," *Journal of Criminal Justice*, Vol. 21, No. 2. pp. 131–142.

YOUNG, JEFFREY. 2006. "Waters Seeks to Sway AIDS Group on Prisoner Testing," *The Hill*, September 12, p. 5

ZANER, LAURA. 1989. "The Screen Test: Has Hollywood Hurt the Corrections Image?" *Corrections Today*, Part 51, pp. 64–98.

ZINGER, IVAN, CHARAMI WICHMANN, and D. A. ANDREWS. 2001. "The Psychological Effects of 60 Days in Administrative Segregation," *Canadian Journal of Criminology*, Vol. 43, pp. 47–83.

ZUMBRUN, JOSHUA. 2007. "Celebs Put Their Best Foot Forward," *Washington Post*, July 18, pp. C1–C2.

ZUPAN, LINDA. 1986. "Gender-Related Differences in Correctional Officers' Perceptions and Attitudes," *Journal of Criminal Justice*, Vol. 20, pp. 297–309.

ZUPAN, LINDA. 1992. "The Progress of Women Correctional Officers in All-Male Prisons," in I. L. Moyers (ed.) *The Changing Roles of Women in the Criminal Justice System*. Prospect Heights, IL: Waveland Press, pp. 232–244.

ZUPAN, LINDA L. 2002. "The Persistent Problems Plaguing Modern Jails," in Tara Gray (ed.) *Exploring Corrections: A Book of Readings*. Boston: Allyn & Bacon, pp. 37–63.

ZUPAN, LINDA L. and BEN A. MENKE. 1988. "Implementing Organizational Change: From Traditional to New Generation Jail Operations," *Policy Studies Review*, Vol. 7, pp. 615–625.

ZUPAN, LINDA L. and BEN A. MENKE. 1991. "The New Generation Jail: An Overview," in Joel A. Thompson and G. Larry Mays (eds.) *American Jails: Public Policy Issues*. Chicago, IL: Nelson-Hall, pp. 181–194.

ZWEIG, JANINE M., REBECCA L. NASER, JOHN BLACKMORE, and MEGAN SCHAFFER. 2006. "Addressing Sexual Violence in Prisons: A National Snapshot of Approaches and Highlights of Innovative Strategies, Final Report." Washington, D.C.: Urban Institute, Justice Policy Center. www.asca.net/public/PSV%20Final%20Report_Oct2006.pdf (accessed August 27, 2007).

Index